No Comfort

ALSO BY DAN PIETSCH

The Greatest Happiness

A tale of love and revenge set in an alternate world and in a different time, somewhere between the Oxus and the Jumna

The greatest happiness is to scatter your enemy, to drive him before you ... to see those who love him shrouded in tears.
~Genghis Khan

http://TheGreatestHappiness.com

No Comfort

A Nightmare of Physical, Psychological, and Sexual Child Abuse;
A Journey to Forgiveness and Reconciliation;
A Story of Courage, Love, and Hope

Dan Pietsch

Cabin Fever Publishing
Idyllwild, California
ᑎ�E

ᑎᖮ
Cabin Fever Publishing
P.O. Box 750
Idyllwild, CA 92549
www.cabinfeverpublishing.com

PUBLISHER'S NOTE
This is a work of fiction. Names, characters, places, and incidents either are the product of the author's imagination or are used fictitiously, and any resemblance to actual persons, living or dead, events, or locales is entirely coincidental.

Manufactured in the United States of America

ISBN 978-0-9842636-0-8

Library of Congress Control Number: 2009910168

For my long-suffering wife, Susan

Carolyn
she heard music

1955–2007

IN MEMORIAM

Acknowledgments

I am indebted to I. F. Cobb for his inspiration and intrepid support throughout the course of this project.

It's better to be good than evil, but one achieves goodness at a terrific cost.

~Stephen King

Foreword

No one keeps a secret as well as a child, and, because of that, many an evil remains forever untold. I am pleased, therefore, that Llewellyn Trout has decided to make public the story of his life—yes, even the secrets of his childhood.

His journal has been an important part of his therapy, and writing it has helped Llewellyn come to terms with dark remnants left by the abuse and neglect he suffered as a child. I asked him to write with honesty and in detail. "Imagine yourself reliving the events," I told him.

That's exactly what he has done.

When Llewellyn suggested sharing his story with others, I encouraged him to do just that. He and I both hope his story will give encouragement to others who are struggling to emerge from the dark shadow of abuse.

J. L. Kent, Doctor of Psychiatry

March 12

I SHOULD HAVE killed Miss Elsa the same day she moved into the apartment above the garage. I didn't know it at the time, but a kid can get away with murder. It would have been so easy. After all, Pop had guns. Lots of guns. And he had showed me how to use them.

But at first me and Misty liked Miss Elsa. We were excited as can be that evening when she said, Come along, sweethearts, we're going out to Flo's Diner. We'll get us some burgers and fries.

When we got to Flo's, the waitress lady talked to us very nice, and she smiled real friendly. You can sit at the table by the door, she said.

Miss Elsa pointed to a booth in a section where the lights were off. We'd rather sit there, she said.

The waitress lady told her, I'm sorry, ma'am, that end of the diner is closed. We've had a bit of an ant problem.

I don't give a darn what problems you've had, Miss Elsa said. I told you we want to sit over there.

The waitress lady shrugged and said, Suit yourself, ma'am.

When we were all scooched in, Miss Elsa made me and Misty fold our hands as she prayed for the food we were about to receive.

Then she smiled at us and said, I like this end of the diner better, don't you, Lewie? How about you, Misty? Over here we don't got folks sitting close by, listening and paying attention to everyone's business but their own.

The waitress lady sure was right about those ants. They were crawling on the table in a long line, and sometimes they stopped and put their heads together. Pop had one time told me that putting their heads together is what ants do when they talk to each other, and I had listened real careful, but I couldn't hear them saying anything, so I didn't know if Pop was teasing about that ants could talk or if maybe Pop could hear better than me because he was a grown-up and I was just a kid.

Anyhow, Miss Elsa said, Don't you worry about those little critters, Lewie. We'll take care of them.

1

She took out from her purse a cigarette lighter, a green one, and on the table next to the salt and pepper and pancake syrup there was a candle in a yellow glass. Miss Elsa lit that candle and soon there was melted wax. Miss Elsa dribbled some on those ants, and she said, Look, Lewie; look, Misty. Look how those little critters squirm. Then she said, Best we put them out of their misery, don't you think?

She fixed the flame on that lighter of hers so it was very big, and she aimed it down on those ants and made them dead.

You want to give it a try? she said to me, and I told her, No, Pop says I'll burn my fucking fingers if I play with fire.

Miss Elsa said to me, Don't swear, Lewie. It's not nice. It's not Christian.

I said, Why not? Pop swears. He's nice. He's Christian.

Miss Elsa looked at me disgusted and with a scowl. She said to me, Well, Lewie, you can stop worrying about that Pop of yours. Look around; he ain't here. Besides, playing with fire isn't dangerous so long as you're careful.

Miss Elsa held the lighter out to me and said, Go ahead, sweetheart, I won't tell.

So I did what she said because, well, I guess it's what little boys like to do; they like to play with fire. I don't know why; they just do. They like fire. Like it a lot.

Miss Elsa showed me how to work that lighter of hers, and she said, Now aim it down on those little critters, Lewie.

So I did, and the fire made them dead. From those ants was a crackly noise and a bad smell.

Miss Elsa winked at me. Don't you worry, she said. Miss Elsa can keep a secret. She won't tell a soul. Not your Pop. Not anyone. And you won't tell, either, will you, Misty?

Misty shook her head, but I knew from the way she looked at me that I had done a bad thing, and, if Pop ever found out, he would hit me because I deserved it. That's what Pop always did when we deserved it; he hit us. Sometimes hard. Sometimes not so hard. You never knew which it would be. Mostly it depended on how much Comfort Pop had drunk.

Anyhow, just about then the waitress lady brought our burgers and fries, and Miss Elsa said, Why don't you sit on my lap while you eat, Lewie?

She lifted me onto her lap, and, as I was eating my burger and fries, Miss Elsa was stroking my legs because I was wearing shorts, and she was stroking them real soft and gentle, and it felt good, and I felt safe and happy sitting there on Miss Elsa's lap.

Miss Elsa said, Oh, Lewie, your legs are so cold. Are you chilly?

I told her, No, I'm not cold, but I guess she didn't hear because she said, Don't you worry, sweetheart, Miss Elsa will warm you up, and she kept rubbing my legs, and she told me, You know, Lewie, when I was a little girl my legs were soft and smooth just like yours. My daddy would hold me on his lap and he would stroke my legs real gentle and he would say, Oh, baby doll, your daddy loves you.

I motioned for Miss Elsa to put her head down to me so I could whisper in her ear.

I got to go pee, I told her.

Well, first you finish up your fries, Miss Elsa said.

I told her, I really got to go bad.

Miss Elsa said to me, Sometimes it helps if you hold yourself down there and squeeze. It makes you not have to go so bad. And she did it to me; she held me and she squeezed, but it didn't help, only hurt, so I tried to eat my fries real quick so I could go to the restroom. But there was still lots of fries left, so I said, Please, Miss Elsa, I really got to go bad. Really, really, really bad, and Miss Elsa sighed and said, Well, then, run along, I guess.

I did run but I didn't make it in time, and I a little bit peed my pants, and when I went back out I was so ashamed.

Miss Elsa shook her head and looked at me very disappointed, and she said, Oh, Lewie, I can hardly believe what I see. Did you really wet yourself? A big boy like you? Oh, my, my, my, Lewie. Your Pop would be so ashamed. So very, very ashamed. Let's hope he don't ever find out.

I said, Please don't tell, and Miss Elsa brushed away some ants and patted the seat for me to sit down beside her, and I did sit down, and she put her arm around me, and then I felt better.

Now, Miss Elsa said; Now it's time for a real treat. And, sure enough, it was a mighty special treat because Miss Elsa ordered milkshakes for us. Vanilla for me. Strawberry for Misty. We were both of us so excited because Miss Elsa even let us to have whipped cream and sprinkles on top.

She said, Of course, my sweethearts, of course you can have whipped cream and sprinkles, and I told her, Thank you, Miss Elsa. I'm glad you've come to live in the apartment above the garage.

Misty said, I like you, Miss Elsa. Thank you for letting us have whipped cream and sprinkles.

Miss Elsa smiled and gave us both a hug, and she said, Maybe it's better if we don't tell Mom and Pop about the milkshakes because, well, sometimes parents don't like their youngsters having sweets just before bed.

Yep, us kids and Miss Elsa had secrets right from the start. Lots of secrets. Miss Elsa made having secrets so much fun. Well, at first they were fun. But later on, they weren't no fun at all. Not one bit.

So, like I said, me and Misty at first liked Miss Elsa. But it was only because we didn't know about the things that would soon start happening. We didn't know about the baths in the claw-foot tub. We didn't know about having to hide under a bed or in the dark basement with the spook man. We didn't know about the switch from the tree out back. Lots of things we didn't know. If we had, maybe one of us really would have shot Miss Elsa on the day she moved into that apartment above the garage.

Sure, we were just kids—me five years old and Misty four—but there were plenty of guns in the house, and me and Misty could both use a gun plenty good enough to kill a person. Pop hadn't let us shoot any of his guns; not yet he hadn't, but he had showed us how to aim and how to load bullets and how never to point a fucking firearm at yourself because, like he told us, if you do, you're likely to blow your goddamn head clean off. Is that clear Llewellyn? You never aim a gun at anything you don't intend to shoot.

Pop liked guns. He had lots of them, but his most favorite was the genuine M-16 rifle that was just like the one he carried when he served in the Marine Corps over in the Nam back in '69.

Yep, back in '69 Pop went off to the Nam, but, unfortunately, not all of him came back. Some gook, he said; Some gook over on the Cambodian border took half his right arm. Took the damn thing and kept it.

Pop may have left half an arm over in the Nam back in '69, but he came home with two things he hadn't had when he enlisted in the Marine Corps.

A Purple Heart medal and a wife. A gook wife.

But a gook wife was okay. Even in Waynesburg, Arkansas, most folks could agree on that. After all, Pop's woman knew her place. She didn't talk back, she worked hard, and you had to admit she had a downright sweet personality.

Pop and his gook wife lived in their house out on Warner Road for many years without producing any children. The general Waynesburg consensus was that it probably had something to do with the two races, Gook and American, that is, not being entirely compatible.

But then I came along and proved that consensus wrong. If anyone still had doubts, the matter was for sure settled when, about a year later, Misty got born.

She got her name from a movie: *Play Misty for Me.* It was one of Pop's favorites.

Fact is, Pop liked pretty much all the Clint Eastwood movies. Clint Eastwood, he used to say; That Clint Eastwood is a real man's man. The guy don't take shit from nobody.

So Misty got her name from a movie that starred a real man's man. And me, I got named Llewellyn. Yeah, go figure. I one time told Pop that Llewellyn was a sissy fag name, and he hit me and said, You watch your language, young man. You watch your fucking language.

Anyhow, Misty looked a lot like Mom. Eyes a little bit slanty and skin a little bit brown. Just what you would expect of someone who was half Vietnamese.

But I didn't look like Mom hardly at all. Which I suppose was just as well, seeing as looking like a gook didn't improve a person's social status in Waynesburg, Arkansas.

My first memories aren't of Miss Elsa and the terrible things she did to me and Misty, starting with the baths in the claw-foot tub, there in the bathroom of our house out on Warner Road. In fact, one of my earliest memories is a happy one of Pop giving me a bath in that same claw-foot tub.

Pop sure did laugh when I passed gas and made the water bubble. He called it turning the water into champagne.

Damn it, Llewellyn, he said, our Lord turned regular Holy Land tap water into communion wine, but here you done turned dirty bath water into genuine bubbly champagne.

I told him, Pop, what's champagne? and he said, Well, Son, it's a kind of bubbly wine that rich folks drink on special occasions. But folks like you and me are most often content with a cold Pabst if we feel like having something bubbly.

I still didn't really understand what Pop was talking about our Lord doing with the tap water, but I figured it must be that Holy Land folks drank bubbly champagne on special occasions after they took a bath.

Anyhow, the two of us, Pop and me, we sure as hell had a fine time laughing about those bubbles in the bath water.

March 13

I N THOSE DAYS, things were pretty good for me and Misty. But that changed when Miss Elsa came to live with us.

Mom was working two jobs. Waynesburg Pharmacy all day and Shemp's Pizza most evenings. I doubt she liked the work, but I don't suppose she minded having an excuse to get out of the house.

Whether Mom liked the work or not, fact is, we needed the money. Pop spent his days down at O'Brien's, soaking up Comfort, and, like he told Mom, what do you think, goddamnit, of course he needed money for the bar tab.

On top of that, Pop needed money so he could leave a tip. How the hell was Chester going to feed his wife and kids if his customers didn't leave no fucking tips?

And then, of course there were incidentals Mom needed to take into consideration. Incidentals such as food, the electric bill, and quarters for the washers down at Suds Laundromat. If there was money left over, Pop would most often use it to make another purchase at the gun shows he and Uncle Stew liked going to.

Pop was always buying and selling guns. He kept the most valuable ones locked in the gun safe right there in the living room beside the television. Looking back, I think he should have kept all his guns locked up, but I guess there was limited space in that safe.

I asked him, Why, Pop? Why do you lock up some of your guns?

He told me, Well, Son, it's because I don't want them stolen, of course. After all, you never know when some low-life cocksucker might break in and try to heist one of those beauties. But, goddamnit, even Charles fucking Atlas ain't going to make off with a gun safe that weighs almost 900 pounds. Hell, Son, that's just a hundred pounds short of a ton.

Yep, Pop laughed away at the thought of some dumbfuck even trying to carry off that safe of his.

So you might say Southern Comfort, Colts, and Berettas accounted in large part for why Mom had to work two jobs.

And Mom's working two jobs is why Miss Elsa moved into the apartment above the garage. She lived there rent-free and ate what she wanted from the kitchen in exchange for watching me and Misty, while Mom was off stocking shelves and cleaning tables and Pop was off telling war stories and getting wasted on Comfort down at O'Brien's.

The apartment above the garage didn't have a bathroom, so Miss Elsa shared the downstairs one with the family. I remember the day she told me, Come in here Lewie. Come on, sweetheart; come take a bath with Miss Elsa.

So I got in that claw-foot tub with her, and I laughed when she washed my toes and tickled my belly. And then I tickled her, too, and she said, Oh Lewie, you're such a funny little boy. Tickle me again.

Me and Miss Elsa soaped each other up till we were both of us squeaky clean. Then Miss Elsa sat there in the water, watching me as I dried myself. She made a moaning noise, and I said, Is something wrong, Miss Elsa? because her face looked like she was in pain, but she told me, Get on out of here, Lewie; just get on out.

Before Miss Elsa came to live with us, we used to take a bath on Wednesday and then again on Saturday evening so as to be clean for the Lord's Day, when we would dress up real nice, me in a suit, and drive into town for the worship service at Waynesburg Baptist. I would take with me my favorite book, *Bible Stories for Young Children*, which had a picture up front of Adam and Eve with no clothes and sharing an apple real nice and not fighting over it, but bushes covering the only naked parts you really wanted to see, and another picture on a different page that showed the poor sinners drowning in the great flood, but Noah standing in the rain and his long hair's not even wet, and he's smiling real happy because he's got a boat and the poor sinners don't.

Most every Sunday, Miss Elsa went with us to Waynesburg Baptist. She sang real loud, and she sometimes called out, Praise Jesus, in the middle of Reverend McKey saying his sermon.

Pop said Miss Elsa was a good Christian and a godly woman.

I figured that must be why Miss Elsa said cleanliness was nigh unto godliness, and she insisted on her and me taking a bath pretty much every day. And before long it wasn't just me that got in the tub with her. Soon little Misty was excited as can be to strip down and get in there, too.

The three of us would have fun making bubbles and floating rubber ducks before getting down to the real business of washing, tickling, and splashing till we were all squeaky clean and next to godliness.

Then one day, Miss Elsa began inviting Miss Veronica over to the house. It was to be our secret.

Miss Elsa and Miss Veronica would take baths together, and, for a while, me and Misty didn't have to get next to godliness every day.

I didn't mind at all not having to take a bath.

Misty was glad, too. I don't like Miss Elsa no more, she said. I'm glad we don't have to get squeaky clean with her.

Miss Elsa and her friend at first locked the door the whole time they were in the claw-foot tub, but me and Misty could hear them giggling and carrying on, and we knew the two of them must be having a great time splashing, tickling, and getting squeaky clean.

But of course me and Misty couldn't go on forever getting dirtier and dirtier, so it wasn't long before we were brought in again for daily baths.

There wasn't much room in the tub, so Misty sat between Miss Veronica's legs, and I sat between Miss Elsa's. She stroked mine real gentle like she had that night at Flo's Diner, and she whispered to me, Oh, sweetheart, Miss Elsa loves you.

When we were squeaky clean and next to godliness, me and Misty got sent out, while Miss Elsa and her friend stayed in the tub with the door locked, getting even more squeaky and godly.

One time I passed gas and made bubbles in the bath water. Miss Elsa obviously didn't know about our Lord turning bath water into bubbly champagne, and she didn't laugh about it like Pop would have. She made me stand up in the tub, and she spanked my bottom, and she told me I was a naughty boy for doing such a thing. She said to me, Lewie, you should be ashamed. You are a disgusting little boy. Disgusting and filthy.

One day the two women had been drinking from Pop's bottles of Comfort, and when it came bath time, they had me and Misty do things that made us embarrassed.

At first, we still giggled, but it wasn't any more a fun giggle, and pretty soon me and Misty didn't giggle at all—not one bit we didn't.

Misty was becoming angry. Even if she didn't say so, I could see it in her eyes, and I was becoming angry, too; so when Mom came home one night, I told her about the baths and I said, Me and Misty don't want to get squeaky clean with Miss Elsa no more.

March 14

THE NEXT DAY Miss Elsa looked mad. Really, really mad. She took Misty in the bathroom and locked her there. Then she got a big knife from the kitchen and made me come with her out in the back yard.

I want you to help me choose a tree to cut a switch from, she said.

I didn't know what she was talking about, but I did as I was told, and I pointed to the tree that had the tire swing me and Misty liked to play on.

Miss Elsa slapped the back of my head so hard, and I saw spots in my eyes, and she yelled at me and said how the heck was she supposed to cut a switch from a tree when she couldn't even reach the branches.

So I pointed to a different tree, and she must have liked it better because she didn't hit me, and she nodded and cut from it a long skinny branch.

This one will do just fine, Miss Elsa said as she cut away all the leaves and all the bark.

I didn't know why she had cut that stick. Pop used to hit me now and then, and he hit Mom and Misty, too, when we deserved it, but only always with his hand. Just his hand. Never anything else. Never with a stick. So I didn't know what I was doing when I helped Miss Elsa choose that stick she was fixing.

When she was finished, she made me carry it back inside and to the bathroom, where Misty was quiet as a mouse and not crying or begging to unlock the door like I would have done if it was me that got locked up.

Miss Elsa unlatched that door, and we went in with Misty.

Look what your brother helped me fix, Miss Elsa said, taking the stick from me. Now you'll see what happens to you, young lady, when your brother's a naughty boy and tells secrets that's supposed to be just between us and no one else.

She made Misty lift her dress that had ruffles like a princess and then lower her panties that had pink flowers and butterflies.

Now bend over and grab your ankles, she said to Misty, and Misty did as she was told.

Then Miss Elsa started in with that switch.

She hit Misty once. . .twice. . .three times.

Miss Elsa counted those hits. Out loud she counted them.

One. . .two. . .three.

Count with me Lewie, she said. Count with me. We're only going up to seven, but the counting don't start till you count with me.

She hit and then she hit again, but I didn't say nothing, so the counting didn't start. Then she hit again, and this time I counted. I didn't talk count,

I scream counted.

One. . .Two. . .Three. . .Four. . .Five. . .Six. . .Seven

Seven. It doesn't seem like much, but let me tell you, seven is forever. Seven is like when you wake in the midnight and you see the spook man in the dark corner and you are so afraid your voice gets stuck inside so you can't call out to Mom and Pop, and you are afraid to move in case the spook man will see you, and so you lie there all the dark night just watching and waiting. And even that's not how long seven is when you are counting and watching Miss Elsa hit your little sister with a stick you chose from the tree, but not the tree with the tire swing because how can Miss Elsa reach the branches, and it's all because you were a naughty boy, naughty and wicked, and you told a secret that was supposed to be just between you and no one else. That's how long seven is when you scream count.

Seven is forever long.

One. . .Two. . .Three. . .Four. . .Five. . .Six. . .Seven

Misty never made a sound.

When it was done, I ran from the bathroom, and I was still scream counting, Eight. . .Nine. . .Ten. . .Eleven. . .

I ran to the bedroom and curled up on my bunk that was below Misty's, and I was still scream counting. I counted till I didn't know my numbers any higher, and then I began sobbing so hard I couldn't catch my breath.

Soon Misty came in and curled up beside me. She put her arm across my shoulder, and me and her lay there and we went to sleep.

March 15

AFTER THE BATHS stopped, the hide-and-seek games began. They weren't fun games. Not fun at all. Not one bit. I remember the first time we played that game. It was Miss Elsa's birthday, and we all clapped for the cake that had birthday writing on top and candles, too, and Miss Elsa on accident spit on the cake because she was blowing the candles so hard.

But still she couldn't make them go out, and she looked funny because her cheeks were puffed and her eyes were popping, and because of that I laughed at her. I tried not to, but it came out anyhow.

Miss Elsa said it was not nice of me to laugh and I was a naughty boy, and how dare I be so rude, and if I thought it was so easy to put out all the candles, Well, then, let's see if you can do any better yourself, young man, and we'll see who's laughing then.

Miss Elsa took my hand, and she made me with my fingers pinch the fire on those candles to make them go out, and it burned my fingers and made them hurt—made them hurt really, really bad—and I wanted to cry, but Misty was looking at me in a way that was like talking to me, and she was saying, Don't cry, Lewie; don't cry because that's what Miss Elsa wants you to do, so be strong and don't cry. And having Misty look at me that way made me brave, and I didn't cry, and it made me feel good inside and not a crybaby like usual.

But by not crying I had made Miss Elsa angry even more, and I knew it was on account of her being afraid that if I was brave enough not to cry, then maybe I would be brave enough to tell Mom and Pop what had happened.

So Miss Elsa said to me, If you should happen to be asked, young man, you're to say you were careless and disobedient and you touched the burner on the stove because if you say anything else, well, you know, young man, there are still plenty of branches on that tree out back.

And it was now that Miss Elsa made up the new game. The hide-and-seek game. She said it was a birthday party game.

She made me and Misty take off our clothes. Then her and Miss Veronica hid their eyes and counted to ten, going back and forth between them as they called out the numbers.

Ready or not here we come, Miss Elsa said, and me and Misty real quick scrambled under our bed that was a bunk bed, and we lay there naked, shivering, and trying not to sneeze from the dust bunnies that kept tickling our nose. All we wanted was to get found quick and make the not-fun game be over.

I don't like this game, Misty whispered to me, and I told her, Shush, because I could hear Miss Elsa and Miss Veronica coming in the hall.

But those two ladies were in no hurry to find me and Misty. They searched one corner of the closet, then the other. Inside the big wooden toy chest Pop had made out in his workshop. Under the pillows and behind the dresser. Finally the two of them sat down beside each other on the bed. Me and Misty could see their feet side by side on the floor right in front of our face.

I wanted to get found and make this not-fun game be over, so I made a little noise in my throat to give those ladies a hint where to find me and Misty.

Miss Veronica said, You know, Elsie, I think those two rascals have all along been hid right here under this bed.

I was so afraid. Having someone just about to find you in a game of hide-and-seek is supposed to be an exciting kind of scary, but this kind of scary was different. It wasn't fun at all. Not one bit.

All sudden like, Miss Elsa's hand shot under the bed and grabbed my arm, and Miss Veronica grabbed Misty's leg, and they pulled us out, and we were screaming.

Misty bit Miss Veronica and got away. I kicked with my foot, and it hit Miss Elsa's nose and made her bleed. She screamed and she jumped away.

They locked me in the room and went to get Misty. I hid under the bed again, but when they brought Misty in, Miss Elsa grabbed my leg and pulled me out. She and Miss Veronica spanked me and Misty's bare bottoms—not with a stick from the tree but with a belt of Pop's, very hard, and they told us we were naughty and wicked because we had bit and we had kicked, and, moreover, children like us ought to be ashamed.

Oh, we were ashamed, alright—we were so ashamed—me and Misty were. And because of that we never told anyone about the things that happened to us. Everything was a secret, and I was good at keeping secrets; Misty, too.

When the spanking was over, I was crying like a crybaby, not brave at all anymore. But not Misty. Misty never cried. The women left us alone in the room, and we crawled under the blankets and Misty curled up beside me, and we went to sleep.

March 16

T HINGS GOT WORSE. Lots worse. Miss Elsa and Miss Veronica made me and Misty do things that I can't tell you about because I'm still too ashamed.

But I can tell you there was no more giggling. Not me and Misty at least, we didn't giggle. Didn't giggle, not one bit.

But Miss Elsa and Miss Veronica giggled lots of times as they sat watching us, and me and Misty had to be there naked in front of them while they giggled and pointed and whispered in each other's ear.

They made me do bad things to Misty. And when I said to them, No, I won't do it no more, Miss Elsa told me, Young man, I have a mind to take you out back and cut us a switch from the tree, and if we do that, it'll be you who does the hitting. Is that understood?

What terrible things they made me do to Misty. I didn't understand, but I knew it was naughty and wicked and I should be ashamed.

I was just a kid and didn't even know why girls and boys were different. It was just because they got born different for some reason. If you got born a boy, they gave you a boy name and you wore boy clothes; if you got born a girl, they gave you a girl name and you wore girl clothes. Simple as that.

I didn't even know where babies came from. When I one time asked Pop about it, he said that babies were a gift from God and why the fuck was I asking questions like that, anyhow?

As I was doing those things to Misty I sometimes cried. But Misty never did. Never once.

It got worse when we started the chasing games.

Like terrified little animals, me and Misty tried to keep away from those two ladies. They chased us through the house, and we were screaming and we were naked, and I tried to run outside but Miss Veronica locked the doors, and they hunted us down, trapping us in corners only to let us slip away, then chasing us over sofas, and under tables.

It was worst when they got us trapped in the stairwell, Miss Elsa at one end, Miss Veronica at the other end, me and Misty in the middle, and then the women chased me and Misty up and down, up and down, up and down until all of us were tired and out of breath. Then the two women closed in and grabbed hold of me and Misty. They dragged us into the bedroom, me screaming and kicking but Misty just doing what she was told, and they threw us down on the bed with our legs hanging over the edge and they spanked our bare bottoms and told us how naughty we were.

One time I tried to escape out a window, and I almost made it, and for that, I had to go with Miss Elsa and get a switch from the tree. And this time it was me who had to do the hitting because if I didn't, Misty would get fifteen hits. But if I did the hits myself it would only be ten.

After I did the hits, I went into the bedroom and curled up on the bed and was crying like a crybaby and was shivering, but Misty didn't come in and lie down beside me with her arm across my shoulder like before, and it was all on account of me trying to escape out the window, and, because of it, I could hear Miss Elsa locking Misty in the basement, all dark and with the spook man, so I went to go down and be with her, but the basement door was locked, so I went to find Miss Elsa and tell her, Let Misty out. Let her out right now. Please let her out.

But Miss Elsa had gone away to I don't know where. I thought maybe it was to her apartment above the garage, so I went there, but no one answered the door, so I rattled the handle and went in, and I was scared because I had never been in there before, and it was dark and the curtains closed, and I think the spook man hiding in the closet, but there was a dim light on top of a big glass thing like they keep goldfish in, but this one not with water and fish, but, instead, a snake bigger than any one I ever saw before, but Miss Elsa wasn't there, and I hoped when she came back the snake would bite her and make her dead.

So Misty had to stay in the basement all day. I sat by the door and she sat on the other side, and we talked, and I told her, Misty, don't be afraid; the spook man isn't real, but I knew it wasn't true what I said because I had seen the spook man lots of times, but I hoped Misty would believe me and not be afraid.

Near evening, Miss Elsa came back and unlocked the door before Mom or Pop got home. She said to Misty, Young lady, you can be glad, I don't leave you locked down there for days at a time like my daddy used to do to me. You can thank your lucky stars I'm not like him.

March 17

THEN CAME THE day I bit the nipple off Miss Veronica.

Miss Elsa had made me sit cross-leg on the floor, and she told Miss Veronica, Sit on his lap. Sit on his lap and make him play the kissy game.

So Miss Veronica hitched her skirt way up around her fat waist and sat down on my lap, facing me. She was so heavy and it hurt my legs. Miss Elsa stood watching, laughing and clapping. Miss Veronica undid her shirt and pulled out one of her breasts and held it in my face.

Play the kissy game, little Lewie, play the kissy game, she said in a sing-song voice.

I was so scared, and I tried to pull away, but the wall was behind me. And I tried to stand up but Miss Veronica was too heavy on my legs. And I tried to move away to one side, but there was Miss Veronica's arm stopping me. And I tried to move away to the other side and there was Miss Veronica's other arm stopping me.

And then she held her huge breast in front of my face.

The kissy game, the kissy game, she kept singing, and I could smell her breath, and it was like Pop's when he comes back from drinking Comfort at O'Brien's.

Miss Veronica shoved her breast up against my face, covering my nose and mouth, and I couldn't breathe, and I got panicky, and I struggled and struggled, but I couldn't get away, and I still couldn't breathe, and I knew I was going to die, and I did the only thing I could think to do—though, matter of fact, it wasn't thinking at all, but just doing what came natural, sort of like the instinct of a frightened animal, desperate to survive.

I opened my mouth.

Opened it wide.

And then, hard as I could, I bit down.

I heard a shriek, and then there was blood. So much blood. I had something soft and sort of rubbery in my mouth, and I tried to spit it out, but just then a hand slapped my face and in surprise I on accident swallowed.

Blood was pouring from Miss Veronica's breast and she was screaming and she dropped down on her hands and knees and was searching like as if she had dropped a cat's eye marble or something special like that on the floor and she was trying to find it. And then she turned to me with a look like she was afraid of me and she started to scream, Spit it out you naughty boy, spit it out or I'll hit you again. Spit it out. Spit it out.

And that's when we saw Misty standing there in the door with one of Pop's guns in her hands.

I would have been scared if I was Misty. I would have been so scared I wouldn't have been able to hold the gun without my hands being all shaky. But not Misty. I don't think she was afraid, not one bit. Her voice was just regular. Not screaming like mine would have been.

Get out, she said to those ladies. You both get out or I'll shoot you and make you dead.

That day with Miss Veronica's blood splashing dark red on the green linoleum, and Misty all cool and collected and pulling the hammer back on that 22 gun, just like Pop had showed us how, those ladies had good reason to be scared. Miss Veronica was smart: she left our house and never came back. But I don't think Miss Elsa took Misty serious enough.

She should have.

At the time I didn't know anything about breaking points. I didn't know what could happen to a person, even a little kid, when you get pushed too far.

But I know now, and I know Misty was near her breaking point.

March 18

GUNS. THAT WAS the only kind of gift I ever got from Pop. Birthdays and Christmas, too, always guns. But up till now, it was always toy ones; not even BB or pellet, on account of Mom wouldn't allow it.

But when I turned six, Pop put his foot down and said, Enough is enough. I'm getting the boy a real gun. It's his right as an American.

So he took me down to Tanner's, and I got to choose between a Savage Mark 1-G and a Marlin 15. I chose the Savage. I liked the name better: Savage—it sounded good.

The next day me and Pop went out shooting. Misty begged if she could please come along, and Pop said, Hell, no. Why on earth would a sweet little thing like you want to go shooting?

But Misty looked at me and I could tell from her eyes that she was scared to be left alone with Miss Elsa. Scared worse than when the spook man is in your room and it's dark midnight.

I told Pop, Let Misty come with us so she can learn how to shoot, and Pop shrugged and said, Well, why the hell not. Ain't nobody going to say that Henry Trout don't believe in equal rights for females. If my daughter wants to learn how to shoot, I'll damn well be honored to teach her.

But Pop had no idea what was going to come about as a result of Misty learning how to shoot. None of us did. Except maybe Misty.

Anyhow, all three of us, me, Misty, and Pop, got in the Chevy, and we set off driving to where Pop said was a splendid place to let off a few rounds. On the way, Pop was drinking Blue Ribbon, and he kept the can in a paper bag, and I asked him, Why, Pop? Why do you keep the can in a bag? And he told me, Well, officially, Son, I'm not supposed to be drinking while I'm behind the wheel, and I prefer not to have any trouble with the cops.

I thought, Those cops sure are stupid, because anyone with half a brain can figure out what it is Pop's got hid in that brown paper bag of his.

Misty said, Why don't you stop drinking for a change, and Pop just grinned and answered that he had to empty a few cans for us to use as

20

targets because if you shoot a can that's full of beer, it will explode and leave a fine mess.

And besides, Pop said, Why waste a perfectly good beer?

We drove a ways on a dirt road, and it was very rough, and I asked Pop, wasn't it bad for the car, and he looked at me and said, Llewellyn, I ain't driving a piece of Jap crap that rattles itself apart. This is a genuine Chevy made right here in the USA, and it can handle this dirt road just fine, don't you worry about that.

Just about then we got to where Pop said was the splendid place to let off a few rounds.

There were lots of squirrels in the trees, and Pop told me, Go ahead, Son, see if you can shoot yourself one of those cocksuckers. Makes no sense shooting empty beer cans when you've got something live to aim at.

So I gave it a try, but I missed every time, and I thought it must be the sights on the gun were broke, and I wished I had told Pop to buy me the Marlin instead of the Savage.

Misty and Pop were standing there watching and grinning away at me, and Pop was winking at Misty because I was missing every shot.

I told Pop, This gun you bought me is a piece of Jap crap, and I said to Misty, Well, you try it, then, if you think it's so easy, and she looked up at Pop, and he nodded and said, Go ahead, my dear. Go right ahead.

So I gave Misty my Savage, and, sure enough, she took out a squirrel with her first shot.

I bet I could do it if I had a better gun, I said.

I've got a shotgun in the trunk of the Chevy, Pop told me. A genuine made-in-America Browning. You want to give that a try?

I should have known Pop just wanted to teach me a lesson, but I said, Yes, let me try that shotgun, because I knew shotguns make it easier to hit your target due to them shooting a bunch of little pellets instead of just one bullet.

When Pop got the shotgun, he asked if I was sure I knew what I was doing, and I was really mad and almost crying by then, so I told him, Of course I do, just give me the gun.

So he loaded a shell and handed me the Browning.

Fact is, of course, I had no idea what I was doing, and the gun didn't knock the squirrel out of the tree, but the recoil sure did knock me on my butt. It surprised me so much and my shoulder hurt and my ears were ringing and I thought maybe I had somehow shot myself. But when I saw Pop standing there, laughing away, I knew I hadn't shot myself, but I wished

I had because that would serve Pop right, and he sure wouldn't be standing there laughing if I had shot myself dead.

Pop walked over, put out his hand, and helped me to my feet.

They say experience is the best teacher, he told me, and I said to him, I don't never again want to shoot a gun.

But Pop said, Be a man, Llewellyn. I'll give you a few pointers, and you'll be a first-class marksman in no time.

So Pop showed me how to hold the shotgun real tight against my shoulder and he suggested maybe I should try shooting with my back up against a tree so the recoil wouldn't knock me over.

It worked, and I got two squirrels before we went back home—one with Pop's Browning and one with my Savage. So the day turned out to be a good one after all, and I liked guns again, and the only thing I didn't like was that Misty got three squirrels and I only got two.

March 19

IT WASN'T LONG after this that I went off to Mrs. Euston's first grade class at Waynesburg Elementary. I got all new clothes and a lunch box with the Hulk on it, all green and his muscles busting out of his shirt. I was excited to go. Happy to get away from the house and away from Miss Elsa.

On the second day, I was allowed to visit Mrs. Euston's class library, and in that library was a story book, and on the cover of that book was a picture of a girl who had slanty eyes and a little bit brown skin sort of like Misty, and there was a wolf hiding behind a bush and with very sharp teeth. I couldn't read the words, but I could read the pictures, and in them the wolf is sneaky and wicked, and spooky in the woods and scary, and dark with trees that have spooky faces and branches like arms. But when the girl gets home there is a fire in the fireplace and candles, and Mom and Pop, and safe.

All sudden like, I knew Misty was that little girl. But for Misty at home there wasn't any fire in the fireplace. There weren't any candles glowing bright. There wasn't no Mom. There wasn't no Pop.

There was just the wolf, and the wolf was already in the house with Misty, and if I didn't go home to keep her safe, the wolf would kill her and make her dead. So at recess I sneaked away while Mrs. Euston was busy scolding a girl who was by the name of Laura Small for saying the "F" word, which didn't seem like a very good reason to get a scolding, and I ran all the way till I got home.

But it was too late.

Not too late so that Misty was dead, but too late because something terrible had happened. Something that I didn't know what it was.

I found Misty seated on the kitchen floor, and in her lap was the little puppy that a few weeks ago Pop had got for free at the pound and gave Misty for a present, but I didn't know why she got a present because it wasn't her birthday, and not Christmas either. The puppy had floppy ears and breath that smelled good when it licked your face, and it was curled up in Misty's lap, and Misty was gently petting it because she loved that puppy.

When Pop gave it to her, she was so excited, and she named it Furball, and Pop laughed and said, Goddamn it, honey, that name sounds like something the fucking cat coughed up.

Misty had asked me to move to the top bunk and let her have the bottom so Furball could sleep with her. Misty wouldn't do anything and wouldn't go anywhere without that little dog.

Right now she was sitting there on the floor with the puppy in her lap and petting it and her eyes staring at the wall in front. Misty wouldn't say nothing. Not even when I talked to her. Not even when I put my arm around her and tried to comfort her. All Misty did was stare at the wall in front.

Misty looked mostly all the same—her nose and her mouth and her ears. But not her eyes. They were still a little bit slanty, like Mom's, but inside they had changed, like as if she got different eyeballs from a different person and it made me scared to see them, and I didn't want to look at Misty's eyes no more.

When it got dark and Mom and Pop still weren't home, I got a blanket and put it over the two of us and over Furball, too, in Misty's lap, and we fell asleep.

In the midnight I woke, and Misty was still beside me. I heard her make a sniff noise like maybe she was crying and then more sniffs and other cry noises, and I thought, Maybe Misty does cry after all, but she waits until the midnight when no one can hear her.

I whispered, Don't cry, Misty. Tell me what's wrong.

Misty whispered back to me, and she said, Miss Elsa had made her help cut a switch.

Did Miss Elsa hit you? I asked.

Misty said, No, she hit Furball and I had to watch, and if I closed my eyes there would be all the more hits.

Why did she do it? I asked, and Misty whispered to me it was because she had told Miss Elsa she was going to tell Pop about that she didn't want no one to take care of her no more—not Miss Elsa, not Miss Veronica, not no one—and because of that Miss Elsa had cut the switch from the tree out back and she had hit Furball.

She hit twenty times and I had to count, Misty told me. Miss Elsa hit twenty times, and she told me, Young lady, you better watch your step or next time something even worse will happen to that puppy of yours.

I whispered, Don't worry, Misty, I'll stay with you tomorrow. I'll protect you. I won't let that lady hurt Furball.

In the morning, Misty was back to like normal. Normal, except that she wouldn't say hardly a thing. Hardly not a word. And her eyes on the inside were different just like the day before.

Pop said Misty was being sullen and insolent, and Mom just shrugged and sighed like, Heaven help us, and then she had to hurry off because Waynesburg Pharmacy was having a sale today and prices had to be changed for all the things that were sale price.

I pretended to go off to Mrs. Euston's class at Waynesburg Elementary, but when I heard the bus coming, I hid behind the bushes like the wolf in the story book but not with sharp teeth, and the bus went away without me.

When I saw Pop leave the house to head on down to O'Brien's, I quick snuck back inside and spent the day there with Misty to keep her safe.

Miss Elsa tried to catch us but we went in the basement and took Furball with us, and we hid in the dark, and Miss Elsa came looking for us, but she couldn't find us, and I could tell she was scared of being in the dark basement, and I was surprised because I didn't know that grownups were afraid of dark places or of the spook man, but I could tell Miss Elsa was afraid, and she didn't look for us down there very long, but she locked the door and we couldn't get out, but we were glad she did lock us there because it was better to be locked in the dark with the spook man than to be in the house with Miss Elsa. Me and Misty held each other tight and the spook man wasn't in the basement that day, and we were safe together; me and Misty, and Furball.

That night when Pop came home, stinking of Comfort, Miss Elsa told about me being naughty and not going to school. She said I had been playing hooky, but she was lying because I wasn't playing hooky and I didn't even know how to play that game, but I did know the right way to say it, and the name was hockey, not hooky, and you had to have ice to play it, but we didn't have ice, so how could I play the game, and Miss Elsa sure wasn't very smart not to know about that. But I didn't tell Pop because I knew if I did, Miss Elsa would tomorrow take me out back to get a switch from the tree, and I would have to hit Misty with that stick and if I went to school, then Miss Elsa would hit Furball with the sick.

When he heard about the hooky, Pop got in a rage and told me to stop being a sissy about going to school. I was a big boy now, he said, and I damn well better start acting like one. Be brave, Llewellyn, and don't you dare bring disgrace on me or on the name of Trout.

I told him, I'm not a sissy, and I don't care about disgrace or about your name of Trout.

That made Pop angry even more, and he said, You sometimes piss me off, Llewellyn. You royally piss me off, and he hit me so hard one of my teeth chipped and cut the inside of my cheek, so I had to rinse with salt water till the bleeding stopped, but my tooth was chipped and my lips were puffy, and because of it I looked funny in the mirror, and I knew that tomorrow the kids at Waynesburg Elementary would laugh and make fun.

March 20

THE NEXT MORNING Misty didn't say anything, but from how she looked at me I knew she was afraid to be left alone with Miss Elsa, and I thought maybe I should stay home again to be with Misty instead of go to school, but I told her, Sorry, I can't stay home. Pop will hit me again.

But the real reason was that a girl in Mrs. Euston's class and who was by the name of Michelle Morrison and very pretty and very nice, and it was today her birthday and her mother was in the afternoon going to bring cupcakes and popcorn and lemonade for all the class to have a party, and me and everyone else was so excited for that party, and if I stayed home with Misty I would miss out.

When I told Misty I couldn't stay because Pop would hit me, she nodded, but she didn't say nothing. I think she knew there was a different reason than what I had told her. I felt bad because I would be going to school and to a fun party and Misty would be all alone at home with Miss Elsa.

But I went off, anyhow, to Waynesburg Elementary, and when I got there, sure enough I saw that book lying on the floor in Mrs. Euston's library, and the girl on the cover looking scared and the wolf poking his head around the corner from the back cover with sharp teeth, and I knew I had done wrong to leave Misty alone, and when it came time for recess I knew I better sneak away again, and almost I did, but then I heard the girl who was by the name of Michelle Morrison, and she was telling one of her friends that there was going to be birthday favors for everyone in the class, and it was something very special but she wasn't allowed to tell anyone what it was, but then she whispered in her friend's ear and I knew she was telling anyhow, and I thought, Maybe Misty will be okay, and Furball, too, until I go home at the regular time and on the bus.

So I stayed, and when afternoon came, sure enough, Michelle's mother brought in cupcakes and lemonade—but not any popcorn because on second thought maybe that would leave too much of a mess for the poor custodian, and we wouldn't want to do that, now, would we, children?

Nicely wrapped in birthday paper there was for everyone in the class a small present, and we couldn't open it until the end of the party, and we had to all open at the same time.

All the girls got princess treasure boxes with plastic locks that really lock and you better not lose the plastic key or your treasure will be stuck inside that box forever unless you break the plastic lock, and that would be a shame, now wouldn't it, children?

Me and all the other boys, we didn't get treasure boxes but, instead, got plastic transformer toys that if you fold the pieces out one way it's a robot and if you fold them another way it's a car.

When school was over, I went on the bus, and the other kids from Mrs. Euston's class were playing with their treasure box or their transformer toy, but not me because I was worried about Misty and why had I stayed at school all day just for a stupid cupcake and a toy I didn't even like.

When I got home it was too late.

Too late for Misty. Too late for Miss Elsa.

I sneaked into the house from the back, where the door didn't squeak like the front, and there was Misty standing in the kitchen with one of Pop's shotguns. She had it tight against her shoulder, and her back was against the wall for support, just like Pop had showed us how to do it so as not to get knocked on your butt from the recoil. The shotgun was a kind that had two barrels, one of them over top the other, and if you pull the trigger twice, it shoots from both barrels but not both at once.

Miss Elsa was kneeling on the floor with her hands folded in front of her like the picture of Jesus in the Bible story book, where he is kneeling and praying to his father which art in heaven hallowed be thy name. Except Miss Elsa wasn't praying but, instead, crying and whimpering.

On the floor over by the garbage bucket was Misty's puppy, and it wasn't moving and it had blood from one eye.

I'm sorry, Misty Baby, Miss Elsa was saying in what Pop would have called a crybaby voice. I swear to Jesus, Baby, I won't never hurt your little puppy ever again. Oh, sweet Jesus I swear I won't hurt it ever again. I'm sorry, Baby. I'm sorry what happened to the poor little thing. And I won't never hurt you, either, Baby. Not you or little Lewie. I'll leave. I'll go away so you won't never have to see me again. I'll go away like Miss Veronica did. Oh, sweet Jesus, please just put down that gun. I promise I won't never hurt your puppy again. Oh, sweet Jesus, I swear I won't.

Miss Elsa sobbed and she whimpered, and she kept swearing to sweet Jesus that she would do anything, anything at all, Baby, anything you ask, but for heaven's sake just put away that terrible gun. Oh, sweet Jesus, just put away that gun.

But Misty wasn't sweet Jesus, and she didn't put away that gun.

She pulled the trigger. Twice she pulled it.

The first time blood splattered everywhere. On the walls, on the cabinets, and on the refrigerator, where there was a picture Misty had drew of her and her puppy, Furball, playing in a park where there was kids on swings and families with picnics and everyone happy.

Miss Elsa looked down at her belly where there was a big red hole and her eyes got wide and scared.

The second time Misty pulled the trigger, Miss Elsa couldn't look down because she didn't have eyes no more and they were gone like most of her forehead. But her mouth was still there, and it was gasping like the blue-gills Pop would catch when he took me fishing out on Lake Pleasant.

And then Misty dropped down the shotgun on the floor, and she turned and looked at me, and asked why hadn't I stayed home with her and helped protect Furball.

And that was the last time Misty ever talked to me. The last time she ever talked to anyone.

Something deep inside Misty had changed, just like her eyes had changed, and it wasn't Misty any more that was in there but somebody else, and it was scary to look at her.

Misty was gone, and the place to where she went was a dark place. I didn't know where that dark place was, but I knew Misty had gone there, and I wanted to bring her back. But I couldn't reach her, and I knew it was my fault because I had gone off to Waynesburg Elementary, all safe in Mrs. Euston's class and with my lunch box with the Hulk, green and busting buttons off his shirt, and the class having a party with a cupcake and a transformer toy.

Yes, I left Misty when she needed me most. I went off and left my little sister alone with the wolf.

I never found out exactly what happened in the house out there on Warner Road that day while I was off having a party at Waynesburg Elementary. Misty never told.

She didn't tell me. She didn't tell anyone.

But I think what made it unbearable for Misty was having to face Miss Elsa all on her own without me being there beside her. Having me beside her is what had given her something to hold onto, and with me gone, the dark current was too strong, and it carried her over to the other side—to the dark side. I was a coward. I had been afraid of Pop, afraid of him hitting me. Afraid that the kids at Waynesburg Elementary would laugh if I had a second chipped tooth and an even more puffy lip. And I was selfish and wanted a cupcake and a toy. I had abandoned my little sister to face the unbearable by herself.

Soon Miss Elsa's mouth stopped moving, and Misty went in the bedroom and sat in a corner, staring into the nothing. I sat down beside her, but it was as if she didn't know I was there. I said to her, Misty, I promise I won't ever again let no one hurt you, but I don't know if she heard me from where she was on the dark side.

March 21

AFTER MISTY SHOT Miss Elsa, Uncle Stew, the cop, he wasn't really our uncle, seeing as he was Pop's second cousin, but we called him Uncle Stew, anyhow, and, being a cop, he tried to fix things up so Misty wouldn't be in too big of trouble. But people from the state came in and said that an in-depth criminal investigation would have to be initiated, though it was most unlikely that charges of any kind would be filed against a minor only just turned five. But, then again, they said, the child obviously would need psychological evaluation.

Those people from the state asked me if I had any information pertaining to the situation with my younger sibling, and I didn't know they were talking about Misty because I didn't know that sibling was how they called her, and I wondered, Don't they know she's my sister? Why do they call her sibling?

But I wouldn't have told them nothing anyhow, seeing as Misty didn't want me to. I knew she didn't from how she looked at me, and her look was scary and from the other side, the dark side, and it made me afraid. But no one else was afraid, I don't know why. Maybe they didn't look in Misty's eyes like I did. I knew Misty wanted all the terrible things that had happened to be our secret and for no one else ever to know, and she wanted that I shouldn't tell, not ever, because of it being shameful and terrible and no one should ever know, and both of us should never tell. And, me, I didn't tell because I was good at keeping secrets, and so was Misty.

So those people from the state said that both of us children would be removed from the home until such time as the situation could be further and more thoroughly investigated.

As for Pop, he would face charges for not securing his firearms so as each and every one of them would be inaccessible to a minor, by which they meant making them so as Misty couldn't have got hold of the over-under shotgun, which is what she shot Miss Elsa with, and I'm glad she did shoot that woman. The policeman, this one wasn't Uncle Stew, said if Pop had secured the guns this unfortunate incident would never have transpired, and Pop was criminally negligent and fully culpable in regard to the death of the deceased, Miss Elsa Hammerstein.

Furthermore, that police officer regretted to inform Pop that he would face charges of possessing illegal firearms, and the aforesaid would be confiscated and Pop would not get them back—not now, not ever. Even the legal guns could not remain in Pop's possession, and because of that, Pop's beloved collection was taken to Uncle Stew's for storage until such time as Pop could determine how best to dispose of them.

For owning illegal firearms and for gross negligence Pop would likely do time in prison. He went to the judge at the court and that's what happened; he got took to the prison for three and a half years, but he could be out in as little as two years, at which time there would be a parole hearing for good behavior.

Misty got took away to a hospital, but I didn't believe it because she wasn't sick, and I told them, Where are you taking her? Let me go along to be with her and keep her safe, but they said, No!

I screamed and told them, Let me go, let me go, let me go! but they held me down on the floor, and I bit one of those men who was holding me down, but Misty never struggled and just let them put her in the green car, and I was biting and fighting, and I did it because I wanted to go with her, but they slapped my face and said it was to break my hysteria, and I thought maybe that's a bone or something, and why are they hitting me to break my bones? but I stopped biting and fighting and was only crying like what Pop would have called crybaby.

They held me down, and I watched them take Misty away.

I was sent away, too, and I lived with people who were nice to me, and they took me to Wonder World Amusement Park, which wasn't maybe quite so big and fancy as Walt Disney World but this park was just as much fun, now, wasn't it, Llewellyn? and I told them, Yes.

But that didn't last long. Mom went before the judge, but it was a different one than Pop and nicer and a lady, and she said that with Pop and his guns gone, the home environment was now safe and healthy for us children. And the judge said it was okay for me and Misty to go home, but there would, none the less, be weekly visits from the Child Protective Service, and Misty would be required to continue her counseling sessions, seeing as the child still refused to say anything about the unfortunate incident with Miss Elsa Hammerstein and still wasn't talking, and no one was quite sure why or fully understood the workings of the child's mind but everyone was confident that in time the poor dear would recover from the trauma.

I knew why it was Misty wasn't talking, and it was because she had been carried away to the dark side. But I didn't tell anyone. That was my secret. Mine and Misty's.

March 22

POP WAS OFF at jail, so there wasn't the expense of Comfort at O'Brien's, and no more buying new guns, so Mom only had to work days at Waynesburg Pharmacy and regretted that she would have to submit her two week resignation at Shemp's Pizza where, anyhow, she got less than minimum and hardly ever more than a few dollars tip, so what the heck.

I still went to Waynesburg Elementary, and Misty was back from the hospital, even though I knew she never was sick in the first place, and Mrs. Euston regretted to inform Mom that I would not be promoted to the second grade, seeing as I had fallen behind due to all the trauma in the home and having been in foster care, poor child.

So me and Misty were both in Mrs. Euston's first grade, but someone had taken home the book with the girl and the wolf hiding and looking around the corner from the back cover and smiling with sharp teeth, but the book hadn't been returned and I couldn't show it to Misty and how much it looked like her in the pictures of the girl.

Mrs. Euston told Mom at a conference how it was frustrating beyond all comprehension to try teaching a child who refused to speak a single word, and Mom reassured Mrs. Euston that Misty was receiving the best possible psychological assistance, and would Mrs. Euston please try to understand that the child had suffered severe psychological trauma. It might take years for her to fully recover, and even then she might be scarred for life.

Mrs. Euston wiped her eyes because she was a little bit crying, and she said she understood how difficult it must be for a girl so young and tender to live with the guilt and nightmares that even a child must suffer after committing murder. But, Mrs. Trout, please understand that your daughter will have to achieve state-mandated educational standards if she desires promotion to the second grade at the end of this school year. And please understand as well, Mrs. Trout, that your daughter must conform to school rules and regulations, just like all the other children.

One day I saw Mrs. Euston scolding Misty, and I told her, You leave my sister alone. And then I said, Misty doesn't have to talk if she doesn't

34

want to, and you better stop sending notes home about her and making her sit on a bench all goddamn recess because it isn't fair.

Mrs. Euston told me, Stop being insolent, young man, and she sent me to Principal Vickers who wasn't my pal even though that's why Mrs. Euston said it was spelled p-a-l and not some other way, and Mr. Vickers told me I would be benched at recess all week for defiance and use of inappropriate language, Have I made myself perfectly clear, young man?

So I sat there on that bench and Misty came and sat beside me, and we watched the kids play four square and tether ball, and they laughed and pointed because we had to sit on the bench and not play, but I was glad because Misty was with me there on the bench, even if she wouldn't say anything.

Everyone, but not me, wanted to force Misty to talk so as she could say things, but I didn't know why you have to talk if you don't want.

Lots of kids at Waynesburg Elementary teased Misty. They called her Miss Mousie because she was quiet as a mouse. I told them, Shut the fuck up you shitholes, and Mrs. Euston screamed and covered her ears, and Principal Vickers sent home a note, but Pop was still off at prison doing good behavior so he could get out in two years for parole, so I didn't get hit because Mom never hit me or Misty, only Pop did, but Mom just shook her head real sad, and she a little bit cried but tried not to let me see and quickly brushed away the tears.

But then the kids at Waynesburg Elementary started calling Misty meaner names and things like gook and chink because she had the kind of eyes like Mom and the kind of skin like her, too. Bobby France called Misty a slant-eyed gook bitch, and I hit his head so hard on the metal bars of the jungle gym that he got stitches and I got suspended from Waynesburg Elementary for a full week and if such an incident of assault should happen to transpire again in the future, well, the family of the injured party would likely press charges, and I would be sent away to juvenile hall, which was like the prison where Pop was except Pop wouldn't be there because it was only for minors, but if I didn't watch it, young man, I was headed for prison just like my Pop.

Those were not happy years for Misty. I was glad Pop wasn't home because he would have scolded her lots of times for being insolent and sullen and he would have hit her when she came home from Waynesburg Elementary with notes about bad behavior and conferences with Principal Vickers, who I didn't like, not one bit. He one time asked me if I could shed any light on my younger sibling's inability to articulate, and this time

I knew what was the meaning of *sibling* but not the meaning of *inability to articulate,* so I just told him, No I can't shed light, because that means, No, I'm not going to tell. Not him. Not anyone. Because I'm good at keeping secrets.

When two years was up, Pop didn't get to come home, so I guess he didn't have good behavior, but he got to come home after three and a half years, and now I was nine years old, and Pop came home for parole, and that meant he had to report in daily, and there were to be no guns at any time in the house or on the premises and all firearms and weapons of any sort were to remain at Uncle Stew's and Pop could not have access to any of the aforesaid.

Also, Pop wasn't allowed to drink Comfort, but he did anyhow.

Mom one time refused to give him money for his Comfort, and that pissed him off, like royally pissed him off, goddamnit, and he hit her, and I told him, Stop hitting her, Pop, so he hit me, too, and told me to mind my own fucking business because my mom was a gook and he should have left her back there in the Nam where she belonged, and if she wouldn't give him money for his booze, he'd just have to get Uncle Stew to sell one of those fine guns to get money so he could buy his own Comfort, and what a disgrace it was when a man had to sell his firearm collection because his wife refused him a few dollars for a bottle of fucking booze.

March 23

IT WAS AUGUST, I know because it was soon to be my birthday, and that's in August, and by now, Pop had been home for a few months from prison, and for my birthday Pop gave me the best present ever—a Weatherby 12-gauge. Maybe Pop wasn't supposed to own guns, now that he was home for parole, but that didn't mean his son couldn't own one, Ain't that right, Llewellyn?

Pop figured that at ten years old a young man should have himself a real gun instead of just a 22, which ain't good for anything much bigger than a squirrel or a gopher; maybe a crow—if you're lucky enough to hit one of those wily little suckers.

Though, that being said, Llewellyn, there's nothing wrong with a 22, and it's a gun any man can be proud to own.

I asked Pop how he got that Weatherby he gave me.

Well, Son, he said. While I was locked up I got to know people. It's sometimes good to have friends in low places.

I didn't much care where he got the gun. I loved that Weatherby. I told Pop, Thanks. You're the best Pop anyone ever had, and that made him smile, and he messed up my hair because that's what he sometimes did when he wanted to show that he liked me.

But Mom just sat there real quiet and didn't say a word.

Four days after my birthday, or maybe five or six, Pop said we were going hunting, just him and me, and we wouldn't be coming back till I had bagged me my first buck. This time Misty couldn't come along. No more guns for that young lady, Pop said.

I took my Weatherby, and Pop took his harpoon gun, which was from the year 1851, and Pop had got it from another one of his friends in low places. That gun was a real harpoon gun from more than a hundred and fifty years ago, and it had been used by harpooners on whaling ships like the Moby Dick, which Pop said was the most famous whaling ship of all time, and he wished he could have been alive back then, so he could sail around the fucking world that they still thought was flat in those days and on a real man's boat like the Moby Dick and not these pansy-ass yachts that they have now days and no one's even allowed to kill a goddamn whale due to the faggots from Green Peace messing with the rights of others.

Being home for parole, Pop wasn't supposed to drive, but, What the hell, Llewellyn we're going to take the Chevy, anyhow. We loaded our guns in the back, and we took a blanket, too, because we could throw it over the two bottles of Comfort on the seat.

Just in case some cop pulls us over for some minor infraction, Pop said, though he didn't figure that was likely to happen, but you can't be too careful now days. Besides, if he got pulled over, Pop was going to be in deep shit anyhow, so what the hell.

Pop sure did laugh that it wasn't even hunting season and here we were going out to shoot us a buck. Hell, we didn't even have a hunting permit because, How can you go requesting a hunting permit when you're on parole and not even allowed to have a firearm in your possession?

We got to where we were going, and Pop pulled off the highway and started driving into the woods. The Chevy wasn't exactly 4X4, but Pop said it could damn well handle the rough terrain better than any goddamn piece of Jap crap.

It was lucky we got where we were going because Pop had been drinking his Comfort, and he had been driving not so good.

Once we were a long way off the highway, we got out of the Chevy and got our guns, me my Weatherby and Pop his harpoon. Pop got out the second bottle of Comfort and he let me taste it because he figured if you're old enough to bag yourself a buck, you're damn well old enough to have your first slug of Comfort. But of course it wasn't my first slug because I had snuck a slug from Pop's bottles more than once or twice, but I hated the taste, and I didn't know how anyone could want to drink something like that.

Before you know it, we saw a buck.

Goddamn, Llewellyn, is this your lucky day or what!

I said, Pop, shush, and he quieted down and whispered, Yeah, I guess we better keep our voices down so as not to scare off that magnificent animal.

And believe it or not, I brought the buck down with the first slug I fired from my Weatherby.

Is that luck, Llewellyn, or is that luck! Pop said.

At first I thought I had missed because in The *Deer Hunter* movie, which was one of Pop's favorites, the deer pretty much just falls down dead, but this here buck instead ran off faster than shit. But it didn't go far, and Pop let out a whoop and we ran to where it was lying there, dead on the ground, and you couldn't even see a hole where the bullet went in, but Pop said it was a shotgun slug not a bullet, and I ought to use the correct nomenclature if I was going to be owning a firearm, and if we turned the buck over we'd sure as hell see a hole, but goddamn, wasn't this a magnificent animal. A ten pointer. We counted them. Not bad, Pop said. Not bad for a boy's first buck. Nothing to be ashamed of, a ten pointer.

We had to leave the buck there on the ground because Pop suddenly realized we would for sure attract the attention of the cops if we went driving home with a buck strapped to the top of the car when here it wasn't even hunting season.

Besides, we had more hunting to do because Pop wanted to bag himself a bear.

I told him he meant a buck, not a bear, because there weren't any bears in these parts, were there?

Pop said sure there were if you looked hard enough. So let's go and try our luck, Son. Goddamn, wouldn't it be a kick in the ass if I bagged myself a bear, Pop said, laughing away about it. He would sure as hell send it over to Slim's Taxidermy in Barkerville, and wouldn't the guys at O'Brien's be jealous as hell when they heard that Pop had bagged his self a bear, and they would come over and see it stuffed in our living room.

A bear, mind you, Llewellyn, a real fucking bear, what a kick in the ass that would be.

Pop wasn't talking so good and not walking so good, either, on account of all the Comfort he had drunk, but we went a long ways and we still hadn't seen any bears, but then we heard a noise in the brush and Pop whispered, That sure as hell wasn't a buck, Llewellyn.

And, like Pop had told me when we were driving here, he had just one shot. Not a shot of Comfort, he didn't mean, but just one single shot with his gun. Just like Davy Crockett, Pop said. When you know you got just one shot, you know you better make it count.

And I tried to stop him in time because I could see it wasn't a bear, but it was too late, and Pop was a good shot even when he was wasted on Comfort and with only one arm. And the man he shot didn't even make a sound or run off like the buck. His knees crumpled and he fell on the ground.

Oh, fucking Jesus, Pop said when we got to the guy who was on the ground, squirming and making gurgle noises.

I told Pop, We better go for help, but he said, Hell no, we ain't going for help. Goddamn it, Llewellyn, I'm on parole. Do you know the kind of shit I'd be in? A parolee out shooting weapons he ain't supposed to have, and hunting without a license, and drunk as a skunk, no less. Jesus, Son, they'll lock me up for years. Probably put me in the chair if this poor cocksucker dies.

And he did die, the poor cocksucker did. He stopped trying to get up, and he just lay there on the ground deader than shit.

We looked around a bit and Pop said it was obvious the poor son of a bitch was just some homeless scumbag. There was some kind of a shack where he lived. Actually you would probably call it more just a shelter and not even a shack, seeing as it was made with branches and a couple cardboard boxes with a green tarp over top, and how the hell did someone get cardboard boxes way out here in the woods, anyhow? Pop wondered.

Inside that shelter, there was a blanket and old coat that the guy obviously used for a pillow when he wasn't wearing it because if you weren't cold enough to need a coat, you might as well use it as a pillow, Pop supposed.

We left the deer lying there, and the dead man, too. We didn't even try sinking his body in a lake or digging a shallow grave like in the movies.

But first Pop took out the whale harpoon from the man's back and wiped off the blood. And then we drove home. We didn't talk much on the way. Didn't talk hardly a word.

This is our secret, Llewellyn, Pop said, one of the few times he talked. You understand that, don't you, Son? You understand that I would go back to prison for a long, long time and maybe even get the chair. And what good would that do, anyhow? It wouldn't bring that poor cocksucker back to life, now would it, Son? Wouldn't help anyone a goddamn bit. What happened out there in the woods was unfortunate, but it was an honest mistake—an accident—and no use crying over spilled milk. I think it's best, Llewellyn, if we just keep this matter a secret between you and me.

I nodded, and I told him, I'm good at keeping secrets, Pop. Real good.

The next day when Pop had sobered up, he got in the car and drove off again. He didn't say a word about where, but he didn't have to. I knew he was going back to where he shot the old homeless scumbag. Pop knew it wasn't smart that we had just left the body lying there. He never said what he did with the body, and I never asked. That's part of keeping a secret. You just pretend it didn't happen.

March 24

AFTER THAT HUNTING trip, Pop began drinking even more. All day he sat there in the living room, staring at the TV, drinking his Comfort and yelling and cussing at the goddamn queers on the soap operas.

When Mom got back from Waynesburg Pharmacy in the evenings, she most times brought burgers and fries. One bag for Pop and one for the rest of us. Me and Misty and Mom would sit in the bedroom and eat our supper, and Mom would lock the door because Pop sometimes flew into a rage at being served goddamn takeout burgers and fries, and he one time hit Mom and dragged her by her hair into the kitchen and told her to fix him a real fucking supper or else he'd kick her gook ass all the way back to the Nam where she belonged in the first place.

And then one night the shit really hit the fan.

All day Pop had been drinking and working on a Colt he got from some idiot who had royally fucked it up by working on the trigger mechanism to lighten the action.

Which isn't a bad thing if you know what you're doing, Son, Pop told me as he sat working on the gun.

But the dumbfuck who had done this alteration went and screwed things up so bad you could barely touch the trigger without discharging the firearm. Hell, you were likely to blow your balls clean off if you were stupid enough to carry a gun like this tucked in your belt.

You remember that, Son, Pop said. Never go sticking a gun in the front of your pants unless you want to blow your goddamn balls clean off.

It was on account of the gun being so fucked up that Pop had got it real cheap, and all he needed to do was fix the trigger and the gun would be good as new.

You just wait and see, Llewellyn, this cocksucker'll be good as new.

But when Pop got the gun all back together, the trigger still wasn't working any better than before, and Pop said, Holy fucking shit, because the gun went off and would have blown a hole in the dining room wall if it hadn't been that Pop had taken the bullets out and laid them on the dining room table, where he had been working on the gun.

When Mom came home from Waynesburg Pharmacy that evening, she had the usual two bags of burgers and fries. One bag with Pop's food. The other one for the rest of us to eat in the bedroom.

We were there in the bedroom eating, when we heard a crash noise out in the living room and then we heard someone slamming against the bedroom door, and I guess the lock on that door wasn't very strong because Pop had no problem breaking it open. We all knew something had gone wrong. Even more wrong than usual. Pop was like one of those demon guys that are on the movies they show at Halloween except that his eyes didn't turn yellow and glow. But there was something different in his eyes that night for damn sure. You could see it there. At the time, I didn't know what true rage was, but I do now, and rage is what was in Pop's eyes that night.

What's this? Pop screamed, holding three paper things in Mom's face, but Mom didn't answer.

Well, I'll tell you, you goddamn gook slut. Tickets is what they are. Fucking Greyhound tickets. Waynesburg to Chicago. One adult. Two kids. Is that where you were planning to run off to, you little gook bitch? Chicago? Run off to Chicago and take my kids from me? Is that what you had planned?

And then he hit Mom. My god he hit her hard. Much harder than usual. Her head kind of snapped and her nose split right open and blood poured out all over. And then Pop hit her again and Mom fell to her knees but was trying to get back up.

And when Misty ran over to protect Mom, Pop hit her, too, and called her a little chicken shit and told her to get the hell out of his way so he could finish off that gook slut that was planning to run off and leave him.

But Misty didn't budge. If Pop was going to get to Mom, he was going to have to go through Misty first.

And I wasn't going to let him hurt either one of them. Finally I was going to stand up to that goddamn son of a bitch that was my Pop. Sort of like Misty, all that time ago when she was pushed to her breaking point, I just snapped.

Stop! I screamed. Stop! And I ran to the dining room table where Pop's fucked up Colt was lying with the bullets beside it, and I put a bullet in the cylinder. Then another one. My hands were so shaky I could hardly do it.

42

Mom was back on her feet now, and she was hugging Misty in her arms, trying to protect her from Pop. And Misty was hugging Mom, trying to protect her, too. Pop just kept on hitting them both. Over and over and over, hitting them, and neither Mom or Misty making a noise, just standing there, holding each other.

Stop, I screamed. And I had never screamed so loud. Not even when I was scream-counting when Miss Elsa was hitting Misty with that switch that I had helped her choose.

Stop! Stop! Stop!

And Pop did. He turned and when he saw the gun in my hand he laughed. You're a fucking fool, Llewellyn. You don't got the balls to kill your own Pop. Put that fucking gun down before you go and hurt someone. But I didn't put it down. Instead, I cocked the hammer.

Pop hit Mom again, and then hit Misty, too, and I could tell it was a challenge. I think he somehow knew I had promised Misty I would never let anyone hurt her, not ever. But Pop didn't think I had the balls to carry through, and he was challenging me. Daring me. Forcing me beyond the snapping point. He wanted me to shoot. I knew he did. I knew he wanted me to pull the fucking trigger and kill his sorry ass—put an end to his pathetic life.

I did pull the trigger, but it was on accident, seeing as the gun's action was all fucked up.

And it wasn't Pop that fell. It was Mom.

Mom and Misty, too, still hugged tight in each other's arms. But arms don't stop bullets. And Misty's head didn't stop the bullet, either, and it went right on through and into Mom's chest.

I turned away. I couldn't look. I screamed. My god, how I screamed. No! No! No! No! Over and over. Over and over. No! No! No! No!

And then Pop came to me, and you know what he did?

He put his arm around me and held me close. Pop smelled good. Like Comfort, but right now Comfort smelled good because Pop was holding me.

I stopped screaming and now I was sobbing. Pop just stood there holding me. And when I calmed down, he sat with me on the bed. I wanted to help Mom and Misty, but Pop said it was too late. They were in a better place, he told me.

I killed them, didn't I?

Pop said, You listen to me, Llewellyn. I want you never to tell anyone what happened here tonight. It's not your fault and you shouldn't take the blame. It's your secret, Llewellyn. No one ever needs to know. Will you promise me?

He took my head and turned it so I was looking at him through my tears.

Look at me Llewellyn. Look me in the eye and promise you'll never tell.

I nodded my head, yes.

Then Pop took me on his lap and held me close. His body was so warm and comforting. So strong and reassuring.

Pop said he had things to tell me. Things he hadn't ever talked about to anyone. Things I had to promise I would keep secret. Things I could never tell to anyone, not ever. Promise on your honor, Llewellyn. Promise you'll never tell a soul.

Pop said it wasn't true about him losing his arm while saving another Marine's life over in the Nam back in '69.

No, Son, over there your Pop fragged an officer of the United States Marine Corps.

I asked what does that mean, fragged? and Pop said it meant that he had killed the officer. Threw a cocksucking hand grenade and killed the son of a bitch.

The officer deserved it. The man had done such terrible things to the people living in the villages. Mom was one of them. The officer was going to do terrible things to her, and it was Pop who had saved her. But Pop had taken a piece of shrapnel from that same grenade that killed the officer and that's how he lost his arm. That grenade took an officer's life. Pop said. And it took my arm as well. But it saved your mom, Llewellyn. It saved your mom, and I brought her home with me to be my wife.

I had questions, but Pop told me I already knew all I really needed to. Of course, the fact was, I didn't really need to know any of it. But Pop needed to tell me. Knowing what he was about to do, Pop must have felt a need to confess his sins. I guess even a Baptist feels that need at such times. And no preacher or priest being present, I had to serve as Pop's confessor.

I didn't really understand what was meant by all of it, but I knew I had promised my Pop that I would keep it my secret and not tell anyone, not forever on my honor.

Then Pop put his arm around me again. He pushed back my hair and kissed my forehead. There were tears in his eyes, too. The first and last time I ever saw tears in my Pop's eyes.

Then Pop smiled at me, and that smile was like the smile of Jesus in my book, *Bible Stories for Young Children,* where he's standing in the River Jordan, raising his two arms up to the sky, but, of course, Pop didn't have two arms to raise because he had left one of them over in the Nam back in '69. The arm he did have was just hanging limp at his side. The smile on Pop's face went away, and he stood there in the bedroom, his eyes closed, his head bowed, his voice just a whisper as he prayed to his father which art in heaven hallowed be thy name; and when he finished, Pop stooped and picked up the Colt revolver I had dropped on the floor.

He walked to where Mom and Misty were crumpled up in each other's bloody arms. Then he put the barrel of that Colt into his mouth and blew the back off his head. He fell over the two bodies crumpled there on the floor, an arm stretched out on one side, a stub on the other like the Bible story picture of Jesus on the cross, but Jesus had two arms and only little trickles of blood from thorns whereas Pop had a hole in his head and blood and bone pieces and other stuff stuck in his hair. He lay there over Misty and Mom like he was protecting them. But it was too late for protecting.

The *Waynesburg Gazette* reported pretty much exactly what I'm sure Pop had in mind.

> It was a murder suicide . . . not unusual in a larger metropolis, but something seldom seen in a small town like Waynesburg . . . a tragic incident in a family that had already witnessed more than its share of tragedy . . . the end of a once-honorable man who was broken in body and in spirit by a war in a far-off place that he both loved and hated. A place he called the Nam.

That's right. My Pop gave his life to protect me. Took the blame for me so that no one would ever know it was me that had killed Mom and Misty. I'll never know exactly what went on in his alcohol-befuddled mind that night when he showed me the greatest tenderness he had shown me in my entire life. But I knew that night that he loved me and that what had happened there with Mom and Misty lying dead on the floor was his fault, not mine. He couldn't change what had been done, but he could take the blame so I wouldn't have to. The cops were fooled. The *Waynesburg Gazette* was fooled. But not me. I knew the truth. But I wasn't going to tell. I had promised Pop. And I can keep a secret real good.

March 25

COMPARED TO MY earlier childhood, the next few years were pretty much uneventful. I was for a short while at two different foster homes, and then the state people sent me back to live with Uncle Stew, the cop. I didn't know at first why Uncle Stew took me in, seeing as it was obvious he didn't like me much, but later on I learned that he got money each month from the state foster care agency. I also found out Mom had had some life insurance through her job at Waynesburg Pharmacy, and, in her will, she had said that whoever took care of her children should get that money, and since it was only me and no Misty, Uncle Stew got the whole amount.

Uncle Stew had an old Winnebago motorhome out back of his and Aunt Marge's house. Its engine was broke, or maybe it was the transmission, I don't remember which, but the inside was in okay shape, and that Winnebago is where I lived until I graduated from high school.

Uncle Stew and Aunt Marge never actually said so, but I could tell neither of them really wanted me living with them. I guess Uncle Stew knew too much of what had gone on at the house out on Warner Road, and I suppose Aunt Marge's imagination suspected most of the rest. I guess they both thought they had good reason to be a bit nervous having me around.

I suppose that's why I wasn't allowed to keep either of the guns Pop had given me. Not the bolt action 22 and most definitely not the Weatherby 12-gauge. Not that Uncle Stew thought I would use either of the aforesaid firearms in the perpetration of any criminal activity, but, well, being an officer of the law as he was, it was his responsibility and duty to take all requisite precautions.

The guns would still be mine, yes, even the Weatherby, but they would be at all times locked up in one of Uncle Stew's gun safes. That satisfied me at the time, but I should have been smart enough to know that Uncle Stew lusted after that Weatherby and, in spite of what I was told, that gun had for all practical purposes been stolen from me by that fine upstanding officer of the law, Chief of Police, Stewart Crawford. I despised the man, but it's just as well he did what he did. It's better for a person like me not to own a gun. I guess I'm just a bit too much like my Pop.

Among the few other things I got to keep from Mom and Pop's possessions was a shoe box of photographs, and I took one of the negatives from it to Waynesburg Pharmacy, and the lady there sent it off for me to get a poster-sized enlargement made, full color, glossy, and suitable for framing, only $29.98 and worth every penny. Yes, definitely worth every penny, and it would be returned via Parcel Post in a sturdy cardboard tube that would protect it during transit through the United States Postal Service, and, by the way, would I like to pay a small surcharge to insure that the beautiful glossy poster would not be damaged in transit?

Of course I paid the extra. I wanted that poster to be delivered without a wrinkle. It was a picture of Pop back in '67 before he went off to the Nam. Back when he had both a left arm and a right.

When, finally, the poster arrived, I hung it on the wall above my bed. And beside it I hung Pop's Purple Heart medal, which I put in a frame I got at Waynesburg Pharmacy. Of the few things I inherited, that Purple Heart was what I valued most.

During those days—those years—I was left pretty much alone out there in the Winnebago. Aunt Marge assured me I was welcome to sit at table and eat meals inside with her and Uncle Stew, but I need not feel any pressure to do so.

I ended up eating most of my meals by myself out in the Winnebago. Sharing meals with folks when you know you're not welcome just isn't much fun. In fact, before long, Aunt Marge began buying me frozen meals. I kept them in the little fridge that was built in below the sink, and I nuked them in the microwave oven that took up most of what little counter space there was. I wasn't allowed to cook anything on the propane stove.

Absolutely not, Uncle Stew told me. There'll be no propane appliances used in that mobile residence. It's for you own safety.

Because of that, winters were kind of cold out in the Winnebago. I saved my money and bought a small electric heater, but it blew a fuse, and Aunt Marge said, what on earth was I thinking, pulling a stunt like that, and I was lucky I hadn't started a fire or electrocuted myself, for goodness sake.

But, fortunately, there was a big enough fuse for the computer Uncle Stew gave me. I suspect he didn't give it to me out of the goodness of his heart but more so that I would keep myself occupied out in the motorhome instead of spending my evenings inside with him and Aunt Marge, watching shows on the big flatscreen television they had just bought—probably with Mom's insurance money. That computer was how I spent most of my free time. If you don't have many friends, a computer can do a pretty good job of providing company.

And, of course there was school, which I didn't much like but actually did pretty well at in terms of grades, except that I didn't do so good when it came to writing, which you can no doubt tell if you're reading this.

Anyhow, I got by with better than passing grades, even if not always by very much, and I stayed mostly out of trouble.

I think it was back in sixth grade at Waynesburg Middle School that I first went to the Marine recruiting office, and the NCO there smiled and gave me a brochure. In fact, he gave me a whole packet of brochures, and he told me to come back after I got my sheepskin, and I said to him, What do you mean, sheepskin?

He just smiled all friendly and told me to stay in school and come back again during my senior year.

Uncle Stew allowed me to get a phone line installed to the Winnebago so I could get internet access, though, as he told me, I would have to pay for the initial installation and the monthly fees as stipulated by the telephone company and the internet service provider.

I guess I was what you would pretty much call a loner back in those days. I had friends, but not many. People stayed out of my way, and that was fine by me. Folks had read the articles in the *Waynesburg Gazette* about the tragic events that transpired at 1828 Warner Road, and, of course, they had heard the Waynesburg gossip—most of it started by Aunt Marge, and, well, I think a lot of folks were just a bit afraid of me.

I remember when that Columbine thing happened, Mrs. Harrison, my sixth grade teacher, told us to write a report about the event. Everyone else's report was about how terrible those boys were to do such a thing—Eric Harris and Dylan Klebold. Mrs. Harrison made us read our reports aloud to the class. Some of the girls started crying as they read what they had written.

But my report was different. I wrote about how it wasn't a good thing what Eric Harris and Dylan Klebold had done, but maybe they had been pushed beyond their breaking point, and maybe some of the kids at the school had deserved to get killed.

Well, Mrs. Harrison wouldn't even let me finish reading my report to the class. Llewellyn Trout, she yelled, You should be ashamed of yourself. You leave my class this instant and report to the principal's office.

Well, I got my ass pretty much chewed out by the principal who was so pissed his face got pink, and spit came flying out of his mouth as he yelled and shook a finger in my face. Then he sent me across the hall to speak to Mrs. Cox, the school counselor, and she asked if I was experiencing any social difficulties or had any feelings of hostility.

By this time I was really pissed because of having been yelled at, when all I had done was write a report I had been assigned, so I made some smartass comment about how I sometimes felt ostracized and isolated. It was a phrase I had heard one of those talk show people mention while discussing the whole Columbine thing. I said it just to irritate Mrs. Cox.

Mrs. Cox didn't know I was just being a smartass kid, so she looked at me kind of strange and told me I was always welcome to visit her office. Any time of the day, she said. She told me I was welcome to just get up and walk out of class any time and come down and see her. No need to get a hall pass or anything.

That evening Mrs. Cox visited Uncle Stew, and I overheard the two of them talking. Uncle Stew assured the counselor that he was quite competent to keep his foster child under surveillance and, yes, Mrs. Cox could rest assured Uncle Stew would certainly do his utmost to insure that all firearms were kept secure and inaccessible at all times.

Mrs. Cox could also rest assured that Uncle Stew would initiate a clandestine investigation of the Winnebago mobile residence out back, which, though currently inoperable did most certainly provided a comfortable and adequate living quarters, and, yes, he would most assuredly search it for contraband or anything of a suspicious or incriminating nature. Moreover, he would investigate the boy's computer hard drive to verify that the young fellow had not been perusing any websites pertaining to the construction of pyrotechnic or incendiary devices.

And for goodness sake, let's also hope he hasn't been learning how to make bombs, Mrs. Cox added.

So being a smartass kid and knowing Uncle Stew was going to investigate my computer, I went and downloaded a bunch of raunchy porn into a folder right smack dab in the middle of my computer screen, where even someone as ignorant as my Uncle Stew couldn't help but find it.

The next day after school, Uncle Stew called me in to his den and asked me to have a seat in the genuine leather recliner. He told me he understood that it was natural for a young male my age to be interested in members of the opposite gender, but that he was, none the less, greatly disappointed in me, and what concerned him most was the fact that some of the photographs on my computer were of other members of the male gender, and he regretted also that he would have to rescind my internet access privileges for a month, but that if ever I had questions regarding gender or reproduction, I should not feel hesitant to seek his advice and counsel, and I could feel secure to confide in him. But I knew that he was feeding me bullshit, because if what he was saying was true, he would never have been searching the Winnebago or my computer in the first place.

Fuck Uncle Stew. Especially for rescinding my internet privileges for a month. Why couldn't he just say he would be taking away my modem for a month? He always talked like a fucking cop.

I think I got some sort of what you might called a perverse pleasure out of the way most of the teachers and some of the kids, and even Uncle Stew and Aunt Marge, over the next few months after Columbine, weren't sure if they should treat me extra nice or just plain avoid me.

I guess nobody wanted to be on my shitlist if ever I went over the edge. Fuck them all. What did they know? I had already been at the edge. I had been there, but I hadn't gone over. Pop had seen to that. He, himself, had pushed me to the edge, but then he pulled me back, just in time. Luckily, I wasn't like Misty: I never got dragged over to the dark side. Almost, I did, but with Pop's help I kept my grip, and the current was strong, but it couldn't take me. Not while Pop held me on his lap that evening there in our house out on Warner Road.

Pop had held me, and that had kept me from being swept away. I didn't even have to hang on by the fingernails trying not to get pulled over to the dark side because I had Pop to hold onto me, and he was stronger than the current.

March 26

WAYNESBURG WAS A small town, but in spite of that, I had hardly ever seen Miss Veronica since that day I bit off her nipple and then Misty scared her away with that gun of Pop's. Occasionally I would see her out and about in town, but she would always cross the street or do whatever she could to avoid me.

But when I started at Waynesburg High, I saw Miss Veronica pretty much every day because she worked in the cafeteria and was the person who gave out the food that everyone complained about but I didn't think was all that bad. She didn't go by the name of Miss Veronica any more, but by Miss Esteban, instead, and she would always look away when I came with my tray, and she always tried to avoid me.

I estimated that she was in her late twenties, and that meant she must have been only a teenager back in the days when her and Miss Elsa would torment me and little Misty. It was strange to think about it now, but back when I was a kid just five years old, someone who was seventeen or eighteen seemed just as much an adult as someone who was thirty.

I knew Miss Veronica was terrified of me. Terrified that I would tell someone what had happened all those years ago in that house out on Warner Road. And I think she realized that I was just as terrified of her.

What if she told what happened? What if kids at school found out about me getting squeaky clean in the bathtub, naked with Miss Elsa, and playing the tickle game. How they all would laugh. What if they found out about me hiding naked under the bed and being chased around the house like a terrified little monkey, peeing because I was so afraid, but not peeing in my pants because I was naked and so was Misty, but I was the one who was leaving the trail of wet spots on the linoleum and the couch and the hardwood floor.

It would have been bad enough if the kids at school knew about those things, but it would have been so much worse if they knew about the things I had done to little Misty. The switch stick I helped choose and the scream counting, or when I hit her ten times because if I didn't Miss Elsa would have done it, and in that case it would have been fifteen hits. And, oh, the shameful, terrible things I did to little Misty as Miss Veronica and Miss Elsa sat watching. You see, it wasn't just for my own sake that I wanted things to be kept secret; it was for Misty's sake, too, because even if she wasn't here anymore, I still had to protect her, and because of that, no one could know any of the things that had happened. Not ever.

So Miss Veronica's secret was safe with me, you can be sure of that. It was kind of like the Cold War, which we were learning about in Mr. Frankfurt's history class, but in this case, it was me and Miss Veronica that had the nuclear weapons. We each knew we could destroy the other, but we also knew that if we did, we would also destroy ourselves. Stalemate is what Mr. Frankfurt called it. Nuclear stalemate. I figured that's what was going on between me and Miss Veronica Esteban: nuclear stalemate.

One day I stayed after school, and I was sitting in the cafeteria, and I thought I was all alone, but then, suddenly, I was aware of Miss Veronica standing there, staring at me, and I was afraid. Almost like I was a little kid again and Miss Veronica was about to sit on my lap and smother me with an enormous breast, and I would struggle to breathe, but I wouldn't be able to, and I would bite down. And there would be blood. So much blood. And something soft and rubbery in my mouth.

It all came back to me, and I was terrified. I felt fear and nausea, and never before had I felt those two things at the same time. Fear and nausea don't often mix, but when they do it's not much fun.

I just sat there, looking up at that woman, unable to move, unable to say a word, and I think I almost fainted, but I wasn't sure, because I had never fainted before, so I didn't know what it was like to faint, but I knew that for a while I lost my vision and everything went dark, and I imagined I was being dragged over to the dark side just like little Misty, and maybe I would see her there. And none of that makes sense now while I'm telling about it, but it sure did at that time, back there sitting in the cafeteria with Miss Veronica staring at me.

She sat down on the bench next to me, and I was trying so hard to bring myself back from the darkness and not be swept away in the current, and I heard Miss Veronica's voice and she said, Llewellyn, I'm sorry.

And as I swam against the darkness I could see her sitting there beside me, and there were tears in her eyes, and she put out a hand and gently placed it on mine, but I pulled away, terrified.

I'm sorry, she whispered. I don't blame you, Llewellyn, but please believe me, I would do anything to change the past. Anything.

She told me that she knew I would never be able to understand. How could I, after all, when she, herself, could hardly understand. But she had been just a teenager, back then. That was not an excuse, of course, she knew that. No, no, no, not an excuse at all, Llewellyn. Her tears were flowing freely, now, and Miss Veronica was wiping her nose on the sleeve of her black Oakland Raiders sweatshirt, and it left silvery slime trails like a slug.

I was ugly, Llewellyn, Miss Veronica said. Ugly and fat. Just like I am now. But when a girl's seventeen, she doesn't feel just ugly, she feels hideous. She doesn't feel just fat, Llewellyn, she feels like a blubbery walrus. Everyone taunts you when you're fat, and what they say to your face hurts enough, but what's so much worse is the things you hear them say when they think you're not listening.

And all the while, all I wanted was a friend. Just one girl who would be my friend, that's all I wanted, Llewellyn. A friend I could share with. It wouldn't matter if she wasn't one of the popular girls. It would be okay if she was ugly. Okay if she was fat. Because if the kids taunted us, the two of us would still have each other, and with each other we could make it through anything. And, oh, if only a boy would have maybe just looked my way with a smile or a good morning, even if it was only when there was no one else around to tease him because he had smiled and said good morning to the fat ugly chick. Oh, Llewellyn, that smile and that good morning would have been enough to carry me through a whole year.

But, I didn't have a friend, Llewellyn. Not one single friend, and there was never a smile, never a good morning. Not until one day at the library, where I was sitting alone because, even though it was the best table in the whole place, everyone went somewhere else when I came and sat down because they didn't want to be at the same table as the fat ugly chick. But that day a woman sat down beside me and smiled, and she invited me to go with her for a burger and a malt at Flo's Diner. And I went with her, Llewellyn, and she told me her name was Elsa—Miss Elsa, she called herself—and she had noticed I didn't seem to have many friends, but, none the less, she liked me, and she wanted to be my friend. She said I was pretty, and she put an arm around me and made me feel I was loved.

By now Miss Veronica was crying so hard she could hardly talk, and her voice came out in gaspy sobs so that it was hard to understand her words.

That woman did something to me, Llewellyn, and I don't know what it was or how she did it, but she made me just as hideous on the inside as I was on the outside. No, not just as hideous, she made me even more hideous on the inside. And I let her do it, but it was only because I wanted a friend, can you understand that, Llewellyn? I only wanted a friend, and Miss Elsa was that friend to me. The only friend I ever had. Can you understand, Llewellyn? Can you understand and forgive me?

I sat there, trying not to be swept over to the dark side. I stared at Miss Veronica, not feeling sorry for her but feeling only fear and nausea, and it was almost like staring into the face of the spook man, and I felt like I was going to lose my struggle against the dark current.

Please, Llewellyn, Miss Veronica whispered through her sobs, Will you please forgive me?

All I could think of was little Misty and the things Miss Veronica had done to her. And so I said to Miss Veronica, No, never. I will never forgive you.

Without another word, Miss Veronica got up and kissed me gently on the top of my head, and I could feel the warmth from her breath, and one of her tears fell onto my head and trickled through my hair, and I felt its wetness on my scalp, and it made me shudder like it was slime from a monster. And then Miss Veronica turned and walked out of the cafeteria.

The next day Miss Veronica was not at the serving line, and the day after that, the whole school was buzzing with what one of the teachers called a morbidly electric excitement because one of the staff bathrooms had been locked and no one would answer from the inside, so they broke open the door, and there, sitting on the toilet, was Miss Veronica, and she had slashed her wrists and was dead, and Betty Crenshaw, who saw when they carried her out, said it took three men to lift her because she was so fat, and her wrists and clothes were all stained brown from dried blood, but her face was gray like dirty sheets.

Of course, it was all over the front page of the *Waynesburg Gazette*—bold headlines and a picture of *Veronica Esteban, High School Cafeteria Worker, Deceased at Age 26,* and the picture made her look not so fat and not so ugly. And on the evening news there was an interview with Police Chief Stewart Crawford, who had investigated the incident, and who said the matter was most unfortunate but, then again, suicide was not uncommon amongst members of the female gender who were experiencing severe mental anxiety.

When I read the article and saw the picture, I remembered Miss Veronica sitting there beside me in the cafeteria, and this time I didn't feel any fear or nausea, but only sadness, and I felt sorry for her, and I wished I had not told her I would never forgive her.

I went to her funeral at St. Joseph's, but there was hardly anyone there, and her mom sat in the front row, sobbing and moaning. I just wanted it to be over quick because I knew Miss Veronica would still be alive if it wasn't for me, and if only I had told her, Yes, I forgive you, she wouldn't have killed herself. Thinking about it made me feel sick to my stomach and I was glad when the funeral was over and I was able to get out of that church. It's not much fun knowing that what you did caused a person to commit suicide.

But the stir and commotion at Waynesburg High over Miss Esteban's suicide was nothing compared to what happened a year and a half or so later, and I wish I had never had any part in the affair.

March 27

I WAS A junior at Waynesburg High, and Mr. Drummond was a new teacher at the school that year. He had just graduated from college, and this was his first teaching job. He was in charge of the computer lab and taught most of his classes there.

He also taught an art appreciation class where we learned about Dali and other artists who painted kind of crazy pictures. I liked it so much I bought acrylics and a canvas, but my painting turned out like crap.

Anyhow, Mr. Drummond turned out to be the nicest teacher I ever knew. Right from day one, kids started calling him Mr. D, and he didn't seem to mind. At first most people didn't like him much, but before long everyone did, the kids and the teachers, too. Mr. D looked and dressed a bit like a nerd, even with nerd glasses, and believe it or not, sometimes a bowtie, even though I think he did that as a joke, but he would look hurt and offended if you teased him when he wore it, so you couldn't quite be sure.

Mr. D liked doing Elvis impersonations. I had never really known much of anything about Elvis Presley, but I checked him out online, and I rented the movie *Girl Happy* and I found it really was amazing how much Mr. D sounded just like Elvis.

Then on Halloween, Mr. D arrived at school dressed up to look like Elvis. Well, Mr. D might have sounded a lot like Elvis, but he didn't look much like him. But he sure did try, with fake sideburns and a white suit with sequins and fake jewels, and a snarl on his lips.

Today you don't call me Mr. D, he said to us. Today you call me Mr. E. Or The King, if you prefer.

He thought it was a funny joke, but most of us were laughing at him more than with him. He didn't seem to mind, though, and I think he was kind of laughing at himself, too.

And then on the night of the school's Christmas dance, the tide really turned for Mr. D. And it turned in ways no one could even have imagined.

And it wasn't all good, but we didn't know it at the time.

March 28

I DIDN'T USUALLY go to school dances, but this time I was hoping that a girl named Jennifer Olander would be there. She was a pretty girl, and I would lots of times lie awake at night and have lustful thoughts about her. I was hoping that maybe she would say yes to dancing with me, but she was with a guy named Randy Bois and I thought, What the hell, there are plenty of other girls just as pretty as you are, Jennifer Olander. Plenty of them even more pretty.

And one of those even-more-pretty girls was named Lindsey Longpoke, and she was at the dance that night, too, and she sure was pretty, but there was no way she was going say yes to dancing with me, and even if she might, she sure as hell wouldn't let me get in her pants afterwards, and, that being the case, who really cared if she would dance with you or not.

Lindsey Longpoke was one of those cheerleader girls, and everyone said she was the prettiest girl at the school, and all the guys had hardons for her, but she wasn't like the other cheerleaders who thought they pissed champagne and shit gold bricks, and if you didn't agree, well, you could just kiss their sweet little ass. Lindsey Longpoke wasn't like that at all.

Lindsey Longpoke was prettier than any of them, yet she didn't think she was better than the rest of us. But none of that changed the fact that I sure as hell wasn't going to have the balls to ask her to dance.

Before long, word got around that Lindsey Longpoke was going to ask Mr. D to dance with her and that she had asked the DJ to play a special song just for them. Everyone wondered if it was true because why would a beautiful cheerleader like Lindsey Longpoke want to be seen dancing with a nerdy guy like Mr. D, even if he was a nice teacher. Especially with him having shown up at the dance dressed like Elvis Presley. We all figured it was a joke, and I was a bit surprised because Lindsey Longpoke was a nice person, and I thought it wasn't right for her to set up Mr. D like that so everyone would laugh at him.

When Lindsey Longpoke and Mr. D walked out to dance, it was almost like some kind of magic or something because all the other cheerleaders suddenly left the dance floor—probably because they didn't like the idea that one of their own kind was going to be dancing with a nerdy teacher, and high school girls being what they are, when the popular girls left the dance floor, all the other girls did the same thing, and the guys sure as hell weren't going to be left out there dancing with each other, so in just moments the dance floor was completely empty except for Lindsey Longpoke and Mr. D.

It was obvious that Mr. D felt a little sheepish as he walked out with Lindsey Longpoke and that he didn't really want to be dancing with her, but he was too polite to refuse when she asked him to dance, and now with everyone standing and staring, he was even more awkward, especially when the song the DJ put on was Elvis Presley singing *Love Me Tender*. But now that Mr. D was out there on the dance floor and everyone watching and all, he couldn't back out without embarrassing Lindsey Longpoke, and so he danced with her, even though he wasn't a very good dancer, and he made sure to hold Lindsey at arm's length the whole time. Everyone laughed when the next song the DJ put on was the Rolling Stones song *Dancing With Mr. D*. Everyone cheered and clapped and everything would have been back to normal except that half way through the song, Lindsey Longpoke stumbled and Mr. D reached out to catch her, and the two of them ended up sprawled on the floor in each other's arms. Everyone went quiet, but then they cheered as Mr. D got back to his feet and, real gentleman-like, helped Lindsey Longpoke back to her feet and then went on with the dance.

March 29

I WAS IN Mr. D's advanced computer class, but it was stuff I already knew. I took the class because it was an easy way to get the credits I needed so as to graduate at the end of the following year.

One day Mr. D asked me to stay for a minute after class, and I thought I was probably in trouble, seeing as sometimes I goofed around in class when I got bored.

But, instead of yelling at me, Mr. D said, Lew, you're doing well in your art class, but why are you bothering to take this computer class? Don't you want to do something to better your mind?

I told him I had already taken auto shop, and, other than that, there really wasn't any elective that I was interested in.

Mr. D sat there a minute, nodding his head and looking serious in thought. Then he said he had an idea and he would talk to the principal, Mr. Bragg, and see what they could work out.

I asked if I could go now so I wouldn't be late for my next class, and Mr. D nodded and said, Why, yes, of course, of course. Sorry to have kept you.

I guess that afternoon him and Mr. Bragg must have worked something out, because next day Mr. D asked me to stay again after class.

Don't worry, he said. I'll give you a tardy pass if you need one.

Mr. D said the choice would be mine, of course, but he had made arrangements so that, if I wanted to, I could switch the times of my computer elective with my algebra class, and that way I would be able to come to the computer lab during the time Mr. D had his prep period.

If you do that, he went on, I'll be able to teach you a bit of programming. JavaScript, and maybe we could even get into a bit of C++.

Mr. D said he would be busy doing lesson plans during his prep period, of course, but he had an easy-to-follow textbook I could use, and he would be there to answer any questions I might have.

At first I was a bit hesitant because I kind of liked having an elective where I could be a slacker and still get an "A" without having to even pay any attention. Still, I did kind of like the idea of learning how to do programming.

Would I have to do any homework? I asked, and Mr. D shook his head. Not unless you want to, he said. But I won't be surprised if I see you taking the textbook home with you every now and then.

So the next day I made the schedule change, but it had been pouring rain all morning, and when I went to the computer lab, power was out, and Mr. D was sitting there, working in the light that came through the window, which was hardly any at all.

I'm afraid we're out of luck today, Lew, he told me. I think the power lines somewhere must have got hit by lightning.

So Mr. D sent me off to the library, and I sat there, looking out the window and hoping the rain would stop because I had to walk home and I would get soaked if it kept on like this.

But it did keep on like this, and I was soaked and dripping before I got half way home, and I heard a car coming behind me, but I didn't even bother to move over because I was already so wet it wouldn't much matter if the car drove through a puddle and splashed water all over me.

I heard the car slow down, and I just ignored it and kept walking, but someone called out, Come on, get in. I'll give you a ride, and I recognized it as Mr. D's voice.

No, I'll get your car all wet, I told him, pointing down at my soggy clothes.

Don't worry about that, Lew. Come on, get in.

I didn't really want to, due to the fact that, if someone saw me, all the next day I'd get teased because getting a ride in a teacher's car has got to be even less cool than having your mommy come pick you up after school instead of you having your own car and being able to drive yourself wherever it was you damn well wanted to go, which is what all the popular kids did, of course.

But I couldn't hardly turn down Mr. D's offer when he had been so kind to me, not just offering me a ride but also going out of his way to get my schedule changed and giving up some of his own prep time to help me out, so I went around to the other side of the car and got in.

No car of your own, yet, I guess, Mr. D said, and I shook my head kind of sheepishly.

What kind of car does your family have? Mr. D went on.

I knew he was just trying to be friendly and make light conversation, but, goddamn, I wished he wouldn't.

I don't have a family, I told him, and I hoped he wouldn't ask what had happened to them, but of course he did do just exactly that. And what the hell was I thinking, because for some unfathomable reason I told him the truth.

I killed my mom and sister, I told him. Then Pop shot himself to make it look like the whole thing was a murder suicide.

Mr. D laughed and said, You tell a good story, Lew, but I could tell his laughter was forced, and I think he was wondering deep inside if maybe I was telling the truth.

That evening Uncle Stew came out to the Winnebago and, as usual, walked right on in without knocking, and he said to me that Aunt Marge had seen me arrive home that afternoon, and Uncle Stew wanted to know why the hell was that new teacher giving me a ride in his car?

I told Uncle Stew it was on account of the rain and Mr. D not wanting me to get wet, even though it was pretty much too late for that, seeing as I was already soaked, but it was kind of him to offer, anyhow, I thought.

But Uncle Stew said I should be careful who I got a ride from, even if it was a teacher because lots of crimes are perpetrated by a person's closest acquaintances, and besides, he had heard about the ridiculous incident between that Lindsey Longpoke girl and Mr. Drummond.

A teacher like him ought to know better, Uncle Stew said. The man had best watch his step if he doesn't want to find himself in hot water.

A few days later, I was in learning JavaScript during Mr. D's prep period when the phone on the wall rang, and Mr. D answered it. He got flustered and then he looked at his reflection in the window so he could adjust his bowtie and make sure his hair was not too messed up, and he said he had to leave for a moment because some parent was at the office complaining about her kid getting an "F" on a test, so Mr. D told me to keep an eye on things, and he would be back as soon as possible, and then he hurried off down the hall.

A little while later I sneezed, and a big glob of gunk got sprayed out onto my computer monitor, so I went to get a tissue from the box on Mr. D's desk. And I really wasn't meaning to be minding anyone's business but my own, but somehow it caught my eye what was on Mr. D's computer, which he hadn't bothered to turn off, I guess because he was too flustered by having to deal with an angry parent, and the computer hadn't gone into hibernate, and there in front of me on the screen was an email, and at the top was the person's name that it was to, and the name was Lindsey.

I didn't really take notice, but when I got back to my computer and had wiped the gunk off the monitor, leaving a big smear that would gross someone out if they knew what it was from, I suddenly wondered if it was Lindsey Longpoke that the email was to, and it seemed strange that a teacher would be sending an email to a student, and I shouldn't have done it, but my curiosity got the better of me, and I went back to see what the email was about.

It didn't say her last name anywhere, but it was obvious I was right about the email being to Lindsey Longpoke because it mentioned about the incident of her and Mr. D falling on the floor during the Christmas dance, and it also mentioned about how Mr. D had enjoyed meeting with Lindsey at the restaurant over in Placerville last week and that he hoped they would be able to meet there again sometime soon.

Just about then, Mr. D came back into the room and I didn't want it to look as if I was snooping where I had no business, so I pretended I was at the desk to get another tissue, and just then the passing bell rang and I hurried off to my next class.

It seemed kind of strange that a teacher would be sending an email to someone like Lindsey Longpoke, not so much because it was strange he would be sending it, but more because it seemed strange that someone like Lindsey Longpoke would be meeting a nerdy person like Mr. D at some place way over in Placerville.

Still, Lindsey Longpoke was no interest of mine except in my teenage fantasies, and I didn't give the matter much thought until a couple of evenings later when I happened to be in the house and Uncle Stew and Aunt Marge were watching a television preacher on their plasma flatscreen, and it wasn't something she often did, but Aunt Marge said, Have a seat Lew, and she pointed to a fancy but not very comfortable chair for me to sit on. So I sat down, and she said, Have you ever watched the Reverend Jimmy Cochran?

When I told her No, Aunt Marge explained that Reverend Jimmy—that's what she called him—had a big church out in California. Something like fifteen thousand members. He's a true man of God, and he always has a good message. Sit and watch with us, Lew. It'll do you good.

So I did, and I thought Reverend Jimmy Cochran was pretty much just as boring as Reverend McKey at Waynesburg Baptist, but his church was a whole lot fancier—a whole lot fancier and a whole lot bigger. More like an indoor sports stadium. Reverend Jimmy wasn't at all like Aunt Marge's usual television preachers, who were at least interesting to watch as they smacked old wheelchair ladies on the forehead and made them faint and get the Holy Ghost, and then those old ladies would get up, healed, and go pushing out the wheelchair they had come in on, while everyone clapped and called out Praise Jesus.

Anyhow, Aunt Marge told me, You know, Lew, Reverend Jimmy Cochran's suits are all made of pure silk. And his shirts, too. Everything the man wears is pure silk. Can you imagine!

And me, being a smartass teenage kid, the words just sort of came out and I said, Even his underwear?

Aunt Marge scowled at me and shook her head like she was deeply disappointed, and she said, What kind of question is that, Llewellyn Henry Trout? Reverend Jimmy is a man of God, and it's just not right to be asking what kind of underwear is worn by a man of God, and I told Aunt Marge, Sorry. It just sort of came out. Sorry.

Anyhow, after the Jimmy Cochran show was over, the news came on, and the news guy was telling about some kid who had disappeared and was feared dead, and the cops were questioning her fourth-grade teacher as a person of interest in the alleged kidnapping and possible killing of the aforementioned juvenile. Then the on-site news guy interviewed a neighbor of the teacher, and the lady was saying she could hardly believe such a thing could be true, because, Well, goodness me, that Mr. Polski is always such a fine, respectable fellow who attends Trinity Lutheran every Sunday and is married and has such a nice family. Well, goodness me, who could imagine!

Uncle Stew said Yeah, yeah, the sicko perverts always seem so nice and normal to everyone. But folks could never really know what kind of strange shit might be going on in the basement of the residence right next door to your own, and that's why you have cops to ferret out the scumbags and get them locked up where they belong.

Later that night I was lying awake out in the Winnebago, and my mind got to thinking lustful thoughts like it pretty often did at night, and it was Lindsey Longpoke I was thinking those lustful thoughts about, and then I began to think how it didn't seem strange that me and half the guys at school had hardons for Lindsey Longpoke and probably dozens of other guys were, just like me, right now lying awake and thinking lustful thoughts about her, but the idea that a teacher like Mr. D might be doing the same thing, well, that just didn't seem right. So my imagination got me thinking about all kinds of possibilities. I could just imagine the news guy on Uncle Stew's plasma flatscreen telling about the police over in Placerville finding the mutilated body of a high school girl lying in a ditch and authorities searching the area for clues as to what had happened to the alleged victim, and suspecting the body was that of a female student from Waynesburg High who had been reported missing but whose name was not being released until next of kin had been notified.

It was hard to imagine a nice person like Mr. D doing anything like that, but then again, nobody imagined it of that teacher, Mr. Polski, who went to Trinity Lutheran and had such a nice family but was now a person of interest in the alleged kidnapping of a fourth-grade girl, and I began to wonder if maybe I should tell someone about the email I had seen.

And I thought, what if it was Misty rather than Lindsey Longpoke. It would be my responsibility to do something. I liked Mr. D, but what if Lindsey Longpoke really was in danger. After all, a teacher just shouldn't be meeting secretly with a student. It just didn't seem right.

I could have told Uncle Stew, seeing as he was a cop, but he was also an asshole, so I didn't tell him. Instead, I thought maybe I could mention something to Mrs. Flax who was the counselor at school, and that's what I did the next day. I told her I didn't want to get anyone in trouble, and that, please, if she wouldn't mind, to keep this confidential.

Mrs. Flax nodded and said, Of course, Llewellyn, you can rest assured that everything you say to me will be kept strictly confidential, so I told her about having seen the email on Mr. D's computer and about him meeting with Lindsey Longpoke over in Placerville and that the two of them were hoping to meet at the same place again sometime soon.

Mrs. Flax said I had done the right thing by coming to her and she would send for me if she had further questions.

Well, I thought when Mrs. Flax said things would be kept confidential it meant that she wouldn't tell anyone without at least asking me first, but obviously that's not what it meant because it wasn't more than half an hour later I was called out of class to see Mr. Bragg, the principal.

Mrs. Flax was in the office with Mr. Bragg, and the two of them looked very serious and not smiling real friendly like usual.

Have a seat, Llewellyn, Mr. Bragg told me, pointing to the chair next to the one where Mrs. Flax was seated. He told me that he had been informed of the accusations I had made, and he hoped I understood the gravity of such charges, but that I had done the right thing because a male teacher had no business corresponding intimately with a female student, much less meeting with her clandestinely.

I told him that I wasn't making any accusations or charges but only had told Mrs. Flax about the email because I wasn't sure what was the right thing to do.

Well, young man, you've done the right thing, rest assured of that, but things like this have to be handled discreetly. Discreetly but thoroughly, you understand, and that's why I'm asking you not to say a word about it to anyone.

I felt like telling him there was no one in the world better at keeping secrets than I was, and it was obvious that Mrs. Flax was just the opposite, but I figured this was not the time or place for smartass remarks, so, instead, I just nodded.

I don't want to get Mr. D in trouble, I said, and Mr. Bragg said he understood my concern, but it was likely Mr. Drummond had a perfectly good explanation, and, that being the case, well, there was nothing for anyone to worry about, now, was there?

That made sense, but I was beginning to wish I had not said anything to Mrs. Flax. Why the hell hadn't I just kept quiet about the whole thing.

Mr. Bragg went on to say that he wondered if it might be possible for me to print out a copy of the email from Mr. Drummond's computer without anyone knowing I had done so.

I said how did he expect me to do something like that?

I was beginning to realize, however, that I had started something, and now there was nothing I could do to stop it. Kind of like a boulder on a hill and you've started it rolling, and it's not going to stop until it gets to the bottom. The only chance I had of ending this whole thing was to get a copy of that email and then maybe everyone would understand there really wasn't any need for anyone to be worried.

So the next day when it was Mr. D's prep period, it had been arranged for him to be called down to the office so I would be left alone in the computer lab.

And don't feel rushed, Mr. Bragg had told me. Feel free to take as long as you need because Mr. Drummond will be kept occupied in the office for the duration of the period.

So once Mr. D was gone, I turned on his computer, and, sure enough, there in the sent folder was a copy of the email to Lindsey Longpoke. In fact it looked like there were a few of them to her, but I had only told Mrs. Flax about one of them, and that was the only one I was going to print, and so that's all I did print.

I felt so guilty when Mr. D returned just before the passing bell, and I was ashamed of myself, because I knew my face was red and my hands were shaking, and I hoped Mr. D didn't notice because, when you feel guilty, you think everyone knows the truth about what you have done.

Mr. D just gave a good-natured sigh and said something about how was a teacher supposed to get ready for the next day's lessons when a school administrator makes him waste his whole prep period down at the office. He smiled and patted me on the shoulder. Get yourself a job as a programmer, Lew, he told me. Don't even give any thought to becoming a teacher.

Other kids were coming into the room now, so I hurried down the hall in the opposite direction so Mr. D or anyone else wouldn't know I was on my way to the office. And I felt like Judas in the Bible story book, with his face all sly and evil, but me not sneaking to the chief priest but instead sneaking down the back way to the office.

When I got there, Mr. Bragg didn't give me a bag with silver coins, but he patted my shoulder and said, Well done, young man, and I'm sure I don't need to repeat myself that this is to remain strictly confidential. I walked out without even answering him because the asshole didn't have to worry about me saying a word. I was ashamed of myself, and there was no fucking way I was going to tell anyone about what I had done.

March 30

THE NEXT DAY, first thing in the morning, there was a school assembly with some lady who had hair like Marge Simpson, but not blue, and she had a PowerPoint presentation to show us how bad it was to use drugs.

She was talking into the squealing microphone, and she said to us, You know, kids, pot's for losers, and, is anyone here today a loser? and everyone called back to her, I am! I am! Yeah, me, too! and she just looked flustered and went on to show more PowerPoint slides that no one was paying any attention to.

She was showing us a picture of some homeless guy who she said was indigent, whatever the hell that meant, and she told us that's how we would all end up if we smoked pot and kept our current smart-aleck attitudes, and just then three cops came into the auditorium through the front door right up by the stage, and Uncle Stew was one of those cops.

Right away, I knew why they had come, and sure enough, with everyone in the whole school watching, they put handcuffs on Mr. D, and he was embarrassed and his face was red, and you could tell from his eyes that he was wondering, What the heck is going on here? and all the kids were wondering, too, but they were wondering what the *fuck* was going on and not what the *heck* was going on, and I was the only one who knew the truth, and this time it was like another picture in the Bible story book where the soldiers are taking Jesus away to the cross but Jesus in the picture looks loving and forgiving but Mr. D just looked embarrassed and confused and a little bit scared, and me feeling like Judas but hoping that it didn't show on my face with evil eyes and a sly grin, and I was ashamed that I had betrayed Mr. D by sneaking behind his back without him even knowing it was me who had done it.

I saw Lindsey Longpoke seated just across the aisle, and her face was white and her eyes were big and a little bit scared.

At first everyone was quiet and you probably never heard a school auditorium quiet, but if you ever do, you'll realize that in a school auditorium even the quiet has an echo. When they had taken Mr. D away, there at first were whispers, then everyone was talking at once, and the Marge Simpson lady had to give up and put away her PowerPoint projector because no one was paying her any attention, and no one wanted to listen about drugs or homeless guys who were indigent but only wanted to talk about what had just happened to Mr. D.

Everyone except me, that is. I didn't say a word.

I again glanced over at Lindsey Longpoke, and she wasn't saying a word, either, but just sitting there with her eyes still big but now there were tears in them and running down her cheeks, and she happened to glance back over at me and our eyes met, and in that moment I could tell that she knew, and I was ashamed and quickly turned away.

That afternoon I was called out of class to Mr. Bragg's office, and Uncle Stew was there along with a man I didn't know. I was so ashamed I could not even look at any of them, and I had to sit down quick because it was another one of those times when I felt the nausea and the blackness and the current tugging at me and trying to pull me over to the dark side.

Mr. Bragg nodded in the direction of the man I didn't know and said it was Dr. Longpoke, and hearing that made me even more ashamed, and I felt the current tugging harder.

Uncle Stew explained that he had taken Mr. Drummond down to the police station for questioning but had released him on his own recognizance. Uncle Stew was wondering, however, if I had any further allegations in regard to any manner of misconduct I may have observed Mr. Drummond to have been engaged in.

I didn't even answer him but just kept trying to swim against the dark current.

Mr. Bragg explained that Dr. Longpoke would like to speak with me, and I shrugged. I expected him to chew out my ass for what I had done, but he didn't.

You did the right thing, lad, he said to me and I could tell from his accent he was from England or Scotland or Australia or one of those places over there, and he went on to say that it was his desire that this whole sordid incident should not be blown out of proportion. He said he had to give thought to the reputation of his medical practice and, more importantly, to the reputation of his daughter, Lindsey, with whom I might be acquainted. A long, drawn-out investigation would not mend matters and would only bring grief to all involved, and surely everyone in the office here understood that the last thing any of us needed was a court case or for the news media to get hold of the story.

Do you understand what Dr. Longpoke is saying, Llewellyn? Mr. Bragg asked.

I just sat there looking at them, not saying anything.

Dr. Longpoke has asked that all charges against Mr. Drummond be dropped. All he requests is that Mr. Drummond's employment at Waynesburg High be terminated and that Mr. Drummond agree to leave Waynesburg discreetly and immediately and have no further contact with his daughter. Is that understood, Llewellyn?

I nodded.

Can we have your word that nothing will be said to anyone about this unsavory incident?

I nodded again.

Very well, then, Dr. Longpoke said. On behalf of myself and my daughter, I extend my appreciation, and as an expression of that appreciation, I would like to offer you this.

Dr. Longpoke had taken his wallet from his pocket and he removed from it a one hundred dollar bill. Here, take it, he said, holding the money out to me.

All I could do was sit there, saying nothing and wondering how many hundred dollar bills Dr. Longpoke had offered the men in that room as an expression of his appreciation for them keeping quiet about what he called the whole sordid and unsavory affair.

I shook my head and quickly left the office. I didn't want the money. Mostly, I didn't want the men to see that I was crying.

It was the period I normally went to Mr. D's room to study JavaScript, but as I passed by today, the room, usually so brightly lit, was now dark, and all the computers were off.

After a slight hesitation I went in. It was quiet and dark in there, and it was a place where I could pull myself together and get the tears out of my eyes before going back out where people could see me.

I sat down at one of the computer tables and after a few moments, my eyes adjusted to the darkness, and I became aware that I was not alone.

Mr. D was seated at his desk, his face buried in his hands.

I'm sorry, he said, looking up at me, and I could tell from his voice that he had been crying. He said I'm just on my way out, Llewellyn. I came in to collect a few personal items from my desk.

He stood up and rummaged through a drawer, shoving a few odds and ends into his pockets.

I sat watching him and found it almost impossible to speak. I finally managed to whisper, Mr. D, I didn't mean for all this to happen.

And all Mr. D said in response was Why, Lew? Why did you do it?

And then he walked out of the room and I was left there with no lights on.

March 31

D R. LONGPOKE MAY have had enough money to buy off Mr. Bragg and Uncle Stew, but obviously he didn't manage to buy off the reporter at the *Waynesburg Gazette*, so the next day, right there on the front page was a picture of Mr. Drummond, who had allegedly already left town discretely and without delay or incident after yesterday having been arrested during a school assembly and, thereafter, taken down to the police station for questioning in regard to alleged misconduct with a female student at the school.

The article said that out of respect for the student and her family, names would not be mentioned, but then it went on a few paragraphs later to say that a clandestine affair had been going on between this student and Mr. Drummond ever since the night the two of them had danced together at the school's Christmas Gala. How fortunate it was Mr. Drummond had been apprehended before he did any physical harm to the girl, though, unfortunately, as is usually the case in situations where a teacher uses his position of authority to manipulate and abuse a student, the psychological scars were likely to last a lifetime.

So why the hell didn't they just come right out and say the student's name was Lindsey Longpoke? Everyone had seen her dancing with Mr. D that night at the Christmas dance. Everyone knew exactly who the student was.

To everyone's surprise, Lindsey Longpoke showed up at school that day in spite of the newspaper article. It must have not been much fun for her, but she kept her head high and pretended she didn't hear any of the whispers, and she acted like she didn't notice how everyone fell silent whenever she came near.

The Drummond affair, as it had already come to be called, was the only thing anyone was talking about, and the rumors were flying.

Mr. D was a convicted child molester.

Yes, but he had failed to register as a sex offender because then he would never have gotten hired as a teacher.

It seems the perverts always go into teaching.

That or the Catholic Church, and, after all, wasn't Mr. D both a teacher and a Catholic?

Lindsey and Mr. D had been heard having sex in one of the stalls of the girls' bathroom on the night of the Christmas dance.

Yes, and Lindsey was pregnant by Mr. D and was likely to have an abortion.

No, no, the abortion had already been performed.

Heaven help us, most likely by girl's father, himself, seeing as he was a doctor.

It was all absurd, of course, and it was cruel, but, like I said, Lindsey Longpoke acted as if she didn't hear a word of it, and she kept her head high. I tried to avoid her because I was ashamed of myself, and I remembered the way she had looked at me the day before as Mr. D was being arrested, and how I had known from her look that she knew it was me that had told about the email.

I know what I would have done if I was Lindsey Longpoke. It would have been one of those Columbine things, and the name Llewellyn Trout would have been the first one on the shitlist.

With Mr. D not being there, I didn't have anywhere to go during the period after lunch, when I usually went to the computer lab to learn JavaScript, and I sure as hell wasn't going to go to the office and request to be assigned another class, so I just went and hung out in the cafeteria. I was sitting there all alone, and it was kind of like that time when Miss Veronica showed up out of nowhere, but this time it wasn't Miss Veronica, but, instead, it was Lindsey Longpoke standing there. And like Miss Veronica, she sat down beside me.

Why did you do it, Llewellyn? she said. Why? What did I ever do to you to deserve something like this? What did Lawrence ever do to deserve something like this?

I knew that by Lawrence she was talking about Mr. D, but I didn't know what to say to her, so I just sat there without saying a word.

We loved each other, Llewellyn. Why did you have to go and destroy that?

I didn't mean to. My voice came out just a whisper. I only wanted to help, I said. I didn't want anything bad to happen to you. I wanted to protect you like I would if you were Misty.

I knew Lindsey Longpoke didn't know who Misty was, but that's what words came out when I spoke.

Lawrence is a gentleman, Llewellyn. He would never do anything to hurt me.

But he is an adult, Lindsey. He is an adult, and you're just a kid.

I'm eighteen years old, Llewellyn. And Lawrence was less than five years older than me. Less than five years. Do you realize that my dad is seven years older than my mom? Seven years, and no one thinks there's anything terrible about that. They love each other, and that's all that matters. And I love Lawrence, and there's nothing I ever wanted more than to spend the rest of my life with him. But he knew what was best for us, and he insisted that we wait until I graduated from high school before telling anyone about our relationship. After that he was going to give his resignation here so he could move out to California to be with me while I got my degree at Stanford.

By this time I was feeling nausea just like the time Miss Veronica was sitting beside me right in this very same place, but now there wasn't any fear, only nausea. That and a feeling of how terribly sorry I was for what I had made happen to Lindsey Longpoke and to Mr. D, whom she called Lawrence.

Can't you go and be with him? I asked. Do you know where he went?

Lindsey Longpoke shook her head. He wouldn't tell me. He sent me this email, though. I printed it out. Do you want to read it?

I didn't really, but she took out a folded-up piece of paper from her pocket, and it had an email printed on it, and there were spots where the paper was wrinkly and the ink was smeared, and I knew it was from tears, and she unfolded it and put it in front of me.

I was a little bit embarrassed because you aren't supposed to go reading other people's love letters, but Lindsey said, Go ahead, Llewellyn; read it. It's not the first time you've read one of Lawrence's letters to me.

So I did, and it told how much Mr. D loved Lindsey and that he was sorry beyond measure for the pain and embarrassment he had brought her. His love had blinded him, and he had acted foolishly. He would miss her, but he was being forced to leave because Dr. Longpoke had insisted on it, and the only alternative was to stay and face possible criminal charges, and, even though he was confident he would have been found innocent of any wrongdoing, it would have brought great pain and embarrassment to everyone involved, which, unfortunately, would have included his beloved Lindsey.

So he had given his word to Dr. Longpoke that he would leave town and have no further contact with Lindsey, and Mr. D intended to honor his promise. Lindsey was the most wonderful person he had ever known, and he would miss her deeply. His life would forever have an empty place in it. But he wished Lindsey all the best, and he knew that she would find someone else who would be an even better husband to her than he could ever have been. He knew it might take some time for her to get over what had happened here, but time heals the deepest of wounds, he said, and when the time came that it seemed right to her, he hoped Lindsey would put him out of mind and find someone else.

And then with a smiley face after the sentence instead of a period, he said that, when that time came, Lindsey really should get to know that Llewellyn Trout boy. Mr. D said he was certain Llewellyn had no ill intentions and only did what he thought was right and necessary, and it was Mr. D's own fault that he had been so careless as not to delete all traces of sent emails. Lew, he went on to say, had a good mind, even if he didn't always use it to its full potential. But above all the boy had a good heart, and Mr. D hoped Lindsey would take time to get to know him.

My hands were shaking so much I could hardly fold the paper and hand it back to Lindsey Longpoke. But she shook her head and said, Keep it.

I looked at her, and there were tears in my own eyes, but none in hers. And what I saw made me afraid because in her eyes I could see that Lindsey Longpoke had been taken over to the dark side.

The next day Lindsey Longpoke was not at school, and that afternoon an assembly was called and everyone was whispering and wondering what was going on, and when Mr. Bragg took the microphone, everyone went even more quiet than when Mr. D had been taken away in handcuffs.

Mr. Bragg regretted that it fell on him to announce to the student body that the night before Lindsey Longpoke had taken her own life, and if any student felt the need to talk with someone regarding the tragic events of the previous few days, we were welcome to come to his office at any time or to the office of Mrs. Flax, the counselor, because there were to be no copycat suicides during his watch, and that was all he had to say except that school was cancelled for the remainder of the day. But everyone be back regular time tomorrow morning and don't think this is an excuse not to do your homework, is that understood?

Everyone started whispering and everyone said, poor Lindsey, and how sad it was, but they were all the same people who just the day before had been spreading horrible rumors about Lindsey Longpoke and Mr. D, but

74

today they were oh, so sad, and wondering how she had killed herself, the poor dear. That's what everyone really wanted to know, of course. How had Lindsey Longpoke killed herself? Everyone wanted every gory detail.

It wasn't until a few days later that we learned Lindsey Longpoke had taken the rubber tube from her father's stethoscope, put it around her neck, and strangled herself.

Everyone said how unfortunate and how tragic it was that a young life had been destroyed by a man who should have known better, but had, instead, toyed with the affections of a young girl just to fulfill his own selfish lusts, and if it were up to them, that Drummond man would be brought back to Waynesburg and made to face justice. The fault was his. The worst of prisons was better than what he deserved.

But I knew who was really at fault. I still had the printed email with Lindsey Longpoke's tear stains on it, and I knew the truth.

But I sure as hell wasn't going to tell anyone. I'm good at keeping secrets.

April 1

TOWARD THE END of my senior year, I visited the various armed forces recruiting offices in town. At first I was gung ho to become a Marine like Pop, but an NCO at the Air Force office gave me a glossy brochure that told how in the Air Force there was opportunity for me to become a nuclear weapons apprentice, learning, as the brochure explained, how to work on Cruise missiles, short range attack missiles, and numerous types of gravity weapons.

I didn't know what the hell a gravity weapon was, but the idea of working on nuclear bombs interested me, and Sergeant Oxcox assured me that the United States Air Force offered unlimited opportunities for a young man such as myself. The Marine Corps, he said, was a fine institution, but I might want to consider the possibility that the Air Force might better suit my personality and aptitudes.

I think the guy was politely saying that the Marine Corps would chew the asshole out of a wimpy geek such as myself. I figured he was probably right.

So I signed up Air Force.

Uncle Stew, when he heard, said he was pleased I had a desire to serve my country, but he couldn't help being somewhat disappointed in my selection of the Air Force over the Marine Corps, which, after all, was the service he and Pop had served in during the Vietnam Conflict.

I mean, even Becky McKey, daughter of Reverend McKey at Waynesburg Baptist, had enlisted in the Marine Corps, and if a female such as herself had what it took to be a Marine, then certainly a male of the species ought to have pride and determination enough to claim the title of United States Marine.

God damn Uncle Stew. Why did the asshole always have to talk like a fucking cop? Because he was one, I suppose. If you're an asshole, you talk like an asshole. If you are a cop, you talk like a cop. Uncle Stew was both.

Anyhow, I had already signed the Air Force papers, and there was no going back.

Becky McKey and I were both scheduled to leave Waynesburg somewhere about the middle of September, and a couple weeks before that, the folks at Waynesburg Baptist gathered for a picnic in Pixley Park across from the church to wish us both the best of luck.

As was always the case at church picnics, there was plenty of food. Mrs. Parton made sure I got some of her potato salad, which, she told me, with a comforting hand on my shoulder, was a recipe she had shared with Mom back when Pop first brought her to the United States from Vietnam. Mrs. Parton hadn't wanted to be intrusive or patronizing, of course, but she wanted Mom to know how to cook American food in order to properly feed my Pop, who was, after all, an American and would, of course, prefer to eat American dishes rather than Vietnamese. Mrs. Parton had assured Mom that, with just a bit of practice, even a Vietnamese woman ought to be able to master this basic potato salad recipe. Then if Mom could just learn how to boil a hotdog and toast a bun to put it on, well, she could serve that up along with the potato salad, and my Pop would be able to enjoy some real American cooking.

I didn't even try to be polite, and I told Mrs. Parton that when Mom cooked Vietnamese it was the best food our family ever ate. Mrs. Parton scrunched up her nose and said something about how if she stretched her imagination she could begin to understand how a person might enjoy eating rice, but it gave her the willies to think how anyone could bring theirself to eat raw fish and seaweed. Oh, goodness me, even the thought is downright unsettling, you know. That's what I call it, Llewellyn, downright unsettling.

The stupid fuck. I just smiled and ate her goddamn potato salad, glad that I was about to be leaving Waynesburg.

After everyone had eaten, there was a softball game.

Vets against the rest, Reverend McKey announced.

The Reverend was a man proud to count himself among those who had served in the military, though he regretted having served during a time of relative peace and had, therefore, been unable to engage the enemy in active combat. He had kept several of his Army uniforms, and he was wearing one of them that day at Pixley Park instead of his usual shirt and tie.

Officer Hooper Jr., one of the policemen Uncle Stew was the Chief of at Waynesburg Police Station was in uniform, too, but his round, pink face grew red when Reverend McKey reminded him that wearing a police officer's uniform was not the same as a veteran wearing a uniform of the United States armed forces. Hooper Jr. protested, however, and finally it was agreed that he should be allowed to play on the vets' team. After all, Uncle Stew reminded everyone, Ever since the Twin Towers, we all know that heroes come in uniforms of all kinds.

Having already signed our enlistment papers, both me and Becky McKey played on the vets' team. Becky McKey kicked ass and hit several home runs, whereas I never made it past second, and then at the end struck out just when all bases were loaded. You could tell that folks were kind of embarrassed of me for being such a wimp, but at the same time, they seemed maybe even more embarrassed that Becky McKey was such a butch. Of course no one who attended Waynesburg Baptist would mention the word "butch" at a church picnic, so they just whispered that Reverend McKey's daughter, Becky, she certainly did have a powerful swing, didn't she?

After the game there were speeches. Waynesburg Baptist had gathered here at Pixley Park to send off two of its own to serve in the noble cause of freedom and democracy. How proud Henry Trout would have been to be here today and celebrate his son's embarkation on a career in the United States military. And, yes, Waynesburg Baptist could be proud, as well.

There were tears and hugs for me as well as for Becky McKey. Everyone was sad to see the two of us leave.

Sad, but oh so proud.

Then came ice cream sundaes followed by everyone gathering to sing *Onward Christian Soldiers.* Finally, Becky McKey sang solo all stanzas of the *Marine Corps Hymn,* which I had a hard time not laughing when she did, and I heard Mrs. Blox laugh two times, though she pretended she was just blowing her nose.

Thank god no one asked me to sing the *Air Force Song* because I sing like shit, and even if I had a voice like that Josh Groban guy, I would have felt like a goddamn fool singing about going off into the wild blue yonder, climbing high into the sun. Besides, those were the only two lines I knew of the song, and what the hell would I have done when I came to the end of them?

Reverend McKey concluded with a prayer for me and for Becky, his daughter. May Llewellyn be ever courageous, and may Becky ever remember to honor her country while maintaining the purity of her God-given body. And, of course, God, bless all the brave men and women serving their country and may we all be victorious in our fight for freedom in those godless Moslem countries of the Middle East.

Then as an apparent afterthought, Reverend McKey asked Stella Roche to lead everyone in singing *God Bless America.*

That picnic was Waynesburg's farewell to the last of the Trouts. There were no tears on my part. I was happy to be finally leaving Waynesburg. Happy to be leaving the folks at Waynesburg Baptist. Happiest of all to be leaving Uncle Stew and Aunt Marge. I wasn't going to miss them any more than they were going to miss me.

But obviously Uncle Stew and Aunt Marge were going to miss the monthly checks they had been getting from the state foster care agency because a couple days before I was scheduled to leave, Uncle Stew introduced me to a kid who would be taking my place in the Winnebago out back.

The kid's name was David; he was six years old and very proud of the Nike shoes he had received for his birthday. And he was excited to be coming to live in what he called a real home. I felt sorry for him. He would find out soon enough what kind of home it actually was.

Little did he know.

For that matter, little did I know. I had always thought I'd had it bad. But not compared to what David had to look forward to.

Poor kid.

April 2

A FEW WEEKS later, I left Waynesburg and went off to become an Air Force nuclear weapons specialist.

But things didn't work out exactly as I had planned. Not as my Air Force recruiter had planned either. But I suspect he was less disappointed about the change than I was.

Toward the end of basic training, I was told the Air Force no longer needed my services in the area of missile maintenance, so instead of being trained in the intricacies of missile weapons systems, I could now look forward to learning the fine art of filling out forms, moving mail, and doing word processing.

Yes, I was to become a US Air Force mail clerk. More officially, a US Air Force Information Management Apprentice. Less officially, a US Air Force titless WAF.

I sure as hell wasn't going to write home and tell the folks in Waynesburg about the change in plans. Wouldn't Aunt Marge love starting the gossip.

Here, Becky McKey goes off to kill Islam terrorists in Iraq, while poor Llewellyn gets stuck sorting mail. Goodness me, wouldn't his poor old Pop roll over in the grave if he heard that one. Poor Llewellyn. Well, it was his own choice, you know. He could have become a Marine if he wanted to.

Yeah, sure.

Anyhow, mail clerk was to be my Air Force destiny.

Basic training complete.

Off I went on a Greyhound bus.

I learned how to fill out forms. How to compose email.

Whoopee shit.

Mail clerk training was finally over!

Transfer paperwork was finally complete.

Then FIGMO!

I was sent off to work in the mail room at a small base somewhere out in the middle of the goddamn Mojave Desert.

Talk about going from bad to worse.

Talk about going from worse to FUBAR.

Just be glad it's not Thule Greenland or Bumfuck Egypt, the smiling NCO said as he handed me my PCS orders.

When I pressed him for more information, he said he didn't know much about the place. A barracks and a couple radar domes, I think. Probably keep track of the planes out of Edwards. Maybe the Shuttle, I'm not really sure.

Well it turned out the guy was right about the barracks but not about the radar domes. There wasn't even one of those. There was no runway. No airplanes. Everything looked old and run-down. Drab and industrial. What the hell kind of Air Force base was this, anyhow? It sure wasn't like anything in the glossy brochures the recruiter had given me to take home and peruse at my convenience.

In fact, I learned that they didn't usually even refer to this place as an air base. An installation is what it was more often called. An Air Force installation out in the middle of the goddamn Mojave Desert.

There were a couple office buildings and several radio towers of some sort that had around them high cinder-block walls topped by bales of barbed wire; there was a chow hall, a motor pool, and a building with apartment style living for married personnel and families. There was a closed-down bowling alley and an NCO Club as well. That was about it. That and the desert.

I was pleased to learn I would have a room of my own in the barracks, and, better yet, that I wasn't going to have to do any latrine duty. In fact, I wouldn't even have to clean my own room, other than doing the basics like making my bed each morning. Senior Master Sergeant Leroy explained it all to me as he showed me around.

You see, he told me, There's a cleaning service here on base, and for just thirty dollars a month, a maid takes care of cleaning your room and the common areas of the barracks. It's a Mexican gal, and she does a damn good job of keeping the place spotless for us.

Sergeant Leroy next took me over to the NCO Club. It's not much, he said, But out here in the middle of nowhere you make do with what you got. At least it's air conditioned and there's always plenty of cold beer and lots of ice to cool the harder stuff. It's open to everyone: airmen, NCOs, officers.

Officially, of course, no alcohol was served to anyone under twenty-one. But the good news was that out here in the desert, the no-underage-drinking regulation was pretty much ignored so long as you didn't go over an unofficial three-drink limit, which applied, of course, only to enlisted personnel under the legal drinking age. After all, what else was there to do out here in the godforsaken desert, now that the bowling alley had been closed due to a malfunction of the ball return mechanism. You got to give the enlisted personnel some kind of recreation, even if it means bending regulations a bit on the drinking age, Sergeant Leroy told me.

So that evening at the NCO Club I sat drinking beer with a couple guys who worked at the motor pool. They laughed and kidded me when I told them I was the new mail clerk.

We got ourselves a new titless WAF working the mail room, said the guy who was in charge of the motor pool. His name was Staff Sergeant Sanchez, and he told me I was the flat-chestedest, butt-ugliest titless WAF he had ever seen. But you don't got bad legs, and I bet you've got a nice warm pucha, he said, laughing and slapping my back.

I asked him what was he talking about. I figured it was some kind of Mexican word. What does pucha mean? I wanted to know.

Staff Sergeant Sanchez laughed even louder. Fuck hole, is what it means, my gringo friend. Or if you like it translated to more polite, medical terminology, you could say it means pussy.

That gives you a pretty good idea what kind of guy Sergeant Sanchez was. And believe it or not, his first name was Jesus, just like our Lord, except he didn't pronounce it the way our Lord did, but like Hay-soose.

Staff Sergeant Hay-soose Sanchez talked with a Mexican accent, whereas our Lord, I figured, if he had been still alive nowadays, would probably have had a pretty much regular American accent. He sure as hell wouldn't have called himself Hay-soose—of that much I was damn sure.

When I told everyone at the NCO Club my name was Lew, they assumed it was short for Lewis and that's what they started calling me:

Lewis. I sure as hell wasn't going to correct them and tell them that Lew was actually short for Llewellyn.

Back at the barracks I had signed up on the roster for weekly maid service at the only time slot still open. 0-six-hundred, Monday morning.

And when that time rolled around, I was still groggy as I stumbled out of bed and answered the door with nothing on but my boxers.

Mermaid cleaning service, said the woman standing in front of me.

Goddamn, I was embarrassed to be standing there almost naked.

This sure as hell wasn't the cleaning service I had been expecting. I had figured my room would be cleaned by some chubby, middle-aged mother-type Mexican woman wearing black janitor-type utility shoes, a frumpy gingham dress, maybe an apron, and a little cap that's kind of like one of those that a nurse wears perched on top of oily hair that's all pulled back in a bun.

But here standing in front of me was an eighteen, maybe nineteen or twenty year old girl who was sure as hell the exact kind of woman Reverend McKey had in mind on those occasions he would preach on the evils of women who intentionally incite a man's lust of the flesh.

About the only thing that was as I expected was that she was Mexican. She wore white go-go boots that went up to her knees and a lime-green dress that barely covered her panties, which I later discovered had a topless mermaid embroidered on them. She had a topless mermaid embroidered on her dress, too, right above that lovely left boob with the words Mermaid Cleaning Service embroidered right beneath.

I felt myself turning redder than a sloe gin fizz, and I stammered something about having forgotten I was scheduled to have my room cleaned.

The girl looked at me and smiled—goddamn, she sure did have a pretty smile, and there was a playful sparkle in those big dark eyes of hers.

You want me to come back later, Airman, she asked me.

Damn, she didn't even talk like a Mexican. Her accent was just regular American.

You want me to come back later when you aren't standing there in your boxers and sporting a morning woodie?

That just made me blush all the more, and I could tell she was having a good time making me feel stupid. I told her, No need to come back. I just moved in a couple days ago and there isn't really anything that needs cleaning.

The girl told me she would be back the following Monday. Same time she said. Six o'clock, sharp. Make sure you got clothes on, Airman.

That evening at the NCO Club, everyone laughed as I sat drinking Coors and telling about opening the door half naked and finding the mermaid girl standing there.

She sure is pretty, I said.

Goddamnit, Lewis, said the motor pool guy whose name was Jesus Sanchez. That mermaid is more than beautiful. Hell, I'd eat a mile of her shit just to see where it came from.

I told Sanchez I wasn't sure I would go that far.

Well, Sergeant Jesus Sanchez said to me, Tell me at least that you didn't send that sweet little puta away without inviting her in to chew on your churro.

I wanted to know what was a churro. It seemed I was going to be bilingual in Mexican if I kept hanging around Sergeant Jesus Sanchez for long.

A churro is something us Mexican guys got but you white boys just wish for.

Well, that didn't tell me exactly what a churro was, but it wasn't hard to figure out what Sanchez was referring to Mexican guys having. That made me blush and Jesus laughed all the harder.

A churro's kind of like a Mexican doughnut, he said.

The other guy from the motor pool, whose name was Frank, laughed and said to Sanchez, So you Mexican guys got something round with a hole in it?

Fuck, no, Frank, Sanchez said. What you're talking about is a white boy's doughnut. Mexican boys got doughnuts that are long and strong. And Mexican girls just love to dip them in hot chocolate before putting them in their mouth.

Jesus laughed again. He always laughed when he thought he was being funny. He bought me another beer. A Corona. He said it was a genuine Mexican beer that would put pelos en los huevos.

Frank said that meant the beer would put hair on my balls. Speaking of which, he went on, We got a pool going here at the club. Maybe you want to join it, Lewis. We call it the ball pool.

A football pool? I asked.

Everyone laughed, especially Jesus Sanchez. No, Lewis, he said. Frank's talking about our ball-the-mermaid pool. Everybody puts in ten bucks and every penny goes to the first one who manages to fuck that mermaid girl. We got seventy bucks so far. What do you say, Lewis, do you want to bring it up to eighty?

I wasn't sure I wanted anything to do with this, but I figured it would just be easier to put out ten dollars and let things slide.

Everyone cheered when I pulled out my wallet and laid two fives on the bar.

You got to bring back a pair of her panties, Sanchez said. You got to bring them back as proof.

How are you going to know they're hers? I asked.

Because nobody else in the world has a topless mermaid embroidered on their panties, that's how, Sanchez said.

She's got a mermaid, even on the panties? I asked.

Yep, Sanchez said. Frank swears he saw it once when the sweet thing was bending over, cleaning under the pinball machine. Isn't that right, Frank?

April 3

NEXT MONDAY MORNING, I was up and fully dressed when the mermaid girl came to clean the room. I was a bit uncomfortable being there as she worked. It felt kind of like having a servant or a slave or something like that. The girl said her name was Calli, and she was friendly and talked as she went about cleaning. Goddamn, she was pretty, and she sure did talk a lot.

She had been working at the installation for almost a year. She had a son but no husband because the father got scared off when she told him there was a baby on the way. She couldn't really blame the guy, though, seeing as she was only sixteen at the time and he was only fifteen.

Mermaid Cleaning Service was Calli's own company, and she had a business license to prove it. As of yet, she was the one and only employee, but not for long, she assured me; within a year or two, she figured she would have a dozen or more people working for her. And a few years after that, she'd have franchises all across the country. Hell, why not the whole world? She had seen this show on TV about a luxury hotel in Dubai or somewhere like that over in Saudi Arabia or Kuwait or wherever the heck it was, and wouldn't it be kickass if Mermaid Cleaning Service could get the janitorial contract for a place like that. And, not to change the subject, but Calli wondered if I would mind her cleaning my room next Sunday afternoon instead of on Monday morning. Monday was her son's birthday. He was turning four, and Calli wanted to take him to LA for his first trip to Disneyland.

I said it didn't matter to me if she did the cleaning a day early. Besides, even if I had cared, how the hell can you say no to someone who wants to take her four-year-old kid to Disneyland for his birthday?

Next Sunday afternoon, when Calli showed up to do her cleaning a day early, I asked if she was looking forward to her trip to Los Angeles.

She shook her head. Don't think I'll be able to go, Lewis. My car isn't working so good. Patrick is going to have to wait till another time for his trip to Disneyland. Tomorrow we're going into Boron and doing the birthday pizza thing, instead. I think my car will make it that far.

I asked Calli if she would like for me to have a look at her car. I took auto shop back in high school, I said. Maybe I can figure out what's wrong.

Calli smiled that sweet fucking smile of hers but told me she didn't want to be a bother.

Hell, it's not a bother I told her. I like doing that kind of stuff.

Well, Calli sure as hell did drive a crappy car. It was an old Buick with a cracked rear window and fake sheepskin seat covers. It didn't take me long to figure out that one of her spark plug wires was bad. I wondered if I might be able to get one over at the motor pool.

When I asked, Staff Sergeant Jesus Sanchez told me I couldn't have one, due to that being a misappropriation of government property. That's called stealing, Airman, he told me. People go to jail for stealing from Uncle Sam.

I said I didn't want a new one. I was just wondering if there might be an old one lying around that might have a few miles of life left in it.

Sanchez told me he had just replaced a few wires during routine maintenance. The old ones probably worked okay, but I still couldn't have one, seeing as they belonged to the government.

Motor pool Frank said, For chrissake, Sanchez, let him have a wire. They're just sitting there in the trash to be thrown out. Go ahead and take one, Lewis, he said.

He handed me one of the old wires and said, Don't worry about Sanchez. He's on the rag today.

Sanchez said, Fuck the both of you, but he didn't stop me from taking the wire.

The plug wire was longer than it needed to be, but it seemed to work just fine, and Calli was delighted. She said her son would be excited to learn he would be going to Disneyland after all. You'll be his hero, Lewis, she said to me. Then she hesitated a few moments and I could tell she was nervous about what she wanted to say.

Uh, would you like to come with us, Lewis? To Disneyland, I mean. I got a coupon for half price off the admission.

I was a bit flustered just like I think she was, but I sure as hell wasn't going to turn down an offer to spend a day at Disneyland with a girl beautiful enough to have given me lustful thoughts more than once over the past few nights.

I pretended to think about it and not be too eager, and then I said, Yes, sure, that would be great; I would enjoy going.

So Calli came by early the next morning to pick me up in her Buick. I was kind of disappointed and at the same time kind of relieved that she wasn't wearing the short green dress and the go-go boots that were her Mermaid Cleaning Service uniform. Instead, she was in Levis and a sweatshirt that had Pooh Bear on it. I wondered if, maybe, she had mermaid panties under those jeans of hers. I sure wouldn't mind finding out.

Her kid started crying when Calli told him I was the person who would be coming along to Disneyland.

What's the matter, honey? Calli asked.

Her son sniffed and said, But, Mama, you told me he was a hero.

Calli laughed. I told him you were a hero for fixing my car, Lewis. I think he figured you'd be some kind of superhero like Spider-Man or something.

Goddamn, I felt like a piece of shit. I mean, what the hell kind of person makes a four-year-old kid cry on his birthday. Fortunately, he stopped crying when I told him I would buy him ice cream when we got to Disneyland.

Strawberry swirl? he asked, and I told him whatever the hell kind he wanted, but then I said, Excuse the French, because Calli had looked at me like, Watch your language in front of a little kid, Lewis.

Once Patrick had stopped crying, Calli wanted to take some pictures of him before we started out. After all, a kid only has one four-year-old birthday in all his life, and if you don't get it on film now, you never will.

She didn't have film, though, but, instead, a digital camera, and it was obvious it must have been brand new because Calli didn't know how to work it. I explained how to use the zoom and the portrait mode, but Calli looked at me like, What the heck are you talking about, Lewis, so I told her, Forget it. Just go ahead and push that button there.

Calli smiled. Then she took so many pictures that, even without using the zoom or the portrait mode, she sure as hell must have got at least a few good ones.

Then we climbed into her Buick with Patrick sitting in back and Calli hoping the cops wouldn't stop her because she didn't have one of those child safety seats for him. It seemed we hadn't gone more than a couple miles, but it was probably more like ten or twelve, when Calli pulled in to a Shell station. The car needed gas, and Patrick already needed to take a piss, or like he said it, he had to go pee-pee.

I was left working the pump while Calli took Patrick inside the minimart to do his pee-pee. But the two of them came back out just a few moments later.

Here, let me do the gas, Calli said. Would you mind taking Patrick in to use the men's room? He's not going to hold it much longer, and there's someone in the women's room and the door's locked.

Hell, I felt a bit stupid taking someone's kid to use the restroom, and I tried to make some kind of lame excuse, but Calli looked at me like, Come on, Lewis, don't be such a jerk. What's the problem, she said. It's not as if you got to hold his thing for him. He can go himself. I just don't like sending him in alone. There's too many perverts out there.

I shrugged and took Patrick to the men's room. I mean, what else was I going to do? The kid was obviously about to pee his pants.

When Patrick was done, he insisted that I hold him up at the sink so he could wash his hands. I sighed and held him up, but instead of drying his hands afterward, the little twerp flicked water in my face.

I pretended to fly into a rage and did a gorilla impersonation. Patrick let out a squeal of delight and darted out the door with me in pursuit close behind. Calli was there with her camera, and she took a picture of us just as I scooped Patrick up into my arms and did a loud gorilla roar that made him let out another squeal of delight.

When we got back to the car, Calli handed me the camera so I could see the picture.

Goddamn, Calli, I said. The poor little guy looks like he's scared to death of me.

Of course he is. Wouldn't you be scared if you were being chased by a big ugly gorilla?

I'm not a big ugly gorilla.

Well, I guess you're not really a gorilla. And you aren't very big.

Patrick laughed when I told him it was his mother's way of calling me ugly.

I think there's something a little bit wrong, Calli said as she pulled back out onto the highway.

It was obvious pretty quick that there was something more than a little bit wrong. The Buick's engine raced, and the car wouldn't shift up out of first.

Can you fix it? Calli wanted to know.

I shrugged and then shook my head. I don't think so.

Can we make it to LA?

Not a chance, I said. But you might make it home if you put your flashers on and drive real slow.

Patrick started to cry when he realized that he was not going to Disneyland.

Mama told me you fixed the car, he said looking at me with distrust and anger. Why did you tell Mama a lie?

Goddamn, I felt like a piece of shit. I mean, that's just the way you feel when a four-year-old kid blames you for fucking up his birthday.

Calli tried to help her son understand that it wasn't my fault. Mr. Lewis did fix the car, honey, she explained. But now a different part is broke, and that's too bad, but it's not Mr. Lewis's fault.

Patrick wasn't buying it, though. I wish you hadn't come, he said, scooching across the back seat to be as far from me as possible.

Calli made a helpless sort of smile and patted my leg. Don't you worry, Lewis. Patrick doesn't hold a grudge for long.

Calli lived in an old Airstream trailer stuck out in the middle of nowhere about three miles from the base, which, itself, was in the middle of nowhere. I told her she better drive directly back home. I could walk the three miles to the base, no problem, but I wasn't sure the car would make it that far.

When we got to the Airstream, Calli asked me to at least come in for a soda before I set off.

The Airstream looked old and run down from the outside, but inside, Calli had fixed it up real nice. It was a little bit messy, though, and there sure were a lot of toys scattered around.

Calli told me not to feel bad when I accidentally stepped on a Spider-Man action figure and broke off one of its arms. But Patrick, of course, started crying again.

Hell, I said. I'm really screwing up your son's birthday.

It's not your fault, Lewis. I tell him to pick up after himself, but he never does. And I'm always too tired when I get off work to do anything about it.

You leave your kid alone here while you're at work? I asked. That's not a good idea, is it?

What the heck am I supposed to do, Lewis? It's not as if there's a daycare just down the road.

As I was about to leave, Calli went into the bedroom and returned a few moments later.

They're for you, she said, holding a pair of panties out in front of me. They even have Mermaid Cleaning Service embroidered right across the butt. A picture of a mermaid, too.

I kind of blushed and stammered something about why was Calli giving me a pair of her panties.

Oh, come on, Lewis. Do you really think I don't know about that pool you guys have going back at the NCO Club?

I felt myself blushing even more. I said to Calli, But the two of us didn't even . . . well, what I mean, you and me didn't . . . We didn't do what you're supposed to in order to . . .

What's the matter, Lewis, Calli said to me. Are you trying to say you didn't get laid?

I kind of nodded.

Well, I know that, and you know that. But no one else does. So what's the problem? Calli held out the panties. Here, take them. Win yourself that pool. Count it as pay for helping me with my car.

I grinned and shoved the panties into the pocket of my jacket.

What's the pool up to, anyhow? Calli wanted to know. A couple hundred bucks?

Eighty.

Dang, Calli said with a grin. Are you telling me you guys set up a ball-the-mermaid pool and eighty bucks is all you can come up with? How do you think that makes me feel?

That night I claimed my eighty dollars. Everyone cheered and slapped me on the back. Everyone except Jesus Sanchez, that is. He got pissed, I think because he was Mexican and Calli was Mexican, and he thought that a white boy like me shouldn't be balling some Mexican chick.

Anyhow, I bought everyone a round, but Sanchez said something about I could shove my beer up my culo. Whatever the hell that means, but of course it wasn't hard to guess.

The next day I was working in the mail room when Major Dennis, the base commanding officer, came in. He was real friendly and not at all like I would have expected a commanding officer to be. He started a conversation and asked how I liked being stationed out here in the boonies. I told him it was okay but that yesterday I had hoped to go to Disneyland. Unfortunately, however, Calli's car had crapped out, and screwed up our plans.

Major Dennis said he was sorry to hear that, and after thinking about it for a moment, he said he would talk with Sergeant Sanchez and see if it could be arranged for someone at the motor pool to give Calli a ride to work each morning till she could get her car fixed.

That night when I was at the NCO Club, Jesus Sanchez came in, even more pissed off than usual.

They got me working as a goddamn chauffeur, he said to motor pool Frank. Major Dennis told me I have to give that goddamn mermaid girl a ride to and from work every day.

Motor pool Frank said he would have thought that Jesus would enjoy giving a ride to a foxy chick like that.

Fuck you Frank. Do you really think I like being chauffeur to Lewis's goddamn slut? When I re-upped it was to be a mechanic, not to be a taxi service for some sleazy little puta.

It was obvious that Sanchez was pissed off and looking for a fight. Anyone would do, but he really disliked me for some reason, and I sensed he was egging me on—trying to get me to say something that would give him an excuse to beat the shit out of me.

I got up and left.

The following morning as I was having breakfast at the chow hall, Sanchez came and sat next to me. He seemed in a better mood, and he even apologized for the night before. He had with him a flyer he had printed up showing his car and information about it. I'm putting my Impala up for sale, he told me. After breakfast I'm going to be posting this flyer on the bulletin board over in the mail room.

I took a look at the flyer.

You interested in buying a car? Sanchez said.

I don't think so, I told him.

Why not, Lewis? You don't know how to drive?

I shrugged and said, I do, but I don't have money for a car.

Well, this is a good deal, Lewis. You're missing a real opportunity, but the choice is yours.

Sanchez said he would keep the car himself, but he needed to send money to his mom, who was still living down in Mexico. She's poor, Sanchez said. She don't have much money and she needs to see the doctor to get medicine for her liver.

I'm sorry to hear that, I said.

Well, then, buy the car, my gringo friend, Sanchez told me. If you want to help, buy my car.

All that day I kept thinking about how great it would be to own a car. As I was sorting the mail into everyone's boxes over at the mail room, I kept glancing at the bulletin board where Sanchez had posted his flyer. The best part was that he was only asking $850 for the car.

With the little bit of savings I had and with what I had left of the $80 I had gotten for the ball-the-mermaid pool, I had enough for the car with a bit left over for insurance and stuff like that.

That night at the NCO club, I asked Sanchez about the car again. He told me, Lewis, it's a great driving machine. It don't look like much, that's true. But it runs good. Real good.

When I woke the next morning, I was the proud owner of a 1987 Chevy Impala. White, Auto, PS, PB, Mint, New Tires, Black vinyl top, $850 OBO, No Reasonable Offer Refused.

It didn't take me long to realize I should have checked things out more carefully before taking Sanchez's word for it that the car ran like it was new off the showroom floor.

Never buy a car when you've had a half-dozen or so shots of Tequila.

The night before over at the NCO Club, Sanchez had been in a good mood, and he was feeling generous with his money.

You ever tried Tequila? he asked me.

I shook my head.

Well, then, my gringo friend, let me introduce you to the drink of my Aztec ancestors.

I didn't really like the taste, but I tried to be polite. Sanchez was in a rare good mood and I didn't want to piss him off.

It's good shit, isn't it Lewis? he said. Here, let me buy you another.

At the time I didn't know why the bartender was letting me drink so much or why Sanchez had become so friendly. I was a fool not to figure things out when I saw Sanchez slide the bartender a twenty. At the time, I thought he was leaving a hell of a big tip, but I felt kind of stupid now as I thought about it and realized that Sanchez hadn't been leaving any regular tip, and it wasn't out of camaraderie that he had kept buying me drinks.

I wasn't wrong in thinking that Sanchez, being a mechanic at the motor pool, ought to know better than anyone whether or not the car was in good shape. Where I went wrong, of course, was in trusting Sanchez to tell me the truth.

I saw Sanchez that afternoon, and I asked him about the fluid that left a wet spot on the pavement any time the car was parked for more than a few minutes. It looks like brake fluid, I told him.

Sanchez laughed. Ah, don't worry about that, Lewis, he said. There's a little leak in the master cylinder. Just top it off every now and then with a bit of DOT 3 and you won't have any problem.

A couple days later when I turned the key, the car wouldn't run. Well, it turned over okay, so I knew the battery was good, but the engine wouldn't stay running.

Sanchez shrugged when I asked him about it. Maybe check out the ignition system, he said. They sometimes act up a bit, you know. It's common on that kind of car.

I told him I was beginning to think he had sold me a piece of shit.

What are you saying, Lewis? Are you calling me a liar?

I told him, No not really, but I don't think you told me the whole truth.

Well, puto, if you had asked me, I would have told you. But I don't recall you asking nothing about the master cylinder or the ignition system or much anything else, for that matter. How do you expect to get an honest answer if you don't ask no honest questions?

It took me more than a month and most of a paycheck to get the car running again. And even then, it would sometimes die unexpectedly.

April 4

ONE MORNING I went to the barracks common room, where there was a plasma flatscreen and a couple vending machines. Sanchez was there in nothing but his boxers. He was sprawled out on the couch, watching an *I Love Lucy* rerun.

Calli was in the room, cleaning.

I put my coins into a vending machine. It took my money but didn't give me a soda. I hit it a couple times, but still no luck.

Careful with that machine, Sanchez said. No need to get violent with it. The thing's been empty for a week.

Why didn't you tell me before I lost my money? I asked, and Sanchez just shrugged and lay there grinning at me.

Shut that fucking thing off, he yelled when Calli plugged in her vacuum cleaner. Can't you see I'm watching TV?

I'll only be a few minutes, Calli said.

I said to fucking turn it off, Sanchez yelled. You can come back and finish when this show's over.

Calli said she had a lot to get done today, and would Sergeant Sanchez please be patient with her. But Sanchez got up and yanked the vacuum cleaner's plug out of the wall.

Let her do her work, I said. Sanchez was really pissing me off.

Fuck you, Trout.

I didn't argue. I just plugged the vacuum cleaner back in. And that's when Sanchez really came unglued. He sprang out of the couch and put a fist into my gut. It didn't hurt much but it knocked the breath out of me, and I stood there, gasping for air.

Sanchez pulled the vacuum plug again.

Calli put an arm around my shoulder until I could get my breath back. Don't worry about it, Lewis, she whispered. I'll come back later. She gathered her cleaning supplies and left me alone in the room with Sanchez, who was lying there again, sprawled out on the vinyl couch, a shitty grin on his goddamn face.

I told him, Fuck you, Sanchez.

He just grinned all the bigger. You'd like that, wouldn't you, my gringo friend. But I'm afraid you're going to have to find yourself someone else to fuck. This here Mexican don't like girlie boys. Now get the hell out of here, you little puto, before I knock the shit out of you instead of just your breath. Why not go take a drive in that fancy car of yours. It is running, isn't it?

I walked off feeling like a fool. Fuck that sack of Mexican shit.

It was a month or two later that Calli one day showed up late for cleaning my room. Her eyes were puffy from crying, her lip was cut and swollen, and it was obvious she had been smacked around a bit.

She went about her work and at first wouldn't say a word.

I said, Come on, Calli, tell me what's wrong, and she started to cry. She sat down at my desk, hid her face in her hands, and sobbed. When she was finally able to talk, she told me it was Sergeant Sanchez that had hit her.

She said that last evening when she went home, Patrick had acted real strange and hadn't wanted to stay up for popcorn, which was always a favorite treat of his. Instead he had gone to bed right after dinner. As Calli tucked him in, she had felt his forehead, but he wasn't feverish. Are you feeling okay, honey? she asked him, but instead of answering, he started to cry.

Finally Calli was able to get him to talk. He was so afraid she would be angry. So afraid she would be disappointed.

I didn't obey the rule, Mama, he told Calli. I disobeyed the rule. I opened the door, and I'm not supposed to.

Did you let someone in the house? Calli asked, and Patrick nodded.

Calli asked who it was, but Patrick wouldn't tell. I'm not allowed to, he said. If I tell, he's going to take you away and I'll be all alone and no one will be here to take care of me.

Calli told her son that he didn't have to tell her anything. It's okay, honey, she said. You don't have to say a word. I'll just make some guesses. How will that be? If I'm right, all you do is nod your head. If I'm wrong, you just shake it. That way you won't be telling. We'll just be playing a guessing game. Do you think that would be okay?

Patrick started by just nodding and shaking his head, but before long, he was talking without Calli even having to ask any questions. He told everything that had happened.

Sanchez had come to the Airstream, and Patrick had let him in. Sanchez had sat with him on the couch, cuddling him in his lap and stroking his hair as the two of them watched television cartoons.

It just gives me the creeps, Lewis, Calli said to me. Sanchez had no right to come into my house. He had no right to sit there watching TV with my son. It's not right for a man to come into someone else's house uninvited and sit watching cartoons.

Calli went on to tell me that this morning when Sanchez had come by to give her a ride, she had confronted him regarding what had happened. That's when Sanchez got really pissed and slapped her.

He told her he had done nothing wrong. He had come by to see her, and when she wasn't home, he had spent a few minutes watching the end of a cartoon Patrick had been watching on TV. He said he hadn't even sat down on the couch and he had no idea why Patrick would be making up lies like that about him.

I remembered all those years ago, sitting on Miss Elsa's lap as she stroked my legs, there in that booth with the ant problem at Flo's Diner, and I thought about Sanchez sitting on the couch, holding Patrick on his lap, stroking the boy's hair, probably with one hand while who knows what he was doing with the other, and I knew in my heart this was more serious than Calli realized.

I said, You got to do something about this, Calli. You got to go talk to Major Dennis. You got to tell him about what happened. It's a serious thing what Sanchez did. Real serious. I'll go talk to Major Dennis if you don't want to.

Calli looked up at me, and I could see fear in her eyes. No, Lewis. Please. You have to promise me you won't.

Someone has to tell him, Calli. I don't think you understand. It's for your son's safety. This is more serious than someone just coming over uninvited and watching cartoons in your house.

No, Lewis, please don't tell anyone. Please promise you won't say anything to anyone. Please, Lewis, I beg you. I beg you not to say a word. Not to Major Dennis. Not to anyone. Please promise.

I said I wasn't going to say anything if she didn't want me to. I mean, if anyone can keep a secret, it's me. But I told her, Be careful, Calli. Be really careful. Don't ever let that man around your kid when you're not present. Tell Patrick he can never open the door again. Not ever. Not for anyone. Calli, you have to tell your son he can't ever again let the wolf in the house.

Calli looked at me and kind of crooked smiled, and I could tell she didn't really understand what I meant about letting the wolf in.

I asked Calli why she had come in to work after getting smacked around like she had.

She just shrugged. What the heck am I supposed to do, Lewis? I can't stay home and have Patrick see his mother all beat up and crying. What else am I supposed to do? Tell me, Lewis. Just tell me!

I told her to go wash up. Get yourself pulled together, I said. I remembered Pop telling Mom to do that before sending her off to work at Waynesburg Pharmacy on mornings after he had beat her up.

I told Calli I would give her a ride back home, but she said to me, I have to work, Lewis. I need the money. How else am I going to afford a new transmission for my car?

I told her, To hell with the money, Calli. If you won't think about yourself, then at least think about your son.

Calli smiled, but her eyes didn't sparkle.

When I drove her home, I left my car for her to use. It's not running real good, I told her, but it should get you back and forth to work, no problem. I don't want you having to rely on that fucking Sanchez anymore.

Calli said she didn't feel right about using my car. I'll walk to work, Lewis. I don't mind. Really I don't. It's only a few miles.

I grinned at Calli and said, Yeah, like you're going to walk the whole way in go-go boots? You'll twist your ankle in under a week, I guarantee it.

Calli smiled back at me, but she didn't argue. Thanks, Lewis, she said, and she reached out and took one of my hands and kissed it.

That night at the NCO Club, Jesus Sanchez was what Pop would have called pissed and drunk as a skunk. He was obviously looking for a fight. Preferably a fight with me, as usual. In the end, his being drunk ended up working to my advantage.

I don't think it was so much that Sanchez wanted to hurt me. It was more that he wanted to humiliate me, and, to his brain, I think there was nothing more humiliating than to get beat up in front of a bunch of people. I was pretty sure that's what he had in mind for me.

If he had just wanted to hurt me, Sanchez could have stepped up in some dark alley, though I guess there weren't many of those out in the desert, and he could easy enough have beat me bloody.

End of story.

But in order to humiliate me, he had to do it in public, and it had to look as if I was the one who had provoked the fight.

Sanchez muttered something about that I should chinga tu madre, and I told him, Goddamn it, Sanchez, if you're going to cuss at me, at least have the balls to do it in American instead of Mexican.

Go fuck your mother.

That's better, I told him. I knew he was determined to draw me into a fight, and I just wasn't going to give him the satisfaction of success.

I had recently taken to using Pop's Purple Heart medal as a keychain fob, and as I was fishing in my pocket for change to pay for my beer, I pulled out my keys and placed them on the bar.

Sanchez nodded at the keys and said, What's a wuss like you doing with a Purple Heart? I thought they were for war heroes.

It's my Pop's, I said. He was a war hero. He was injured in Vietnam.

What did he do? Get his dick blown off?

Well, Sanchez could have insulted me all night. He could have called me all his goddamn Mexican swearwords. I would have just done my best to ignore him and stay out of a fight. But when he took to insulting my Pop, well, that was like 9/11; I couldn't any longer just sit there and not respond.

But I still wasn't going to let Sanchez lure me into throwing the first punch. I was going to get him to do that.

Insult me if you want, I said to him. But you don't insult my Pop, you shitty Mexican culo.

I didn't know if I pronounced it right, but Sanchez understood me just fine.

He slammed his Corona down so hard the bottle broke. You might say he leapt from his barstool, but, fact is, he was so shitface drunk that it was more like he stumbled from his barstool. And then he swung at my face. I may not be especially strong, but I'm pretty quick, and I ducked. The swing went wild, and Sanchez stumbled over himself and went down. He fell into the bar, smashing his face on the edge of the glass top. It took a moment or two, but suddenly there was blood. Lots of blood. And a crooked nose on Sanchez's face.

Staff Sergeant Jesus Sanchez didn't bother to swear. Not in English. Not in Mexican. He just let out a bellow of anger as he lunged at me a second time. But I was waiting for him, and, again, I managed to move out of his way. He stumbled and fell, hitting his head on the hardwood floor. Goddamn, it sounded like he had cracked his fucking skull. He struggled to his feet. It was obvious he wasn't going to give up. The poor bastard just couldn't learn.

Nonetheless, he was more furious and more determined than ever, so, as he swung at me a third time, he actually connected. Instead of hitting my face his blow landed pretty much harmlessly on my shoulder. You would think my natural reaction would have been to hit back.

But instead I just laughed.

If I had taken a swing, the fight would probably have stayed at that level—two guys fighting it out with their fists. But being laughed at was more than Sanchez could take. He grabbed up the broken Corona bottle from the bar and came at me, holding it by the neck and slashing the air with the jagged piece of glass just like in the movies. I guess that's what really got my adrenalin going.

There was one of those floor-standing metal ashtrays there by the bar, and I picked it up and swung it, protecting myself from Sanchez as he came at me with his broken bottle.

And that's how I took him out. I hit him on the side of the head and knocked him unconscious. He went down hard and lay motionless on the floor.

April 5

THE NEXT MORNING I was told to report directly to Major Dennis. I figured, shit, now I was really in trouble. But there had been a whole NCO Club full of people who had heard Sanchez provoke the fight by calling me Mexican swear words and by insulting my Pop. They had all seen the guy come at me with a broken beer bottle.

We don't tolerate fighting at this installation, Airman Trout, Major Dennis said, looking up at me from across his desk. But a man does have a right to protect himself, and from what I've been told, your use of force last night was justified. Nonetheless, there'll be no more fighting. This will not happen again. Do you understand me, Airman?

I nodded.

You stay out of Sanchez's way. That's all, Airman Trout. You're dismissed.

I did stay out of Sanchez's way, and things went well for quite a few months. But I was a fool to think my troubles were over. Sanchez had humiliated himself, but it was me he blamed. He was going to have his revenge.

It was not long after my twentieth birthday that I was one day told to report again to Major Dennis.

Well, shit, I thought. What is it this time?

Major Dennis wasn't smiling as he looked up at me from across his desk.

Airman Trout, I'll get right to the point, he said. The Air Force these days is pretty tolerant about a person's sexual orientation. I'm not supposed to ask, and most times even if I heard, I would just pretend I hadn't. But when someone goes around saying he prefers young boys, well, that's something I just can't overlook.

Holy shit! What the fuck was going on here? I just kind of stood there staring stupidly at Major Dennis. But I wasn't feeling stupid, I was feeling scared.

Well, Airman Trout?

It isn't true, sir. Who told you that? Suddenly I knew the answer to the question even without Major Dennis saying anything.

It was Sanchez, wasn't it?

That's not important right now.

Like hell it's not important, sir. I have a right to know who's accusing me of something like that.

It would be better if you don't say anything more right now, Airman Trout. I can arrange for you to talk with a military lawyer if you like.

Talk to a lawyer? No I don't want to talk to a lawyer. You don't need a lawyer unless you've done something wrong, sir. And I haven't done anything wrong.

God fucking damn. What the hell was going on here? I had been taken completely by surprise. No, I didn't want to talk to a lawyer, but there was another son of a bitch I sure as hell was going to talk to.

I walked over to the motor pool and found Staff Sergeant Jesus Sanchez seated behind his desk. I guess when you're in charge of the motor pool you get your own desk. Especially if you're named Jesus.

On the other hand, Frank, who did all the work, didn't get a desk, just a chest of tools.

Sanchez sat there with his feet up on his fucking desk and a shitty grin on his acne-scarred face. What can I do for you, Lewis? he asked.

I know what you're up to, Sanchez, I told him.

Well, baboso, tell me, then, what exactly is it I'm up to? Sanchez said, wiping his nose on his shirt sleeve. His nose had healed a little bit crooked from that night he beat himself up over at the NCO Club.

You're spreading rumors about me, Sanchez. You're accusing me being some kind of pervert who likes little boys. You're the pervert, Sanchez. You're the one who cuddled up on the couch with Calli's little kid.

Sanchez pushed his chair back from his desk and reached into a drawer. He pulled out a box of chocolates, opened it, and held it out to me.

Fuck your chocolates, I told him.

Sanchez just smiled and shrugged. Suit yourself, my gringo friend, he said, taking a truffle, shoving it whole into his mouth, and chewing real loud.

It's not true, Sanchez. You know that.

Sanchez shrugged. What's truth got to do with anything? It wasn't true what those pretty little girls said back at the Salem witch trials, now, was it?

You learned about the Salem witch trials when you were in school, didn't you Lewis? Truth isn't important. What people believe is all that matters.

I folded my hands behind my back to hide the tremor. This was crazy. Just fucking crazy. Crazy like it must feel if you were somehow a person in one of those Dali paintings I remembered from Mr. D's Art Appreciation class back at Waynesburg High.

Fuck you Sanchez. Truth does too matter. This is America, not goddamn Mexico. I have my rights. You can't go accusing me of things that aren't true.

Sanchez sat there grinning and once again offered me a chocolate. I hit the box out of his hand, sending the candies scattering across his desk. I expected Sanchez to beat the shit out of me, but he just kept on grinning as he put the candies back neatly into place.

No one's going to believe you, Sanchez. People will know you're just making it all up because you don't like me.

No doubt you're right, Lewis. No doubt you're right. You had better hope so. They put child molesters in prison, you know. And I hear it's not much fun for them there. Nobody likes a child molester. Nobody.

April 6

THAT SAME AFTERNOON I was called again to report to Major Dennis.

He told me to have a seat. I had declined to have a lawyer, which was my right, though Major Dennis believed it was, perhaps, foolish and naïve on my part. He assured me that I could at any time change my mind and request legal representation. But until such time as I did, I should be aware that anything I might say could and would be used against me.

I told you, sir, I don't need a lawyer. I haven't done anything wrong. Sergeant Sanchez is just saying things about me because he doesn't like me.

It's not just Sergeant Sanchez that's saying things, Airman Trout.

Tell me who, then, sir. Tell me exactly what the hell is going on here.

Major Dennis reached into the drawer of his desk, pulled out a photograph, and laid it in front of me.

Is that a picture of you, Airman Trout?

Of course, sir. That's obvious. That's me and Calli's kid.

Well, Airman Trout, Miss Moreno has reported to me that you touched her son inappropriately. Actually, she did not say it so politely, Airman Trout. She wasn't so politically correct. She was much more specific. Would you like to know exactly what she has accused you of?

Jesus Christ, things were getting stranger by the moment. I guess so, sir, I said.

Miss Moreno's son says that when the two of you were in a public restroom, you asked him to display his penis, well, he calls it his pee-pee. And then, Airman Trout, he says that you asked if you could touch it. He told you, no, but you did it nonetheless. Do you have anything to say for yourself, Airman Trout?

Only that it's not true, sir. Not a word of it.

Then how do you account for that photograph?

Jesus Christ, sir. Me and the kid were playing. Just goofing around.

It looks to me like you're coming out of a public restroom, Airman Trout. Are you telling me that you and Miss Moreno's son were playing in a public restroom?

It's not how it looks, sir.

No, Airman, it certainly is not how it looks. Not at all. Have a look at the boy's face. Is that the look of a boy who has just been playing? The look of a boy who has just been having fun? To me the kid looks scared. If looks have anything to do with it, I'd say the kid is scared to death of you.

Well, sir, I know it doesn't exactly look like it, but . . .

Airman Trout, it's obvious the boy's not having fun at all. Whatever happened in that restroom obviously wasn't something he found enjoyable. It was something that terrified him.

I was just pretending, sir. Pretending to be a gorilla.

At this point, Major Dennis told me he suggested that I say no more. The choice was mine to make, but he had advice for me, and he hoped I would listen carefully.

The charges were serious. Very serious. More serious than I may as yet have had time to reflect upon. The Air Force, he told me, preferred not to be involved in scandal. But if forced to deal with an ugly issue such as this, the Air Force would come down on me like a shitload of fucking bricks.

Airman Trout, charges such as this bring shame on the entire Air Force when they go public. The goddamn news media love nothing better than to smear shit like this on TV screens all across the country. Hell, not across the country, Airman Trout, across the whole goddamn world.

Major Dennis assured me that the Air Force would go out of its way to make it absolutely clear to the whole world that it did not go easy on someone accused of child molestation.

They'll make an example of you, Airman.

But, sir.

Are you a religious man? Major Dennis asked me.

Well, sir, I guess so. I'm a Baptist.

Well, that's close enough, Airman Trout, so I guess you know what they did to Jesus Christ.

I shrugged. I didn't know what the Major was getting at.

They nailed his sorry ass to a goddamn cross, that's what they did.

I guess so, sir.

Was he guilty, Airman Trout?

No sir.

Did being innocent help him?

No sir.

Do you understand what I'm trying to get across to you, Airman Trout?

I sat for a while without speaking. I felt dizzy and light headed. I was glad I was sitting down.

I think I understand, sir.

That's good, Airman Trout. Because it is vitally important for you to understand the seriousness of the accusations that have been made and the seriousness of your current situation.

Major Dennis went on to say that Calli, Miss Moreno, as he called her, was not insisting on pressing charges. All she really wanted was to see me gone. And the Air Force, of course, would prefer not to bring an incident like this into the public eye. So, if I was willing to sign papers attesting to a lesser charge, the Air Force would be willing to send me on my way and let things drop with nothing more than a dishonorable discharge.

What kind of lesser charge, sir?

Major Dennis told me that if I was willing to admit to charges of having made blatant and unwelcomed homosexual advances on adult personnel both military and civilian, I would be given a dishonorable discharge and sent on my way.

Think long and hard about it, Airman Trout. Making unwelcome homosexual advances is not a criminal charge, and you wouldn't even have a criminal record. You'd be getting off easy. Real easy. I suggest you not make a hasty decision.

I can't do it, sir, I said. None of the charges are true.

Major Dennis shook his head gravely.

I believe you, Airman Trout. I would personally see to it that you got nailed if I thought the accusations were true. But unfortunately, there's a mother and child willing to testify against you. And if that's not damning enough, you have a Staff Sergeant who, other than that instance in the NCO Club a while ago, has an honorable if not spectacular Air Force record and is willing to testify that you actually bragged to him about the incident with the child.

But, sir. I was pleading. My voice was like what Pop would have called a crybaby voice. It's just not right, sir. None of it's true.

The choice was mine, the Major told me again. I could demand my right to talk to a lawyer, but if I did that, God, himself, couldn't guarantee that things might not escalate out of control. There would likely be no turning back. He advised that I might well find myself looking at years of prison time. Not that you wouldn't get a fair trial, he said. But if things don't go well for you, the powers that be will come down on you so hard you'll wish you could trade your position for that of a Jew at Auschwitz.

106

I didn't know what to do. I didn't know where to turn. I needed help. Real help. I was a young man, just turned twenty and with no experience in anything of this sort. One thing I did know: things were serious, and I knew I was in over my head.

That evening I walked over to Calli's place. I was sure I would be able to clear things up. If only I could talk to Calli and Patrick, I was sure I could get to the bottom of things. Somehow there had been a terrible misunderstanding, but certainly everything could be set straight.

When I got to the Airstream, I found the car I bought from Sanchez parked out front. Calli had long ago gotten her own car fixed, but my Impala was leaking brake fluid so bad it wasn't safe to drive. I hadn't bothered to get it fixed; It wasn't worth fixing. I wondered why had I been such a fool as to try helping Calli by loaning her my car. Here, I had tried to help her, and she had shown her appreciation by accusing me of molesting her son.

When I knocked, there was a long delay before the door opened, and when it did, it was only a small crack. Calli looked out at me. She had obviously been crying. I asked if I could come in.

No, Lewis. Go away. I don't have anything to say to you.

Just tell me, Calli, is it true that you accused me of molesting your son? Is it really true?

Go away, Lewis. I don't want to talk to you.

Jesus, Calli, please. I'm going to get dishonorably discharged because of this. Maybe even do time in prison.

Calli was crying again now, but she just closed the door, and I heard the deadbolt click.

April 7

T HE NEXT MORNING I told Major Dennis I had decided to take his advice. He nodded gravely and said that he knew all along I was a sensible young man.

I figured you'd do the wise thing, he told me, and he said he would have hated to see me get myself in over my head.

I said to him, I'm there already, sir.

Major Dennis had obviously been pretty sure what I was going to do, and he had already drawn up the appropriate paperwork. He had me sign it right then and there. It was not standard procedure, he told me, but he had made arrangements for the matter to be handled swiftly, judiciously, and discreetly so as to avoid the usual bureaucratic procedures that might have led to unnecessary embarrassment to myself, the Air Force, and the mother and child involved.

I didn't know then, and I don't know now whether things were handled as they were because Major Dennis sincerely wanted to help me, whether it was primarily to avoid embarrassment to the Air Force, or if having a scandal of this sort occur under his watch was simply not in the best interests of Major Dennis' career plans. Most likely, I figured, it was a bit of all three.

Major Dennis may have avoided embarrassment to the Air Force, but that didn't help me much. What the hell was I going to tell folks back in Waynesburg? I mean, really, what was I going to say?

Was I supposed to call and say, Hi, Uncle Stew, I'm getting kicked out of the Air Force for being a pervert pedophile. But don't worry, Uncle Stew and Aunt Marge, none of it's true. They're just making it up.

Shit. I mean, really, shit!

I finally decided it was best to be honest and explain my situation. I did it that evening in an email to Uncle Stew.

Within a few hours, I got a response.

Uncle Stew and Aunt Marge were both sorry to have received my transcription of events as I had reported them to have transpired. Sorry they were, and extremely disappointed. Uncle Stew wanted to be able to trust me, but, as a loyal American, he also had to trust his government, you know, and, well, Llewellyn, if an officer of the United States Air Force had accused an enlistee of having perpetrated some manner of homosexual perversion, much less pedophilia, well, then, a person had to consider that there might be some truth behind the allegations. There was, he feared, more to the story than I was willing to admit, and Uncle Stew was disappointed that I did not feel free to confide in him.

He recalled with pain the incident of the pornographic images on my computer, and it gave him cause to question my honesty as well as my orientation in terms of gender.

And even if none of the charges were true, I had still brought shame upon myself. I was an American, after all, and it is a cowardly thing for an American man not to stand his ground and fight for his honor. I had my rights, and I would have received a fair trial in accordance with stipulations of the Unified Code of Military Justice. Yes, even if I was innocent on all counts, there could be no doubt that I had taken the coward's way out.

Uncle Stew gravely regretted having to inform me that I was no longer welcome at his and Aunt Marge's residence, and, should I decide on returning to Waynesburg, I would be on my own. It was his advice, however, that I not return. After all, the citizens of Waynesburg were loyal Americans, and they would be unlikely to give a warm welcome to me or any other party dishonorably discharged from the armed forces, regardless if that party be a pedophile, a homosexual, or merely a coward who lacked the courage and conviction to stand up to his accusers.

Aunt Marge would be sending an additional love offering in the sum of $45 to the Green Branch Ministries of Reverend Jimmy Cochran, her favorite television evangelist. Enclosed with the offering she would include a request that the Reverend's prayer team call upon Almighty God that I might find strength against the temptations of Satan. Aunt Marge hoped I would consider making it a regular habit to watch the Reverend's weekly television broadcasts. She was sure it would help me find blessing and forgiveness for any sins I may have committed. Remember, Lew, God is merciful and he loves you.

You're like a son to me, wrote Uncle Stew, and he wished me the best of luck, but he suggested that I seek counseling and that, perhaps, I could get involved in a good Bible-teaching church, where I could find a wholesome and morally-healthy environment. Once I had a new address, would I please let him and Aunt Marge know, so they could send me a UPS box with the few possessions I had left in the motorized residential vehicle parked out back, though Uncle Stew regretted to inform me that, for the wellbeing of all parties concerned, he would be unable to return to me either the 22 or the Weatherby 12-gauge firearms. Once I was settled in somewhere, maybe someday he and Aunt Marge would be able to stop by for a visit if they happened to be in the area.

Love, Uncle Stew and Aunt Marge

April 8

SO ON A bright sunny day, the only kind they have in the Mojave Desert, I took a bus headed for Bakersfield. I left my Chevy Impala parked out at Calli's place. She could keep the piece of shit if she wanted it. I knew it wouldn't get me far, and it would cost more to have it repaired than it would to buy a car that was already in decent running order.

When I bought the bus ticket, the guy at the window said, Bakersfield? Why the hell would a young man like you want to go to Bakersfield? Anyone with brains is trying to get the hell out of that place just as quick as possible. Fact is, most anyone with brains has got out already

I shrugged.

You aren't a fly, are you? said the man behind the window.

What? I said. I didn't know what the guy was talking about. I just wanted him to give me my ticket.

Well, you know what attracts flies. I don't for the life of me know why, but they swarm to it just like certain folks swarm to Bakersfield.

It's got to be better than Waynesburg Arkansas, I said.

The guy behind the window shook his head sadly. Well, don't say you weren't warned.

I thought, This guy's crazy, but, on the other hand, I began to wonder, what the hell was I getting myself into? I mean, I didn't really know why I had chosen Bakersfield as my destination—other than that I didn't have money for a ticket to anyplace much further. A ticket to Los Angeles would have cost about the same, but the thought of living in such a big city made me uneasy. I had googled Bakersfield, and it didn't sound so intimidating, but still big enough that I didn't think I'd have too much problem finding a job, and big enough that I would be able to slide right in, unnoticed. No difficult questions asked. No whispers. No gossip.

With the holiday season just around the corner, stores were busy, but I soon discovered it's not easy finding employment when you have a dishonorable discharge from the Air Force.

Finally I got a job at Pickford Grocery, working midnight to 8 a.m., stocking shelves and cleaning floors. I learned pretty quick that Mr. Pickford had illegal shit going on in a back room there at the store, and I guess he liked having a person such as myself working for him. He knew that a person desperate for a job is likely to keep quiet about anything illegal he might see happen.

He was right about hiring me. There isn't anyone better at keeping a secret.

I was required to wear a ridiculous uniform that was half airline pilot and half janitor, but the cap was more like the railroad conductor ones you see in old-time pictures. Pay seemed low but adequate, and the store's employee entrance was just across the street from the two-story stucco building where I had found a one bedroom, one bath apartment, fully furnished; includes TV and self-cleaning oven, on-premises laundry facilities, and easy access to all the arts and entertainment of Bakersfield, the cultural hub of California's lush Central Valley; available immediately, first month's rent and security deposit due prior to move-in. Call any time, day or night.

I didn't give a damn about Bakersfield's cultural entertainment or a flying fuck about California's lush Central Valley, but the fact that the apartment was located just across the street from Pickford Grocery made it so that I would not have to buy a car. Not right away, at least. And considering my financial situation, that was a good thing.

Mornings in Bakersfield were almost always foggy. The lifeless sky never cleared. There was hardly ever a patch of blue, and the sun was seldom more than a brighter spot in the gray. Life was boring. I knew no one, and without a car there wasn't a way to get anywhere.

About the only good thing was that Mr. Pickford let me buy groceries at an employee discount, and, also, despite my being under twenty-one, he allowed me to buy beer. Though, he said, shaking his finger at me, there would be no employee discount on that, and he would take no responsibility if drinking got me in trouble with the authorities.

So I worked all night, and each morning carried home a six-pack, drank it while watching daytime soaps, and then fell asleep until it was time to wake again a bit before midnight, put on the ridiculous uniform with the railroad conductor's hat, and go back to stocking shelves and mopping floors at Pickford Grocery.

I had been hoping to save money for a car, but now, several weeks after I started working at Pickford, I still had saved only a few dollars. Wages had sounded not too bad when Mr. Pickford offered me the job, but I pretty quick found out that things here in Bakersfield were not at all like the Air Force. There was no chow hall with free food. No free barracks. Not even a free laundry. Instead you had to feed quarters into the goddamn washers and driers so fast you started out with a whole roll of quarters but at the end were lucky if you had enough to buy yourself a Twix bar at the vending machine by the door.

So here, just a month or so before Christmas I had finished paying all my bills and I had just $127 left to get me through the next two weeks.

Fortunately that was enough to buy myself a six-pack of Coors, and as I sat in my apartment that morning, watching the daytime soaps, bored out of my skull, and a good way through the six-pack, I heard something that sounded like a yelping dog. I hit the mute button on the remote and sure enough it was a dog, and I thought maybe the poor thing had been hit by a car out in the street, so I went to see what was going on.

It wasn't a dog that had been hit by a car, but it was a dog that belonged to somebody at the house next door to Pickford Grocery, and a guy was hitting the small black puppy, which looked a lot like the one Misty had got from Pop.

It was just a tiny thing, and the guy was holding it by its ears, which were the big floppy kind, and he was hitting it with a stick. I remembered Miss Elsa with the switch and how she had hit Misty's little puppy with it.

I went over and told the guy, Stop hitting the poor thing, but he just said to me, Get the fuck out of my goddamn yard or I'll call the cops and have them drag your sorry ass off to jail.

Let the poor thing go, I told him. What did it ever do to deserve being treated like that?

The guy said the little bitch had shit all over his new carpet. I'm just teaching it a lesson, and besides, it ain't none of your fucking business, so, like I said, get the hell out of my goddamn yard.

I thought there must be some way to get this guy to stop hitting the dog, so I said, Why don't you sell it to me. I took out my wallet, and there was $127 in it, and I took out $100.

Here, I said, take this. But the asshole shook his head. The dog ain't for sale, he said.

I took out everything I had, all $127, and held that out to him, then I reached in my pocket and pulled out even the few coins I had left after doing my laundry. The guy took the money, and you'd think he would have handed me the dog, but, instead, he drop-kicked it to me as if it was a football, and I knew the dog must have gotten a broken leg or something because it fell right back down when it tried getting to its feet. I lifted it, and it just lay there in my arms, whimpering and the guy said, Mister, you just bought yourself a dog, and he went inside and slammed the door.

I wanted to take the puppy to the vet, but I had paid all my money to buy her, so I went across and asked Mr. Pickford if I could have an advance on my wages, and I explained why I needed it, but he said, no, there would be no advanced wages, but I could work some overtime if I wanted, and I could get paid at the end of the week instead of waiting until the end of two weeks as was customary.

As if that was going to do me any fucking good.

So I took my high school ring down to Gary's Pawn and Payday Loan and got myself $60. It only ended up costing $45 for the vet to fix my little dog's leg. I know it would have usually cost a whole lot more, but I told Dr. Brink what had happened and how the little dog's leg got broke, and he said he would do what he could.

There was paperwork to be done, and I had to fill out the name of the animal and the address where it resided, and I didn't have a name yet for her, so I made one up; Mixy. That's what I wrote down on the form: Mixy. It was because she was a mixed breed; Dr. Brink said he thought maybe part Chihuahua and God only knows what else.

Finally Mixy's leg was fixed, and I took her home to my apartment. She had a cast on her leg pretty much just like a regular human cast, so I wrote my name on it because, well, that's what you do on a cast, you write your name on it, and I told Mixy that soon she would be all better and that Dr. Brink had said that with a bit of luck we would be able to remove her cast after four to six weeks.

Mixy fell asleep with me on the couch that evening while I was watching TV, and I forgot to set the alarm, and I was late punching in for midnight shift, and I knew that when he found out, Mr. Pickford would yell at me, but I didn't give a flying fuck. I was just happy that when my shift was over I would be able to go back and be with Mixy.

But when I got back to my apartment, Mixy was lying on the floor. I picked her up gently, but she didn't move. Her eyes were open and not blinking. I guess it wasn't just her leg that had been hurt when she got drop-kicked. Something must have gone wrong inside her.

I didn't know what to do with her little body. You can't go digging a grave in the asphalt of a paved parking lot, and someone's likely to get pissed if you start digging a hole in their front yard.

I had pawned my ring, but I only had twelve dollars left after paying the vet and the bus fare to get Mixy there and back, but I went out and spent nine of those dollars on a soft blanket, the kind you use for small babies, and I wrapped Mixy in it, then I put her in a cardboard box and real gently placed it in the dumpster out back of Pickford Grocery. I hoped no one saw me do it because I was crying like what Pop would have called a crybaby.

It was Thanksgiving day.

April 9

MR. Pickford GAVE me and everyone else at the store a $25 Christmas bonus, so I went out and bought myself a string of lights and some plastic pine branches to decorate my apartment. As I was returning home, I saw a man knocking at my door. I recognized him as the guy who lived in the apartment right above mine. He always looked kind of strange—pale skin, orange hair, pink lips, and bulging blue eyes, but he was always friendly, and he would greet me any time we passed. I had never really talked to him, though, and I didn't know his name.

Oh, I'm glad you're back, he said when he saw me. I was disappointed when I found your pad was empty. Thought I was going to have to split and come back later.

The man introduced himself as Abe. Just like Honest Abe, he said with a smile. Easy name to remember. Easy name to spell. A-B-E.

I told him my name and instead of shaking my hand, Abe held out his palm to do one of those high-five things. He went on to invite me to attend church with him on Thursday evening.

Why Thursday? I asked. Don't you go to church on Sunday?

Oh yeah, I go on Sunday, too, of course, but my church has a guest preacher here from Arkansas. He's holding four days of revival meetings and Thursday's his last day. Come with me; Lew, you'll get yourself a blessing. The Reverend Blackstone is a true man of God. The Holy Ghost has blessed him with the gift of tongues and great healing power.

It sounded kind of crazy, but, seeing as I wasn't scheduled to work at Pickford on Thursday night, and I had nothing else planned for that evening, I said to Abe, Yeah, sure I'll go.

Cool. Noticed that you don't got wheels. Need a ride?

I told him, I could use a ride, thanks.

Know what you mean, man. No wheels is a real bummer.

By Thursday, I had forgot all about Abe having invited me, but that evening he knocked on my door and said, You ready to cruise on over to Santa Margarita with me?

116

He was carrying a guitar, and when we got to his car, he tossed it in the trunk.

Got to slam that trunk real hard or the lid pops open, he said. Looks kind of funny to be truckin' down the highway, your trunk flappin' open. Abe motioned for me to get in on the passenger side.

He shoved one of those old cassette things into the stereo. You like Buck Owens? he asked, and without waiting for me to answer, he punched the play button and then he said, Not every day you get to cruise in a fine car like a Caddy, I bet.

It was a Cadillac, alright. Vintage 1985 or so, I guessed, and it had once been a fine car, no doubt. But that was a long time ago. Now, the speedometer needle jumped around convulsively, there were rips in the genuine leather seats, and the knobs on the aftermarket AM/FM Polyphonic with Cassette didn't match. One brown. One white.

But there were spotless floor mats covering the carpet, the cracked dash was polished, and the windshield was spotless. It was obvious Abe was proud of his car. I was glad I hadn't made some wiseass comment about it.

Well, here we are, Abe said a minute or two later. Close enough we could have walked, but why do that when you can cruise on over in a Caddy, right?

I looked around kind of surprised. I had been expecting to be taken to a neat, black-topped parking lot outside a probably-white building with stained glass, maybe even a tall steeple. Instead, Abe had pulled into a dirt lot out front of a building that looked more like a saloon than a church. In fact, there, right above the door, were the words *The Watering Hole*. The sign had been painted over, but the lettering still showed through. To the right of the entrance, painted on plywood, there was a newer sign that said *Santa Margarita Holiness Church.* Tacked to the bottom of the sign was a piece of yellow posterboard felt-markered with the words, *Holy Ghost Revival Meeting 7:00 p.m.*

We weren't the first to have arrived, and already a dozen, maybe fifteen cars were in the lot, all parked randomly here and there with no effort to line them up side-by-side in usual parking lot style.

From inside the church, there was the sound of people already singing. Abe pointed to the posterboard sign that said *7:00* p.m. and muttered something about him having obviously gotten the starting time wrong, so we slipped in and found seats on metal folding chairs in the last row.

That's our preacher, Abe whispered. Dig?

Where? I whispered back.

Shhh! Not so loud, man. The foxy dame up front of course.

Holy shit! This Santa Margarita Holiness Church of Bakersfield California had a lady preacher? And she wasn't even dressed in lady-like attire suitable for the house of the Lord. Instead, she was wearing skin-tight blue jeans, a flannel shirt, and a yellow cowboy hat.

Holy shit. A yellow cowboy hat on a lady preacher and in the house of the Lord. What the hell kind of twilight-zone church had this Abe guy dragged me off to? I mean, this was like something out of a B movie.

Her name's Preacher Tina. I'll introduce you after the meeting, Abe whispered.

But by this time it wasn't Preacher Tina that had my attention. My eyes were on the girl seated at the battered piano up front. She looked to be about my age, and, goddamn, she was pretty.

And, good golly miss molly, she sure could play that old upright. She was pounding out a song that reminded me of a music video I one time saw of Jerry Lee Lewis playing *Great Balls of Fire.*

At Santa Margarita Church, there weren't any timid old ladies singing in wobbly voices like at Waynesburg Baptist. No, the people here were on their feet and jumping, making the wood floor shake like a freight train passing through.

And all the while, a girl I was falling in love with was beating the hell out of an old upright piano in a song that sure didn't sound like any church hymn I ever heard.

After a while, Preacher Tina introduced Reverend Blackstone, a man of God and a revival preacher with great healing power, come to us here at Santa Margarita all the way from down south in Arkansas.

Folks were pretty much calmed down, now that the singing had stopped, and up front, the girl at the piano had closed the lid down over the black and white keys, and she was sitting with her head resting in her palms, looking bored as a kid listening to a school nurse talk about lice prevention and dirt beneath the nails.

She looked a little bit like an elf; then again, maybe it wasn't quite so much elf she looked like, but maybe more like leprechaun. Not quite so sweet and innocent as elf. Yeah, definitely not elf. Definitely more leprechaun. And her hair sure was pretty. Kind of reddish-blond, straight, short, kind of scraggly, just covering her ears.

Then Reverend Blackstone, as if he was trying to get my attention off the girl at the piano and like he was warning me that I wasn't supposed to be thinking lustful thoughts about a leprechaun I was falling in love with—especially since thinking those lustful thoughts about her was giving me a hardon right here in the house of the Lord; Reverend Blackstone stomped his foot on the hardwood floor real loud, and he jabbed his black *Holy Bible* into the air.

God's people shout Praise Jesus!

Praise Jesus.

God's people shout Praise the Lord!

Praise the Lord.

And now this B movie got even more crazy. Reverend Blackstone said it had come time for a healing. Was there anyone in the congregation tonight who felt a need for special healing from the Holy Ghost? If so, come forward and receive the anointing.

Yes Jesus!

There was a long pause and then a small stoop-backed woman made her way timidly toward the front, pulling behind her a reluctant girl, who looked to be round about five years old. The woman stood, head bowed, in front of the gray-faced revival preacher, and I thought maybe she had gone forward to have her stooped back made well.

But the lady said something about epilepsy, and she pushed the little girl forward to stand in front of Reverend Blackstone.

The man of God said, No, sister, this child does not have epilepsy. The poor creature is afflicted by demons. But he said it, *The pooah ka-reecha is aff-a-licka-ed bah dee-amons.*

I couldn't take my eyes off the little girl who stood there in front of that revival preacher. She was looking around, bewildered and scared, her eyes searching for someone to come to her rescue, but no one did.

And suddenly I saw it. Just like if someone had snapped their finger, I saw in the little girl's eyes that faraway look like Misty got after she was pulled across to the other side, swept over to the darkness.

Just then the little girl fell to the floor, shaking and having convulsions, and it reminded me of the time back in third grade, when Miss Potts told us, Now calm down, class. Calm down and stay in your seats. Boys and girls, did you hear me?

She told us Elizabeth was having an epilepsy, and there was nothing to be concerned about, and, if we just let poor Elizabeth be, her fainting spell would pass and then we could go on with our *Weekly Reader* story of *Abe Lincoln and the Slaves*. But of course all us kids paid Miss Potts no attention, and we ran over and stood around, staring at Elizabeth Blunt having an epilepsy fainting spell, and then, sure enough, she was soon over it, and we went back to our *Weekly Readers,* but nobody was paying any attention to *Abe Lincoln and the Slaves* because we were all of us staring at Elizabeth Blunt.

It wasn't much different here in the Santa Margarita Holiness Church of Bakersfield California. Everyone hurried up to the front and gathered round and were whispering and saying, surely this was the work of demons in the poor child, and Reverend Blackstone had to put out a hand and tell them, Make room, my friends, make room. Stay back, folks, stay back.

Then he got down on his knees beside the girl, and I thought he was going to pray to our father which art in heaven, but he just started screaming loud as he could for the demons to be gone, Be gone, I say, be gone! And he was pounding away with the palm of his hand on the floorboards, kind of like a referee at a wrestling match but louder and harder.

And that's when I couldn't take it anymore.

Leave her alone, I said, and I was surprised how loud my voice came out because I was feeling shaky on the inside. Leave the poor little girl alone. She has epilepsy, and if you'll just stay back and leave her be, it'll pass. I knew I was sounding like Miss Potts talking to a class of third graders, but that's just how it came out. I guess that's how someone wrote the script for this crazy B movie.

I bent over and picked up the little girl as gentle as I could, and by now she had pretty much calmed down, and I carried her outside, where a buzzing sodium vapor lamp flooded the dirt parking lot in dim yellow-orange light.

Back inside the hot, stuffy church with its bright fluorescents, there was all kinds of noise and commotion going on. I could hear people arguing, people shouting, and some lady crying out, Thank you Jesus.

Outside, the night was quiet and the air chilly and damp with fog. On the ground in front of me, the little girl was coming back to consciousness, and I kneeled down beside her and put my hand gently on her cheek because I wanted to comfort her, but she didn't seem to need any comforting.

She didn't seem terrified or scared, like you might think she would be, but, instead, she just lay on the ground, staring up at me as if I wasn't even there and like she was looking right through me and into the fog that swirled yellow in the sodium vapor lamplight, and in her eyes there was that far away look like Misty had in those days after she killed Miss Elsa and got dragged over to the dark side.

Behind me, the screen door of Santa Margarita Holiness Church creaked open and then slammed shut. I turned and saw the man of God from

Arkansas stumble unsteadily toward where I was kneeling, and I suddenly realized, I'll be goddamned, that son of a bitch isn't filled with the Holy Ghost, he's just had a bit too much Comfort.

It looked like he was coming to get the girl, and I was ready to do anything I could to stop him, but he just said to me, Young man, you are of the Devil, and may God punish you for what you did tonight. Then he walked unsteadily over to an old Chevy pickup and drove off, squealing his tires and shooting up dust and gravel as he pulled out of the parking lot and into the street.

Other people were coming out of the church by this time. Some of them came over to look at the little girl lying there on the ground, but when they saw she was okay and not having a seizure, they lost interest, and they got in their cars and drove away.

Abe came and asked if I needed a ride back home, but I didn't want to leave the little girl lying there alone, so I shook my head and said, Go on without me. I'll walk back. So he shrugged and then drove off in his Caddy with Buck Owens still coming from the AM/FM Polyphonic with Cassette, singing about putting another quarter in the jukebox.

One of the last people to come out of the church was the old stoop-backed lady, and she was walking over to me with another lady, whose arm she was holding because of being old and not very good at walking on her own. When she got over to me, I stood up, smiling and expecting her to be happy to see the little girl was okay and conscious, but, instead, the old lady was scowling, and she slapped my face. Then she took the girl's hand and yanked her to her feet so hard that it made me think, Holy shit, how can you be so strong if you can't even walk over here on your own.

Then she said to me that I was of the Devil and I should be ashamed because I had prevented this poor child from being healed of her affliction.

And then her and the other lady, whose arm she was still holding, dragged the little girl over to a white Oldsmobile that, in the yellow lamplight, was the color of old people's teeth, and they drove off into the fog of the Bakersfield night with just one tail-light working and the exhaust pipe rattling away loose under the car.

I sat down on the low cinderblock wall that was between the parking lot and the sidewalk, and I put my head in my hands, and all of a sudden I found I was shaking, but it wasn't just from the cold.

All I could think was, What the hell had just happened? How the fuck had I gotten myself a part in this crazy B movie, and I had sure done a crappy job of acting my part, whatever part that might be, but, in fact, no matter how good an actor you were in this kind of movie, there wasn't much of anything you could do to improve on things because the whole movie is so fucked up that people laugh at even the serious parts.

And now, sitting here on the cinderblock wall, I wondered what the hell had I done, sending Abe off without me because I hadn't been paying attention when we drove here, and I didn't have any idea how to get back to my apartment, even though it couldn't have been more than a few blocks.

I was wishing I had never come to this crazy church, when I was startled by the voice of someone standing behind me.

You're shivering. You must be cold.

I looked up to see the girl who played piano like Jerry Lee Lewis. The leprechaun I had fallen love with back in that crazy B movie that no longer made any sense.

I just sat there on the cinderblock wall, feeling a bit foolish and awkward, and then I held out my hand to shake the girl's, and I said, How do you do, a pleasure meeting you, and, as soon as I said it, I knew how stupid it sounded—kind of formal, like as if I was talking to the goddamn Queen of England or something. Obviously the B movie wasn't over yet.

The girl shook my hand and smiled, but it didn't seem so much a friendly kind of smile but more an amused kind of smile; about the kind of smile you would expect from a leprechaun, I guess. But it was the prettiest smile I had seen ever in my life, and suddenly I was in love again, even if this was crazier than any movie I ever saw.

My name's Tabby Cochran, the girl said to me, and then she just sort of stood there staring at me, and I knew I was blushing, and I hoped that the yellow light from the lamp would make it so she couldn't tell I was turning red.

Well, aren't you going to tell me what your name is? she said to me.

Trout, I told her. Lew Trout. It sounded stupid, I knew it right away. I mean, it's okay to introduce yourself like that if you've got a name like Bond, James Bond. But Trout, Lew Trout? Come on! Whoever wrote the script for this movie had sure screwed things up for me, screwed them up royally.

Lew, huh? Suppose it's short for Llewellyn.

I nodded. I mean what else was I supposed to do? You can't tell a lie about what your name is.

Yeah, but mostly they call me Lew, I said.

And then Tabby sat down beside me. Close. Really close, and the night was chilly, and I could feel the warmth of her body next to me, and all I wanted to do was put my arm around her and have her put her arm around me and we'd keep each other warm.

Things got to be a bit too much for you in there, tonight? Tabby said. I suppose you haven't ever been to a Pentecostal Holiness revival meeting before.

I'm sorry about what I did, I told her. This whole evening I've felt like I'm in some crazy B movie. I shouldn't have done what I did, but it wasn't right what that man was doing to the little girl, treating her like she had demons in her. I mean she's just a kid, and if you go telling her she's got demons in her, she'll come to believe it.

I remembered Miss Harmony, my second grade teacher, telling how people who lived over in Africa were infested with what are called tape worms living in their intestines and what are called hookworms living in their muscles and crawling around under their skin, and after she told us that, when night came and I was lying in bed, I knew I had tapeworms in me because I could feel them squirming in my intestine, and hookworms crawling under my skin because I could feel them, too, and it was the worst night of my whole life, lying there feeling worms squirming and crawling inside me, and I said to Tabby, how much worse it must be for the little girl to have people telling her she has demons living in her. That's got to be worse than worms.

When I told all that to Tabby, she looked at me kind of strange and said, Llewellyn Trout, I do believe you're a philosopher. Either that or you read too much Stephen King.

I guess I just sat there without saying anything for a while because she said, Well, Llewellyn Trout, are you going to tell me, or are you going to just sit there?

Tell you what? I said.

Are you a philosopher or are you a Stephen King fan?

Neither one, I said. I just feel sorry for the little girl.

I wanted to change the subject, so I said, You play really good. The piano, I mean. You sound a lot like Jerry Lee Lewis. Where did you learn to play like that?

Had a few lessons when I was a kid, but mostly I just learned it on my own.

Tabby told me that Preacher Tina was her mom, and on account of that, she always had to play piano at church.

But I don't mind, she said. I like playing.

I said to her, Holy shit, Tabby, you mean to tell me Pastor Tina is your mom?

Yeah, Tabby said. But we call her preacher, not pastor. Pastor sounds too formal. Sort of like calling her bishop or pope or something like that.

I was shivering again and Tabby asked wasn't I just about half froze?

I nodded.

Why don't you go on home? It's getting late, Tabby said to me.

I told her, I don't really know my way. A guy named Abe gave me a ride, and I wasn't paying attention to how we got here. I told Tabby the apartment was near Pickford Grocery and asked if she knew where that was, and maybe she could give me directions.

Sure, I know where it is, Tabby said. Used to live in those apartments, myself. Want me to walk you home, Llewellyn Trout?

Right then, I couldn't think of anything I would rather do than to spend more time with Tabby, so I said, Certainly, I would appreciate it greatly, and there I was, again, being all formal as if I was talking to the Queen of England.

As we walked back to my apartment, Tabby asked me all sorts of questions. How long had I been living in Bakersfield? Why did I leave Waynesburg? Did I have family back there? Did I like working at Pickford?

Tabby was surprised when I told her I had been in the Air Force. Did you fly jets? she wanted to know. Drop bombs?

I really didn't want her asking a lot of questions because I didn't want to tell her about all the things that had happened with Calli and with Jesus Sanchez and Major Dennis. I was afraid that if I did, Tabby would think I was a child molester or some other kind of pervert. I wanted to change the subject, so I said to Tabby, Why don't you tell me a bit about yourself.

She told me that Tina, that's what she called her mom; Tina had been preacher at Santa Margarita Holiness Church since not long after Tabby was born. About four years later, maybe it was five, Tabby's dad had run off with Tina's brother's wife. Isn't that a shit, Tabby said, My daddy ran off with his own sister-in-law.

Anyhow, Tina and Tabby had never had much money. People in the church gave what they could, but they didn't have much, themselves, and as a consequence, Tina and Tabby had never had much either.

I'm not complaining, Tabby said. I suppose me and Tina have always had pretty much everything we really needed. But I'll tell you something, Llewellyn Trout, I'm not staying poor all my life. I'm already on my way up. Already on my way out. I'm leaving Bakersfield. I've already quit my job, and I'm in the process of making plans for a move to Los Angeles. I've been trailer trash long enough.

We were to my apartment by this time, and Tabby said, wasn't it strange that I was living in the same apartment Tina and her used to live in before they moved into the single-wide trailer that maybe I had noticed in the parking lot at Santa Margarita Holiness.

I felt kind of awkward because, how could I send Tabby to walk back alone in the dark, so I told her I would walk her home.

Llewellyn Trout, you're a goof, Tabby told me. It's only four or five blocks, and I can walk back alone just fine. Do you think I'm scared of the dark or something?

Then I did something really stupid. I said to Tabby, Would you like to step inside for a little refreshment? And goddamnit, there I was again, talking like to the Queen of England, and right away I wished I hadn't said what I did, because now Tabby was going to tell me, no, she didn't want to come in, and I would feel even more stupid than I already did.

But she didn't say no. Instead she said, Llewellyn Trout, you're a gentleman to ask.

So Tabby came in, and I started fixing coffee for her, but when I opened the fridge to get milk, seeing as she wanted some in her coffee, she noticed there was a six-pack of Coors right there in front of the going-bad tomatoes, and she asked why hadn't I offered her a beer instead.

I said it was because I didn't want to be responsible for supplying alcoholic beverages to a little kid.

Tabby wrinkled up her freckled leprechaun nose and told me I was no more legal drinking age than she was.

I said, What age is that? and she said to me, I'm nineteen, almost twenty. Close enough to legal, don't you think?

So I opened a beer for her, and one for myself, and she laughed when mine foamed all over the place, and I said, It's not that funny.

Tabby sat down and said, Wow! this is the same couch I used to sleep on when Tina and I lived in this apartment. Tabby told how she used to fold out the couch every night, and Tina would go off to the bedroom because she didn't want to keep her daughter awake with *Jeopardy* and *Wheel of Fortune* because, after all, tomorrow was a school day and she wanted Tabby to be up bright and early.

When she had finished her second beer, Tabby got up to leave, and again I said I would walk her home, but she told me there was no need to, and what made me think she wasn't capable of looking out for herself?

I told her I was a gentleman, and had she ever heard of a gentleman allowing a lady to walk home alone?

Tabby grinned and said, Llewellyn Trout, what makes you think I'm a lady?

I walked her home, anyhow, and since I didn't have to work at Pickford that night, I decided to drink a few more beers before going to sleep, and then, instead of crawling into my bed like I always had before, I folded out the couch because I wanted to sleep in the same place where Tabby used to sleep, and I lay there imagining she was beside me, and I was thinking lustful thoughts, but this time the lustful thoughts weren't about Lindsey Longpoke, or Jennifer Olander, or Calli Moreno, or any of the other pretty girls, but, instead, about Tabby Cochran, and she was more beautiful than any of them, and, like you might imagine, this crazy B movie I couldn't get out of ended up that night being not G rated, probably not even R, yeah, probably more like X rated, even if it was all in my mind.

April 10

THE NEXT NIGHT I got fired. Mr. Pickford said it wasn't anything personal. Nothing I had done wrong. He simply had no further need of my services. He was sorry, and I was welcome to use his name for a reference. Oh, and, by the way, don't forget you'll need to return your uniform. Please make sure you've had it professionally cleaned.

Well, this was just fucking wonderful. It gave me a warm feeling to know it wasn't anything personal. Nothing I had done wrong. What the hell was I going to do now?

The next day was cold and rainy, and, come evening, I was curled up under a blanket and drinking hot chocolate for a change instead of beer, not because I wouldn't have preferred to be drinking beer but because nobody other than Pickford was going to sell beer to someone underage. Anyhow, I was sitting there feeling sorry for myself when there was a knock at the door, and when I opened it, there was Tabby. She was wearing a red Santa's elf hat on her head, and I thought, Goddamn, now Santa's gone and got himself leprechauns to work for him instead of elfs, but I didn't say it, and what I did say was, May I be of assistance?

Goddamn, you would think it was the fucking Queen of England standing at my door.

I brought something for you, Tabby said. She held out to me a plate covered with plastic wrap. Cookies, she said. Christmas cookies.

And, sure enough, there was no doubt about them being exactly that. Christmas angels with pink frosting and jingle bells with half-melted green and red sprinkles.

Tabby stood there smiling at me with that fucking Santa's elf hat on her head, her clothes half soaked from the rain, and water dripping from her nose, and, goddamn it, I was in love with her all over again.

I took the plate of cookies and asked would she like to come in. I didn't have any hot chocolate left but I could fix a pot of coffee. I said, Just look at you, you're half soaked. Let me get you a towel.

So Tabby came in and I got her a towel to dry her face and a sweatshirt and sweatpants she could change into. If you don't mind them being a few sizes too big, I said.

So me and Tabby sat on the couch eating frosted Christmas angels and jingle bells with melted sprinkles on top and washing them down with coffee.

As we sat there, Tabby said, What's the matter, Llewellyn Trout, do you think I've got cooties or something? Why the heck are you sitting way at the other end of the couch from me?

I just sat there blushing and I guess Tabby didn't think I was going to move to be closer to her, so she moved closer to me, instead, and she put the blanket I had earlier been cuddled up under over the two of us, and it gave me a warm, comfortable feeling, being there on the couch and having Tabby beside me and a warm blanket over the two of us.

I told Tabby I had got fired from Pickford, and she was real quiet for a while and then she said maybe it wasn't such a bad thing after all, because if I didn't have anything holding me here in Bakersfield, why didn't I come with her when she moved to Los Angeles?

Tabby had told me that she was planning to move to Los Angeles, but I had thought it was more or less just wishful thinking. It made me a bit disappointed to think that it didn't bother her one little bit to be moving away to where she would never see me again, and, even though she had scooched close to me on the couch and cuddled up with me under the blanket, it was obvious enough she wasn't in love with me, even though I was out of my mind in love with her.

But I sure as hell didn't want her to go thinking that I gave any more a damn about her than she did about me, so I said, well, maybe I would go with her, but then, again, Bakersfield was home to me and I'd be just as happy to stay right where I was.

Home to you? Tabby said. But you just moved here a few months ago. How can it be home? You know, Llewellyn Trout, I sometimes can't figure you out.

I told her that sounded kind of like a poem, and she looked at me as if maybe I was crazy, and I told her, You know, that sentence you just said, it rhymed. Llewellyn Trout—figure you out. It rhymes. Kind of like Sam I am, green eggs and ham.

Yeah, I guess it does, Tabby said. She sat there all quiet for a while, then she said, Llewellyn Trout, do you ever write poems? Did you ever write a love poem for a girl?

I was going to tell her, of course not, but she didn't wait for me to answer and, instead, went right on talking.

I remember when I was a kid, she said, Maybe ten years old or so, and this boy named Alex Quaid wrote me a love poem and put it in my desk when no one was looking. I was crazy in love with him, but my desk was such a mess I never found the poem until near the end of the school year, but when I finally found that note, I thought it had been put in my desk just that same day, and I was so happy and more excited than even on Christmas morning, and when it was recess time I went to where a bunch of boys were standing around at the drinking fountain, and I said, Alex Quaid, I love you, too, and what a sweet poem it was. But by that time Alex didn't like me anymore, and he was embarrassed in front of his friends, and he told me he didn't love me and he never had, and I was a stupid porcupine, which, I guess, was because my hair sort of stuck out in all directions back in those days.

Anyhow, I was still crazy in love with him, so I went home, brokenhearted, and I cried all night, and next morning Tina told me not to worry, I would soon get over the young man, and I told her I already had, and I would never love another boy, not ever again in all my whole life, and so there, Alex Quaid.

Me and Tabby laughed away at that story, and then Tabby said, You never answered my question, Llewellyn Trout. Did you ever write a love poem for a girl?

I said, Hell no, real guys don't write poems for girls.

Well, yeah, I know that, Tabby said. They draw their swords and do battle for them, right?

Better than sitting around writing love poems.

But what if you did, Llewellyn Trout? What if you did write a love poem? What would be the title? Who would it be to?

I was getting flustered and I said, Damn it, Tabby. I told you I don't write poems, and she told me, Go ahead, Llewellyn Trout, give it a try. Here's the first line, Shall I compare thee to a summer's day?

Like I said, I was getting flustered because what the hell are you supposed to say when a girl asks you something like that, so I said, What day are you leaving for Los Angeles?

I was relieved that it worked to change the subject, and Tabby said she was leaving on the 1st of January. A new year. A new start. A new adventure. Are you going to come with me, Llewellyn Trout?

I don't know, I said. What would I do if I moved to Los Angeles?

Who can say, Llewellyn Trout? There's all kinds of possibilities. What are you going to do if you stay in Bakersfield?

I told her, I'll work at a place like Pickford till I'm too old to get a hardon, then I'll retire and die, and I figured that was an answer that would get her to be quiet about writing love poems. Besides, I went on, I don't know anyone in Los Angeles, and how am I going to get started there without any money? I asked Tabby how much money she had.

Not much, she replied, but I hear it's pretty easy to make money in LA. You just stand on the street corner in the right part of town, and there's lots of dirty old men from Arabia and places like that, and they'll pay you pretty good for services rendered.

I looked at Tabby real hard, and I couldn't quite tell if she was being serious. Maybe she was just teasing me back for saying I would work till I was too old to get a hardon. But, on the other hand, there were women who made a living by standing on the street corner, and they had to come from somewhere, and maybe Tabby was one of them. Whatever the case, it kind of pissed me off that she would even say something like that, and I said, Goddamn it, Tabby, what the fuck. Are you serious?

What's the matter, Llewellyn Trout? Don't you think I'm pretty enough to make a living as a hooker?

What the hell do I care? I told her. You just go on to Los Angeles if you want. I'm fucking staying right here in Bakersfield.

Tabby nudged me with her elbow, Come on, Llewellyn Trout, lighten up. Don't guys from Arkansas have a sense of humor?

I told her, Back in Arkansas, guys don't like it when the girl they love goes talking about screwing other guys. Not even when it's a joke. And we don't . . .

I cut myself short because, What the hell had I just said? and I hoped Tabby hadn't noticed. But there she was sitting right next to me, grinning away at me with her freckled cheeks all bunched up around that fucking little leprechaun nose of hers and her green eyes dancing. She'd noticed alright. Well, shit.

So, that's it, isn't it? You're in love with me, aren't you, Llewellyn Trout?

Fuck it, Tabby.

Well? Aren't you?

Goddamn it, what kind of question is that? Here, hand me another cookie, would you. I hoped saying that would change the subject again.

Not till you give me a real answer.

What answer?

Are you in love with me?

Give me a goddamn cookie.

Tabby grinned and shook her head. Not till you give me an answer.

Goddamn it, she was enjoying this far too much, and I knew she wasn't going to let it go.

Well, are you?

Am I what?

You know what. Are you in love with me?

Yeah, I guess I am. Now give me a cookie.

I thought you might be, Llewellyn Trout. I hoped so.

Tabby handed me a pink-frosted angel, and just then her cell phone rang, because they always go ringing when no one wants them to, but this time I did want it to because it changed the subject.

Tabby put the phone on speaker, and it was her mom, and would Tabby please get her butt on home because Tina had just noticed that her laptop was missing and, unless Tabby knew where it had gone, Tina figured it must be that Reverend Blackstone had taken it because he was the only other person who had been in the trailer any time recently.

Tabby said, Well, shit, that son of a bitch. Sorry I got to leave, Llewellyn Trout, but Tina sounded pretty upset.

So Tabby left, but first she kissed me, and she said, Llewellyn Trout, I'm taking you with me to LA, whether you want to come or not. Then she hurried off, and she was still wearing my sweats, and it had stopped raining.

April 11

THE NEXT DAY was Christmas Eve. I was sitting there in my apartment feeling sorry for myself and wishing I had a six-pack, when Tabby came over with my sweat suit all washed and folded real neat. Me and Tina would like for you to come to our place tomorrow and have Christmas dinner with us, Tabby said. That is, unless you have other plans, of course.

Other plans? I guess that's what you have to say to be polite, but Tabby knew damn well I didn't have other plans.

I figured I should be polite, too, so I said, Are you certain your mother wouldn't be inconvenienced?

Tabby laughed. Of course she won't be inconvenienced. I don't think she even knows what big words like that mean. So come have dinner with us, Llewellyn Trout. It was Tina's idea. She'd be disappointed if you didn't come.

Anyhow, the next afternoon, Christmas day, I walked over to Tabby's place. I was surprised to see Abe's Caddy parked out front of the single-wide, and, sure enough, when I went in, there was Abe, sprawled out on the couch. He made room for me and said, Have a seat, Lew. Make yourself comfortable.

So me and Abe sat there drinking hot Christmas punch with only the tiniest bit of rum in it—that's what Tina said was in it, but to me it tasted like there was more than just a tiniest bit—and meanwhile Tabby and her mom worked in the kitchen, which was pretty much the same as working in the kitchen, dining room, and living room all at the same time, seeing as the place was so small.

Tabby was wearing that Santa's elf hat again, and I guess she had dressed up for the occasion because instead of her usual Levis and flannel shirt, she was wearing a dress that hung real loose on her, but real thin, and you could see the shape of her body through it, and she was so damn beautiful that it got me thinking lustful thoughts, and I told myself, Stop it Llewellyn, and to get my mind on other things, I said to Tabby, Can I help in the kitchen, and Abe, said, Yeah, let me help, too, so now all four of us were trying to work in a space not big enough for two.

It was a bit of a procedure getting things set up for dinner. A small Christmas tree was sitting on the dining table, and Abe moved it to the floor in the middle of the living room, being careful, Tina warned him, not to break any of the ornaments.

Next, the dried needles that had fallen off had to be brushed from the table and swept out the door. Finally, Tabby was able to put out four place settings.

Pretty quick it was obvious this wasn't going to be anything like Christmas dinner back at Uncle Stew and Aunt Marge's. No fine china with a gold rim around the edge. No polished silver. No nonalcoholic Martinelli's sparkling grape juice. And no red and green candles with plastic pine sprigs bunched neatly around.

Instead, Tabby set out four paper plates; four Styrofoam cups with a can of Bud alongside each of them; plastic knives, too, and plastic sporks. Then in the middle of the table, where the candles should have gone, went one of those big disposable aluminum foil pans in which a couple chickens instead of a turkey had cooked along with baby potatoes, onions, and carrots.

To finish things off, Tina took out a jar of store-bought beef gravy, nuked it in the microwave, and set it on the table, still in the jar.

Oh, and can't forget this, Tabby said, putting out a can of cranberries: Mrs. Smith's Colonial Style with 40% more inside but only half the calories. Date: expired.

When we finally sat down, I was disappointed when Tina had me sit across from Tabby, instead of beside her, but the dining situation in this trailer was kind of like a booth in a restaurant, with vinyl benches on each side of the Formica-top table, and Tina said for me and her to sit on one side and Tabby and Abe to sit on the other side, so that's what we all did because that's what you do when someone tells you where to sit.

As we ate, I felt a foot nudge mine under the table, and I looked over at Tabby and winked at her, and she smiled back, and it was silly but I slipped my shoe off and I hoped she would do the same thing, and she did, and our feet with just our sox on for a few moments played footsies under the table, and it seemed strange because that foot had a sock on, and Tabby wasn't wearing sox, was she? Then just as I was thinking that, Tabby got up to nuke another jar of gravy and at the same time Tina got up to turn on the outside Christmas lights because no one had remembered to do that this evening, but the foot was still right there on top of mine, and I looked over at Abe, and his eyes got suddenly big and then we both started laughing, and I thought, Holy shit, he thought he was playing footsies with Tina.

Me and Abe, both of us, were turning red as a sloe gin fizz, but Abe with his usually pale skin, bright blue eyes, pink lips and orange hair was probably looking even redder than me, and Tina and Tabby kept asking us, What's so funny, what's so funny, come on and tell us, what's so funny, but you can be damn sure that me and Abe weren't going to say.

After we finished eating, Tina shoved what little remained of the food into a couple Tupperwares. Everything else went into a black trash bag. Sporks, plates, empty cranberry can, everything—even the paper placemats. Then Abe took the trash bag out, carried it across the parking lot, and dumped it into the dumpster out back of Taco Loco.

And then what happened next made me feel really stupid, because it was time to exchange Christmas gifts, and I hadn't brought anything to give anyone because Tabby had told me not to because nobody else was going to be exchanging gifts.

Anyhow Tina got a new *Holy Bible* from Abe, and Abe got a straight razor with a mug of shaving soap and one of those old fashioned brushes to put it on with.

Then Tabby gave me a not-very-neatly wrapped package, and she said it was from her, and what was in it was custom made just for me, and she told me how difficult it had been finding something she thought I would like, but she was glad stores had stayed open late on Christmas Eve.

Anyhow, I unwrapped it, and inside was a yellow sweatshirt with words printed on it, and on the front it said *Hello LA*, and on the back it said, *Bye Bye Bakersfield,* and wrapped in with it was a bus ticket that said *Point of Departure: Bakersfield, CA* and *Point of Arrival: Long Beach, CA.*

And you'll notice it's not round trip, Tabby said, grinning away at me like a leprechaun but still wearing that goddamn hat like an elf. The Greyhound leaves New Year's Day at six a.m., and you better be there on time, Llewellyn Trout, because the bus won't wait for you if you're late.

I just sat there speechless while inside me something happened like had never happened before, and I suddenly knew that if Tabby was going to be on that bus at six a.m. on New Year's Day, I was going to be on it, too, and there wasn't anything in the world that would stop me. Nothing.

I didn't care if that bus was going to Kabul Afghanistan or to Bumfuck Egypt, because wherever it was Tabby Cochran was going, well, that's where I was going, too, and there was nothing in the world I wanted more than to be on that bus, and Tabby meant more to me than anything else ever could, and she wasn't just someone to lie there at night thinking lustful thoughts about, but she was the person I wanted to spend the rest of my life with. And it's strange that a sweatshirt and a bus ticket would make something like that happen to you on the inside, but it did, and I should have said something else, but all that came out was Thank you, Tabby, I like it a lot, and she said, You better be at the station, Llewellyn Trout. Six a.m. sharp.

But Tabby's mom let out a loud wail and said, Oh, no! You didn't go buying tickets ahead of time, did you? And Tabby said, Yes, and, Why? and, Are tickets going to go on sale or something?

Tina said, no, but she hoped Tabby could get a refund, and Tabby said, I don't need a refund, because I'm going to be on that bus, come hell or high water. Besides, I promised Llewellyn Trout I'd take him to LA, and I intend to keep my promise.

Tina said for Tabby just to go ahead and open her present and then she would understand. It was a kind of small present, and I thought probably some kind of ring or jewelry or something, but it ended up being a couple of old keys.

Tabby said, well, actually, she more screamed, What, Tina! You're giving me your truck? And Tina nodded her head and Tabby jumped up off the couch all excited and saying, Thank you! Thank you! Thank you! and then she calmed back down and said, But Tina, I can't accept it, you need the truck.

Tina shook her head. Nope, I won't be needing it no more, she said. You see, me and Abe are getting married, and we figure if we pool our money we'll have enough to buy ourselves a brand new car.

Tabby just stood there for a long time staring at her mom and then she said, Abe? You're getting married to Abe?

Yep, Tina said. Look here. She held out her left hand and pointed to a diamond ring. Abe gave it to me this afternoon. I kept waiting for you to notice.

Abe just sat there beaming, his pink lips smiling and his blue eyes sparkling.

April 12

NEW YEAR'S DAY, I was packed and ready to go when Tabby pulled up bright and early in the truck she got from Tina. Actually, it wasn't all that early, and not at all bright, either, due to the Bakersfield fog.

That's all you got? Tabby asked as she helped me throw into the back of her truck my couple suitcases and a cardboard box I had scrounged from the dumpster out back of Pickford.

That's it, I'm a man who travels light, I told her, and then off we went.

The heavy fog should have kept traffic slow, but it didn't, and everyone was going faster than shit, and Tabby said that's just how things always were on Highway 99 going south out of Bakersfield, though she couldn't imagine what it was that rednecks and Mexicans were always in such a hurry to get to so early in the morning—especially out here in the middle of nothing but farm fields.

I said, Maybe everyone's in a hurry to escape from Bakersfield, and Tabby grinned and said, Well, let's just hope they're not all headed to the same place we are.

That was the first time I had really thought about it, and I realized I had no idea where the hell it was we were actually going. Los Angeles, I knew that much, but anything more specific, I had no clue. So I asked, and Tabby told me she would be staying with her Uncle Jimmy.

He's a pastor at a church in Orange County, just a bit south of LA, she told me.

Tabby had already called and asked her uncle if it would be okay for me to stay a while, too, and he had said of course, I was welcome, because any friend of Tabby's was a friend of his, so if I wanted to, I could stay there until I was able to find a job or do whatever it was I intended to do.

After a long pause, Tabby glanced over sideways at me real quick because she had to keep her eye on the road due to the heavy fog, and she said, Tell me, Llewellyn Trout, what is it you intend to do?

And, shit, before I could really think of anything sensible to say my words just came out like they so often seemed to be doing in this B movie, and what I said was, I intend to marry you, Tabby Cochran, and then I knew immediately what a stupid thing that was to say because here the two of us had known each other for only a bit over two weeks, and there was no way any girl in her right mind was going to say yes to marrying me.

Tabby said, Llewellyn Trout, what did you just say? and I felt really stupid and I said, Fuck it, Tabby, forget I even said that; it just sort of slipped out.

Forget it? What are you talking about, Llewellyn Trout? That's not the kind of thing a girl just forgets. Did you say you intended to marry me?

I said to her, Well, yeah, I did, but it was a stupid thing to say so forget it even happened.

I'm not forgetting anything, Tabby said, and she cranked her window down and reached her arm out and, with big round-and-round motions, signaled for the old white-haired lady riding in the passenger seat of the truck alongside us to roll her window down, and the old lady looked at us like probably Tabby was out of her mind or something, but, none the less, her window slid slowly down.

Tabby put her head out the window and I thought, Shit, she's going to crash this truck, driving crazy like that.

Llewellyn Trout just asked me to marry him, Tabby yelled real loud so she could be heard over the sound of the traffic and the wind.

A scowl went over the old white-haired lady's face, and she cupped a hand to her ear and shoved her head further out the window.

I'm getting married to an honorable southern gentleman, Tabby yelled, but this time even louder. Me and Llewellyn Trout are going to Vegas and getting married.

The white-haired lady scowled and shook her head. It was hard to tell if she had heard or not, but her window slid slowly closed, and the old man behind the wheel sped up, and I think would have pulled over a lane to the left, but there was no going left without running head-on into an on-coming cattle truck, F350, or big rig.

I'll be damned, Tabby said. Those grouches didn't even wish us congratulations.

All I could think was, Holy shit, does that mean she's saying yes to marrying me? And is the wedding already planned, and it's going to be in Las Vegas?

Goddamn, I was back in that fucking B movie, for sure. Come to think of it, I'm not sure I had ever left. And because I needed to do something to get my head straight more than because I was hungry, I said, Let's stop for breakfast.

That meant driving back into Bakersfield, but Tabby said that was okay because we would have to go back anyhow if we were driving to Las Vegas to get married, so a while later, we pulled in to a place called Fred's Diner and Cafe, with neon signs in the windows for cold beer and a painted-on-plywood sign out front that I think was supposed to be of a sweet old grandmother but instead looked more like an evil witch, and she was holding what looked to me like a pie, probably an apple one, and I figured, seeing as witches can't be trusted with apples, maybe me and Tabby better stay away from the pies in this place. And I realized, goddamn, this wasn't just some B movie but more like some Salvador Dali painting, and why in the hell were those kinds of thoughts about witches and apples even jumbling around in my goddamn head?

Anyhow, me and Tabby went in and waited a long time to be shown to a table, and finally a waitress noticed us and yelled out, Anywhere you want, darlings, anywhere you want. This ain't no call-in-for-reservations type joint.

Yeah, we were definitely back in Bakersfield. Maybe that's why it seemed more crazy than a B movie.

We ordered a stack of pancakes, but they weren't blueberry because the waitress said, What makes you think we got blueberries, darling? If you want something like that you should have stopped at a fancy place like Denny's.

While we were waiting for our stack of not blueberry pancakes, Tabby called Tina and explained about me and her getting married, and I had never seen Tabby so excited, and those green eyes of hers were sparkling, and she had that leprechaun grin and was talking so fast I was surprised that Tina could even understand what she was saying, and I heard Tabby tell her mom she would have to ask me, of course, but she was sure it would be fine, and she pushed the phone's mute button and said, Llewellyn, do you mind meeting Tina and Abe in Vegas and we'll all four of us get married at the same time, and for a while I just sat there looking stupid because I wasn't aware of having said that it was okay for Las Vegas to be where we would get married in the first place, and I wasn't sure what was going on here, so I said, You do as you please, my dear, and the reason I said a thing like that, other than it being a southern gentlemanly thing to do, was because in this B movie it seemed as if half the time I was talking to the Queen of England and the other half the time I was just not making much sense at all, and, anyhow, I figured there were times when it was better just to step back and stay out of the way, and I was pretty sure this was one of those times.

When we left Frank's Diner and Cafe, there was a big green puddle under Tabby's truck, and we spent most of the day getting the radiator fixed.

It was late afternoon when we finally left Bakersfield again, and as we got into the mountains, driving toward Tehachapi, it began to snow, and that for me was exciting because I had only seen snow a few times in my life, and I begged Tabby to pull over so I could get out and build myself a snowman.

Let's pull over and make a frosty, I told her.

So Tabby took the next exit, and took it fast so the pickup fishtailed in the snow and almost took us off the exit ramp.

Here, Stop, Stop, Stop! I said, pointing to an open field all covered with new snow, and I knew I was sounding like some excited little kid, but I didn't give a damn because today was maybe the happiest day of my life.

Tabby put on the brakes hard and the truck skidded, coming to a sudden stop just off the road.

Meant to do that, she said, and I told her, Yeah, I bet you did.

Tabby opened her door and tumbled out into the snow, then she scrambled to her feet, and I guess she must have scooped up a handful of snow and tossed it at me because I wasn't watching but was already running across the open field on the other side of the pickup when her snowball hit the back of my head. But it was only hard enough to catch my attention, and I turned and looked at Tabby standing there grinning that leprechaun grin of hers at me, and I picked up some snow, and I packed it real hard and tossed it back, missing Tabby but hitting her truck with a loud smack.

Goddamn it, Llewellyn Trout, make them softer, and don't go hitting my truck. Tabby made another snowball, tossing it and this time hitting me square in the face.

It wasn't hard, but it took me by surprise, and I lost balance and sprawled on my back in the snow.

Tabby stood there looking down at me, laughing and threatening me with another snowball, already made and in her fist.

You surrender, Llewellyn Trout?

Hell, no, never, I told her, and I grabbed Tabby's ankles and pulled her down, and she landed on top of me, still laughing. Then to my surprise, she sat on my chest, legs on either side of me, pinned my arms to the ground, gave me a kiss and then jumped back to her feet, and at that moment I think I was happier than maybe ever before in my life.

Tabby stood there laughing as I waved my arms and moved my legs back and forth to make a snow angel.

It don't look like an angel to me, I said after I got to my feet and stood there beside Tabby, staring at my not-very-artistic creation in the snow.

Yeah. Just kind of a mess, isn't it? Maybe it works better if you let the snow get deeper.

Do you think it's deep enough for a snowman?

Maybe a small one, let's try.

Like the angel, the snowman didn't turn out worth shit. Small sticks and bits of weeds and old leaves were mixed in with the snow, and patches of brown mud, and the balls were all lopsided. Not at all like the snowmen on Christmas cards.

I don't think I like snow, I said. Besides, it's too damn cold. Let's get out of here. Why the hell in the movies when people made snow angels did they get up and just dust snow off their clothes like it was dry white powder and the people were still warm and dry, but, here, I try to do the same thing and my clothes get soggy and I'm freezing.

When we got to the truck, it was obvious we weren't going anywhere. Tabby turned the ignition, but there was nothing more than a chattering click from up front.

Tabby said, Darn it, I left the lights on. This is a piece of crap Tina gave me. Leaky radiator, battery that goes dead in just a few minutes. You got an automobile club card, Llewellyn Trout?

I told her, Are you kidding? I don't even got a car, why would I have an auto club card? So what's next?

Tabby pulled out her cell phone, but no bars. Mine either.

I guess we're stuck here till someone stops and gives us a jumpstart, Tabby said, and she lifted the hood to see if there was anything obvious, but I was pretty sure it was the battery.

Hope someone comes soon, I said, because if not, we're going to freeze our asses off.

But no one did come soon, and Tabby said, What the hell, why aren't there any cars? I wonder if they closed the highway, or something? So we tried the radio in the truck, and even though the battery didn't have power to crank the motor, it still had enough for the radio—at least for a little while. So we listened, and sure enough, the highway was closed in both directions due to accidents.

The news reporter was interviewing Officer Bixby of the California Highway Patrol, and, according to him, it had been ascertained that the highway closure was due to a severe miscalculation on the part of several vehicle operators, one of whom was a juvenile who had apparently misunderestimated the danger of the local adverse weather conditions and had allegedly traversed the highway at an excessive rate of speed, and, unfortunately, had collided and suffered gross bodily trauma, and so you folks all buckle your seatbelts and drive safe in both directions.

And I said, Well, shit, now I for sure don't like snow.

No whining, Tabby said. Stopping here was your idea. Besides, you're supposed to be happy about spending the night in a pickup with a pretty girl like me.

Tabby got a couple blankets from a duffle bag in the back, and they were just a little damp, and she told me to get myself some dry clothes from my suitcases.

So I did, but as I changed, I felt kind of funny doing it there in front of Tabby and all, but Tabby didn't seem to be paying any attention to watching me like I would have been if it was her doing the changing, and by now she had got things all arranged with blankets in the cab of the truck, and I climbed in, and she told me, Crawl in under these here blankets, Llewellyn Trout and keep me warm, but forget any ideas you might have about getting too friendly, because we aren't married yet.

I laughed, and she said, I'm serious, Llewellyn Trout, I'm not doing it till I'm married.

Well, then, that's that, I guess, I said with a grin. Damn, Tabby, you've gone and screwed up my plans for the evening.

You're a goof, Llewellyn Trout. But don't you worry, when time comes, I'll make it worth your waiting.

Actually, I was much too cold to be having lustful thoughts right then, and as I sat there with Tabby, all cuddled up beside me, the only thing I was thinking was, I wish I hadn't been so stupid as to go playing in the snow.

You're a gentleman, aren't you, Llewellyn Trout? Tabby said. One of those honorable gentlemen from the South?

Yeah, that's me, I told her. Kind of like Colonel Sanders—a real southern gentleman, and she said, Llewellyn Trout, has a gentleman like you ever been with a girl? I mean, you know, did you ever . . .

And I said to her, Tabby, I told you I am an honorable gentleman, didn't I?

And it seemed that my answer was good enough for her because she didn't ask any more questions, and I was glad, because I sure as hell didn't intend to be telling her about the first time with Leena Hornsbey up at Fuller Ridge back in Waynesburg.

Or about the times with Jennifer Olander.

And for damn sure not about the time with the woman who I never even knew what her name was because, well, here I am, right out of Air Force basic training, and I haven't hardly even seen a girl for eight long weeks, and I'm taking the Greyhound to the place where I'm going to get trained on how to be a titless WAF, and I find myself waiting in this Greyhound bus station somewhere, I think it was in Oklahoma, and there's a three-hour delay before the departure of the bus I'm transferring to, so I'm sitting there, bored out of my skull, and I go to the news stand to buy a *Popular Mechanics* but end up with a *Penthouse,* instead, and I'm looking at it and hoping no one will notice, but all it's doing is making a bad situation worse, and so I go into one of the restrooms there in the Greyhound station, and it's one of those restrooms with both a man and a woman sign on the door, and a wheelchair, too, and the door has a handle with a lock, and I push the lock button, and I'm in there with my magazine, and I'm having lustful thoughts about that beautiful centerfold, and I guess I didn't completely lock the door, because in walks this woman, and, I think for sure she's going to scream and run out and probably call the cops or something, but she doesn't. Instead, she just comes right on in and makes sure the door is really locked this time.

She's not pretty like that woman in the *Penthouse,* but, then again, she's not butt ugly, either, and, after all, she's real and not just a paper centerfold, and, well, after eight weeks in basic training you make do with what you've got, and who cares if she's not especially pretty and probably about thirty-five years old and I'm only nineteen; like Pop used to say, you make do with what you've got.

So that's what me and that woman do. Right there on the green tile floor. And the whole while, the magazine's lying beside us, still open at the centerfold, and the *Penthouse* Pet staring right back at me.

I guess sometimes you make do more than once with what you've got.

When it's all over, I think, Holy shit, Llewellyn Trout, what the hell have you done? You better unlock that door and then get out of here and run. Run for your life, Llewellyn Trout. Run for your fucking life.

But the woman, all casual and like nothing happened, puts on her clothes and adjusts them in the mirror, which has Mexican graffiti scratched on it, and she makes her dress look all neat and presentable, and her hair, too, and lipstick as well, and then she walks out, and there's a lady outside waiting to use the restroom, and she has a girl with her, and when she sees the woman I made do with coming out and me still in there and the *Penthouse* magazine open to the centerfold and lying there on the tile floor, she makes a *humph* noise and says, Disgusting! Then she hurries away, pulling the girl along behind her, and the girl's crying, Wait, Mommy, wait, I've got to go pee.

Not long afterward, I see the woman I made do with get on a bus, but just before the door closes, she pauses and turns to look back at me and waves, kind of timid like, but I pretend I don't see, then the bus door closes, and she's gone, and I know I'll never see her again, and I think, I don't even know your name, but, after all, how could I because you never said a word the whole time I was making do with you. And come to think of it, I hadn't said a word, either.

No, I damn sure wasn't going to tell Tabby about that one. I'm good at keeping secrets. Even crazy B movie secrets.

The night got darker. And colder. A whole lot colder. A few cars passed by, and I figured probably the road must be open by now, so me and Tabby took turns scrambling out the door each time we heard a car, hoping to flag someone down for a jumpstart. But the cars always kept right on going, and soon we gave up.

We had been listening to the radio for a while, but soon even that went dead, and there was only the sound of the wind outside, and the two of us did our best to keep ourselves warm beside each other under those two thin, almost-dry blankets.

And now we go to breaking news, Tabby said in one of those sing-song-serious TV newscaster type voices. Two young people from Bakersfield have been found froze to death in a pickup truck alongside Highway 58, ten miles west of Tehachapi. Coming to us live from the scene is reporter Llewellyn Trout.

I didn't say anything, but Tabby wasn't going to let me off the hook.

Can you hear us, Llewellyn? Have you got our live, on-the-scene report?

You are not coming through very clear, I said, figuring I may as well play along.

Can you tell us anything from the scene of the tragedy?

Well, the authorities aren't releasing any names until next of kin have been notified, but I can tell you that even in her frozen state, the girl is beautiful, and she has these kick-ass frozen green eyes that melt your heart.

And how about the young man? Can you tell us anything about the young man who is reported to be in the truck with her?

Yes, it appears that he could have gone off and saved himself, but he was obviously an honorable gentleman, and he refused to leave the lady's side, even though it cost him his life.

So he's definitely dead as well?

No doubt about it. He's frozen stiff. Now back to you in the news-room.

Tabby laughed. Froze stiff, is he? Llewellyn Trout, you're a goof.

I put my arm around Tabby and held her close. Damn! the night was cold, but maybe not so cold that I wasn't having lustful thoughts, after all.

It wasn't until almost 8 o'clock the next morning that someone was nice enough to stop and help us. A Mexican guy in an old Durango stopped and gave us a jumpstart. Tabby offered him a five dollar bill, but he wouldn't take it. Keep and give to someone who really needs, he said.

Tabby smiled and said Bueno diez.

Buenos días, he answered with a grin, and then he drove off, his tires making slushy sounds in the melting snow.

April 13

AFTER WE WERE on our way again, Tabby got a call from her mom. Tina said her and Abe were already living it up big in Sin City, and they were worried because they hadn't been able to get through to us.

Tabby said to her, What the heck, Tina, you're in Vegas already? That means you must have been one of those jerks that passed us by last night and didn't even stop to help, and then Tabby laughed and explained what had happened to the truck.

Tina was sorry that her and Abe hadn't seen us, but she was glad everything had worked out. Now at least she knew why they hadn't been able to get hold of us last night on Tabby's cell phone.

Anyhow, Tina said that she and Abe wanted to go ahead and get started on the wedding arrangements. They hoped it could be arranged for today if possible because Abe only had two days before he had to be back at work, and that meant if we could get married this afternoon, tomorrow could be their honeymoon, so if me and Tabby didn't mind, they'd go ahead and start making arrangements.

Tabby said, Go ahead, we should be there sometime around noon. That is, if this darn truck you gave me doesn't break down again.

It was maybe an hour or so later that Tina called back and said everything was a go. Someone had cancelled so a time slot had opened up at the chapel, and if we could make it there by three that afternoon, we could all four of us get married in a double ceremony, which had the added advantage of costing only a little bit more than a regular single ceremony, but me and Tabby didn't need to worry about a thing because Tina and Abe were covering all expenses.

Tabby said that was so generous of them and she wanted to know what kind of a wedding was it going to be. But Tina wouldn't tell. Abe and her wanted it to be a surprise for me and Tabby, but, not to worry, there was no doubt we would both love it.

Tina and Abe had already checked in at a Motel 6, and they had reserved a room for me and Tabby as well. We were to meet them there and then all four of us together would go to the wedding chapel.

When we arrived, Tina seemed to be in a bit of a fluster.

Abe told her, Take it easy, Honeybunch, but Tina said a woman had a right to be a bit flustered on her own wedding day, Isn't that right, Tabby?

Tina was disappointed that me and Tabby didn't have anything special to wear, but she agreed we certainly didn't have time to go buy anything new, and we would just have to make do with what we had, she supposed.

Me, I didn't have a tie, but Abe had an extra, and he was happy to loan it to me, Just don't go spilling on it.

And when I saw what Tabby was wearing, I said, but not too loud, Holy shit, because she was more beautiful than I had ever seen her, and if I wasn't so busy with other things, that dress on her most certainly would have started me thinking lustful thoughts.

There wasn't a lot of time to spare, and soon Tina came out wearing a dress she called lemon chiffon, and shiny green shoes she called key-lime gloss. A while later, Abe came out dressed in a gray polyester suit, oxblood loafers with shiny pennies in them, and a pair of white socks that Tina said were showing just a bit too much, So please loosen your belt, Sugarpie, and pull those pants of yours down just an inch or two. They don't always have to be up above your navel, you know.

Abe mumbled something about the henpecking having already started, but he did as he was told, and then he said, Well, it looks like our wheels have arrived.

I had figured we would all be climbing into Abe's Caddy, and that's how we would get to the wedding chapel—probably listening to Buck Owens on the AM/FM Polyphonic with Cassette, but Abe grinned proudly and pointed to a pink Cadillac that was just pulling up out front of the Motel 6.

Wow, that's how we're getting to the chapel? Tabby asked.

Yep. A pink Cadillac. You're looking at our wedding wheels, my dear, Abe told her. What did you expect with big spenders like me and Tina paying the tab? We went all out with the Elvis Special Deluxe Package. Even paid extra dough for the pink Caddy limo service.

Abe handed each of us a glossy brochure that described the Elvis Special Deluxe Wedding Package in detail.

I glanced at my copy, and, goddamn, what in the hell kind of wedding was this going to be? I hadn't been expecting anything like the few weddings

I had gone to back in Waynesburg, but this was going to be crazy. Not bad crazy, just make-you-laugh crazy.

The Caddy's driver was wearing silky white gloves, and he bowed and made a fancy flourish as he opened the car doors. Everyone piled in. Me and Tabby in back, Tina and Abe up front with the driver.

As we rolled off, everyone was laughing, while Abe read aloud from the brochure a list of what was included with the Elvis Special Deluxe Wedding Package.

Elvis as minister, singing three songs
Ceremony in main chapel
Floral presentation of two roses
Matching boutonniere
24 poses & proofs
Video on VHS tape
Pink Cadillac limo service (optional at additional cost)

Abe, you really did go all out, didn't you? Tabby said.

Abe turned around and looked at us from the front seat. He was grinning away, proud as can be, and he had put on a pair of Elvis sunglasses. He reached into a pocket and pulled out a second pair and handed them to me. I felt kind of self conscious, but Tabby and Tina both said at the same time, Go on, Llewellyn Trout, put them on. So I did, and when I glanced in the driver's rear view mirror to see how I looked, I thought, Why is it I can't seem to get out of this damn B movie?

As the brochure had promised, there were roses and matching boutonnieres waiting for us when we arrived, and when the time came, Elvis, himself, led Tina and Tabby down the aisle, and, the moment I saw him, my heart sank because I recognized him immediately, and it was, of course, Mr. D from Waynesburg High.

But he didn't seem to recognize me; that was fortunate. I guess I had changed a bit in the three and a half or so years since that afternoon when he walked out of the darkened computer lab and said to me, Why, Lew? Why did you do it?

I stood there at the front of the chapel, and I just hoped to god Mr. D wouldn't recognize me, and I quick slipped back on those Elvis sunglasses that I had taken off when we came into the chapel.

The brochure had promised that Elvis would sing three songs, and the first one was *Love Me Tender*, and I remembered Mr. D and Lindsey

Longpoke dancing together to that same song back at the Christmas dance at Waynesburg High, and, now, it was Mr. D, himself, singing the song, and even though he didn't look much like Elvis, even with his artificial sideburns and his white jumpsuit with fake jewels, Mr. D sure did sound a lot like Elvis when he sang.

My sunglasses didn't work for long, and, just as Mr. D got to the part about "we are gathered to witness the coming together," he obviously realized who I was. I could see it in his eyes that he did, and his face first turned red and then became pale, and he stared at me with eyes that seemed first angry and then more like sad. And from this point on, his voice was a bit unsteady, and I don't think anyone else noticed it, but I did, and when the ceremony part was over, Mr. D sang his second song, *I Need You So,* and the whole time I was thinking about Lindsey Longpoke and the rubber tubing from her father's stethoscope, and about Mr. D stopping to give me a ride and not caring that I got his car all wet and muddy, and him going out of his way to arrange for me to learn JavaScript, and I remembered the picture in the Bible story book of Judas with a crooked smile and sneaky eyes. I felt terrible.

I think Tabby sensed that there was something wrong, maybe that I was scared to be getting married, and she squeezed my hand and smiled at me, and I tried to smile back, but inside I wasn't smiling but thinking about Lindsey Longpoke and wondering if Mr. D knew about all the Waynesburg gossip, and I wondered if he had heard about the rubber stethoscope tube, and from the way he was looking at me, I was pretty sure he had.

And then at last *I Need You So* was over, and Mr. D was suddenly smiling again, and the music changed and was happy and Mr. D started dancing, as he sang *Viva Las Vegas,* and the rest of us were dancing, too, and singing along, but I sure didn't feel like dancing, and not like singing either.

Mr. D led us, dancing, out of the chapel, and as he went out the door, the PA system announced, Elvis has left the building.

Then me and Tabby, Abe and Tina, too, had to sign papers that affirmed that we had been officially married in the state of Nevada, and then Mr. D took pictures of everyone and he said they would be mailed to us along with the VHS tape of the ceremony. Then he disappeared into a side room. I was relieved because I figured I would never see him again.

But I sure was wrong about that one.

Altogether, the wedding was over and done in not much more than twenty-five minutes, and Abe said that was just as well, seeing as the guy with the pink Caddy charged by the minute as well as by the mile.

April 14

ME BEING TWENTY and Tabby nineteen, neither of us would, unfortunately, be allowed into the casinos. Abe told us he had heard there was lots of stuff for young folks to do in Las Vegas, he just didn't know what it was or where it was. He said him and Tina might try their luck at the slots tomorrow, but being newlyweds, they had other plans for tonight and that no doubt me and Tabby did, too, and he raised an orange eyebrow and winked a blue eye at Tina, and then his pale face blushed red at his own joke. He pulled out his wallet and handed me and Tabby each a hundred dollar bill.

It's your wedding present from me and Tina, he said. Go get yourself some fancy grub somewhere and enjoy your evening.

I said, That's overly generous of you, Abe and Tina. Thank you so much for your generosity, and then I mumbled something about being sorry about the way that came out but the movie script has really screwed me up.

Tabby looked at me like, What the heck kind of person have I just gone and got married to.

Anyhow, me and Tabby went out to eat, and I had told her about my mom being Vietnamese, so she wanted to go to a Vietnamese restaurant, which ended up being a not very fancy one, but the food was good, and me and Tabby both ordered *Canh Chua Ca Bong Lau,* and Tabby asked what did that mean and how was it pronounced, and I said, Just because Mom was Vietnamese doesn't mean I come out knowing how to speak the language, and Tabby laughed and said, Yeah, I guess it was a dumb question.

When me and Tabby got back to our room, there was a six-pack of Budweiser waiting for us in a bucket of ice, and there was a note on it.

Enjoy, Love Tina and Abe.

Tabby said, Goddamn, don't those guys know that on your wedding night you're supposed to drink champagne, not beer, and her saying that reminded me of Pop and how him and me had laughed about turning the bath water into champagne, and when I told Tabby about it, she laughed almost as hard as me and Pop had laughed when it happened.

Then she said, Tell me about your Pop, Llewellyn. You don't talk much about your family.

And I told her my family was dead, and she said, Oh, I'm sorry to hear that. How did it happen?

I told her it was an unfortunate shooting accident, and I figured she probably would say, Oh, how terrible, Llewellyn Trout, how very terrible, and then she wouldn't say anything more, because that's what most people do, and you know damn well they want to hear more—they want to know every gory detail—but they're afraid to ask.

But Tabby obviously wasn't, and she said, What do you mean, Llewellyn Trout, how on earth do three people all get killed in a shooting accident?

And that's when I told Tabby the truth about what had happened that night in the house out on Warner Road. I told her every detail, and I told her this was the first time I ever told anyone, well, except for Mr. D, and that didn't count seeing as he hadn't really believed me, and then I thought, Why the hell did I just go and tell all that to Tabby because, after all, I had promised Pop it would always be a secret, and I should never have told anyone not even someone who was my wife.

Tabby just sat there on the motel bed for a long time, not saying a word. In fact, she finished a whole can of beer before she said anything, and the whole while I was thinking, Now I've really fucked things up, because Tabby's thinking, My god, what have I done? I've gone and married a murderer.

But when Tabby spoke, she didn't say anything like that; and her voice was real soft and there were tears in her eyes, but not yet running down her cheeks, and she said, I'm so sorry, Llewellyn. It must have been horrible living all these years with a secret like that and never being able to tell it to anyone, and she leaned over and kissed me and hugged me, and all of a sudden, and I don't really know why, but I was crying, and it wasn't just a little cry like what Pop would have called a crybaby cry, but it was a sobbing cry that made my whole body shake, and for a long time I couldn't stop and Tabby just sat on the bed beside me with her hand stroking my head and she didn't say a word. And finally I got myself together, and I was ashamed because here it was mine and Tabby's wedding night, and, instead of being romantic I had gone and told her how I murdered my mom and my sister. Well, shit, I had really fucked things up.

So to change the subject and get my mind on something else, I said, Let's watch TV.

So we did. We watched the end of a movie about some kind of an alien invasion of earth, and it wasn't supposed to be funny, but it got both me and Tabby laughing, and the show that came on afterward was about the mating rituals of the animals of the African savanna, and I said, Let's watch something different, but Tabby had the remote and she wouldn't change the channel, so I got up to do it at the TV, but Tabby with the remote just flipped it right back to the mating lions and antelopes.

I said, Goddamn it, Tabby. You're doing it just to piss me off, aren't you? And she just grinned and said, No, Llewellyn Trout, I'm just trying to get you to come and take this remote control away from me.

So I tried but she wouldn't give it to me and, instead, dropped it down her shirt and told me, Llewellyn Trout, if you want it, you're going to have to get it.

And so I did. And when I had got it, and she was lying there and I was sitting on her, my legs on each side and pinning her down, and I thought, Now I'll show you, so I put the remote down the front of my Levis and I said, If you want that remote, you're going to have to get it, and she said to me, Llewellyn Trout, who says I even want to control the TV? I like the channel that's on just fine, and she was lying there, grinning up at me like a goddamn leprechaun and her freckled cheeks all bunched up around her nose and her eyes green and sparkling and full of leprechaun mischief.

Tabby had said she would make it worthwhile for me to wait till our wedding night, and she sure did, but half way through, or more like half way through the second or third time, we heard a noise from the room next door, and we looked at each other and laughed because we knew that right on the other side of that thin motel wall, Abe and Tina were up to the same thing, and Tabby said, Can't you just imagine Abe naked, and I thought of him with his scrawny arms and legs and his white skin, bulging blue eyes, orange hair, and pink lips. I didn't want to take it any further.

I'd just as soon not imagine it, I told Tabby.

April 15

EVEN THOUGH IT had been late when we finally went to sleep, Tabby wanted to set off for Los Angeles bright and early. It's no use staying in Vegas if you can't go to the casinos, she said.

So we set off, and we were hoping the truck's battery would make it, and I drove for a while, but mostly Tabby drove, and the trip was long and it was getting warm, so I slept most of the way.

I was dreaming about something, but I don't remember what it was, when Tabby reached over and nudged me awake.

Well, we made it, sleepy head, she said. You better wipe the drool from the corner of your mouth. You sure do sleep sound.

I was still groggy and I was wiping my mouth on my shirtsleeve as I looked around. On one side, just down a low cliff was a narrow strip of sand, and beyond that was a whole lot of water that was obviously the Pacific Ocean, but the water was gray instead of blue like I had always imagined, and the sand was just ordinary old brown like a playground sandbox and not white and sparkly like in the movies.

This isn't your uncle Jimmy's place, is it? I said, still only half awake.

Yep. This is where he lives.

I said, Holy shit, Tabby, I thought you said your uncle was a preacher. What's he doing living in a place like this?

There, in front of us was what Tabby called a Mediterranean-style bungalow, but I told her that bungalow might be what she called it, but I called it a BFM, and she said, What's a BFM, Llewellyn Trout? And I told her it was a polite and gentlemanly way of referring to a big fucking mansion.

It was a huge house with an upstairs terrace enclosed by a low wrought-iron rail and decorated with tropical plants growing in enormous pots.

Fancy, isn't it? Tabby said.

I told her, Yeah, especially for a preacher's house.

Well, Uncle Jimmy isn't no ordinary preacher, Llewellyn. In fact, he doesn't even like to be called preacher. Not even pastor. Reverend is what you're supposed to call him. Reverend Jimmy Cochran of Green Branch Ministries.

And I said, Holy shit because, goddamn, I suddenly recognized the name and it was the name of that televangelist preacher that Aunt Marge liked to watch on TV.

As I crawled out of the pickup, stretching my legs and leaning from side to side to loosen up my cramped back muscles from sleeping all slouched over, the door of the mansion opened, and a man walked toward me, holding out a hand and grinning with big white teeth that looked even whiter on account of his skin being tan, but the tan being almost an orange color and you could tell it wasn't real.

He was a big man, not fat, just big, and he was wearing a white silk suit and an open-collar navy blue shirt. Probably silk, too. I remembered Aunt Marge telling me Reverend Cochran wore nothing but silk, with the possible exception of his underwear, which you weren't supposed to ask about, seeing as it wasn't appropriate to ask such questions about a man of God.

And I thought, Sure enough, that's Aunt Marge's television preacher, alright.

I'm Reverend Jimmy Cochran, he said, taking my hand and shaking it real hard. But you just call me Uncle Jimmy. I reckon you must be the young fellow Tabby told us she would be dragging along with her.

Trout, I said, Lew Trout. Goddamn, there I was, once again introducing myself like I was Bond, James Bond. So I real quick said something else so Tabby's uncle wouldn't notice how stupid I had sounded, but what I said came out even more stupid.

A delightful place you have here, Reverend Cochran. My Aunt Marge loves watching you on her flatscreen TV. She sends you money every month.

Well, you be sure to give her my thanks, Reverend Cochran said, smiling and putting a hand on my shoulder. And I don't want you thinking that your aunt's money goes into my own pockets. You see, this place doesn't belong to me. Belongs to the Lord. Property of Green Branch Ministries. I only live here.

The Reverend Cochran smiled real big with his white teeth and then he threw his arms around Tabby in a bear hug that lifted her right up off her feet.

And how's my Tabby Cat he said, putting her down and letting out what I think was supposed to sound like some kind of a lustful cat meow, and then he held her by the shoulders at arm's length, looking her up and down, and he said, My, oh my, Tabby Cat! My, oh my, but haven't you

153

grown to quite a young lady in the few years since I last saw you. Then he did that cat meow again.

Uncle Jimmy invited us in and said he would send Jacob to bring our things from the truck. He had some matters to tend to over at Green Branch Ministries, and he was just about to leave, but he gave me and Tabby cold sodas and then led us upstairs.

Here's your room, Tabby Cat, same as usual. And your friend can have the one next to it. Both rooms open up on the terrace, so the two of you can sit out and enjoy the view till I get back. If you need anything, just call for Jacob.

Tabby seemed kind of like she didn't know what to say, but she said, Well, Uncle Jimmy, actually Llewellyn isn't just a friend.

Uncle Jimmy looked at her and cocked his head kind of funny and said, Well, Tabby Cat, why did you drag him along if he isn't a friend?

Tabby said it wasn't that we weren't friends, but just that the two of us were married, now. We had the ceremony just yesterday up in Vegas.

Uncle Jimmy said, Holy matilda, Tabby Cat, why on earth didn't you say so?

Tabby laughed and said, Well, Uncle Jimmy, I just did say so. Tina got married, too. The guy's named Abe.

Reverend Cochran said, Good golly. So my sister's once again a married woman, is she? I'll be gosh danged. I hope this guy's not a slimeball like her last hubby.

Then Reverend Cochran took a step back and looked Tabby up and down. I didn't quite like the way he was looking at her, but I didn't really know why because there wasn't anything wrong with someone looking at a person, but, still, I didn't like it,

He said, Well, Tabby Cat, if you and this handsome-dansome young fellow have been pronounced man and wife, I suppose the two of you will be wanting to share a room. Why don't you go ahead and set up in whichever bedroom suits you best.

Then Uncle Jimmy said he had to run, but he reminded us that if there was anything we needed, Anything at all, don't you hesitate to call Jacob.

I feel like a movie star or something, being in a fancy place like this with a view out over the ocean, I said as me and Tabby sat on the ocean-view terrace out front of our room. It was getting to be late afternoon and a bit chilly and it wasn't at all the kind of a California beach that I would have expected, all sunny and warm and guys surfing and beautiful girls in bikinis playing volleyball, but, instead, here we sat staring out at a gray ocean under a cloudy sky and only a few people on the beach, all of them bundled up, and instead of sipping drinks in fancy glasses with fruit floating on top and paper umbrellas, me and Tabby were sipping hot cider that had been brought to us by a guy named Jacob, who Tabby said was her Uncle Jimmy's personal valet, which was, in her opinion, just a fancy word for servant or slave.

Tabby had pulled her chair over next to mine, and she reached out to hold my hand, and she said, I think I love you, Llewellyn Trout.

I told her, If you did, you'd get up and fetch me a beer, and she said to me, Only in your fantasies, Llewellyn Trout, only in your fantasies. Besides, you won't find any beer in Uncle Jimmy's house. No alcohol's allowed. No alcohol, no tobacco, and no swearing.

Shit, that's not good, I said.

No whining, Llewellyn Trout. At least the no tobacco part shouldn't give you too much trouble.

I grinned and said, Well, holy moly, what kind of place is this? At least we got a pretty ocean to look at.

You don't got any oceans over in Arkansas? Tabby asked.

I pulled a clove out of my spiced cider and flicked it at her. We have one, but it doesn't got no water due to the global warming.

You want to go walk on the beach? Tabby asked, and I told her, Heck, I want to go surfing. Your uncle got a surfboard?

You're a goof, Llewellyn Trout; you don't know how to surf. Besides, you'll freeze your goddamn ass off if you go out there without a wetsuit. And, being from Arkansas, where the only ocean had dried up due to global warming, I didn't even know what a wetsuit was, and I figured probably it was a California word for swimsuit, so I said to Tabby, Were you expecting me to go out in the ocean naked?

Tabby would have probably laughed and said, Llewellyn Trout, you're a goof, but just then a red Corvette pulled into the drive down below.

Must be Roxy, Tabby said.

On the way down from Las Vegas, Tabby had told me about her cousin, Roxy, and how she had got a brand new Corvette for her fifteenth birthday. She didn't yet have her permit, so, for the time being, she let her boyfriend drive her around in it. She one time drove it herself and got pulled over, but the cop went to her daddy's church, and, because of that, he let her off with just a warning.

Tabby told me, Come on down, Llewellyn Trout. I'll introduce you to Roxy.

Tabby had told me her cousin might seem just bit strange, and that she had gone a bit wild the last year or two, but when I saw Roxy, holy shit, this girl I was being introduced to wasn't anything like I had expected.

Roxy's hair was dyed jet black and looked like it had been cut by some drugged-out kindergarten kid gone wild with a pair of blunt school scissors. She had more earrings than a pirate, and there was a silver spike through her bottom lip that matched the spikes on the collar she wore around her neck. And piercing the belly button exposed below her short, tight top, Roxy had a small silver hoop with a gold cross hanging from it. Centered just below that and just above the top edge of her low-cut jeans was a tattoo that said "Jesus Saves."

Holy shit. What kind of girl was this, anyhow? A preacher's daughter? A pastor's daughter? A reverend's daughter? Here, I had all along thought that compared to Waynesburg girls, Tabby was a bit on the wild side, but compared to this cousin of hers, Tabby was pure as the Virgin Mary.

Still, even with all the bullshit she had done to herself with piercings and tattoos and all, Roxy was still beautiful, and I had no doubt she was one of those girls that the boys at her high school kept in mind for those times when they lay awake thinking lustful thoughts, but I told myself, Don't even go there, Llewellyn Trout. Don't even go there. You're a married man.

Tabby got flustered when she introduced me. I'd like you to meet Llewellyn Trout, my husband, she finally said, and I thought, well, at least I'm not the only one who screws up introductions.

Husband, huh. Ain't that a fancy sounding word for a ordinary looking guy, Roxy said. Is he good in bed?

Roxy went with us out to the terrace, but instead of sitting in one of the wicker chairs, she sat cross-leg on the marble paving stones. She brought out a small baggie and a pack of Zig Zags and then rolled herself a joint. Tabby didn't seem the least bit surprised.

Me, though, I was plenty surprised. What the hell was going on here? Reverend Jimmy Cochran didn't allow alcohol, tobacco, or swearing in his house, but here was his own daughter rolling herself a joint like it was just the everyday thing to do.

After getting it started, Roxy held the joint out to me, but I told her, No thanks, and Tabby said the same when Roxy offered the joint to her.

Roxy grinned. Goddamn there was something about that grin that reminded me of Tabby. Not so surprising I figured, seeing as the two of them were cousins. In fact the two of them looked a whole lot alike, but if Tabby was leprechaun, this girl was more like gremlin. And instead of green eyes like Tabby had, this girl had gray eyes. A pale but deep, rich gray. I had never before seen eyes that color. Something about them made me feel a bit uneasy.

Was Daddy home when you arrived? Roxy wanted to know.

Tabby nodded.

You tell him the two of you were married?

Tabby nodded again.

Was he as disappointed to hear it as I am?

Come on, Roxanne Cochran, give Llewellyn a chance. You might find you like him.

At least tell me you didn't take his last name, Roxy said, glancing over at me. I mean who wants a last name like Trout?

It's not so bad, Tabby said. You get used to it.

You in love with him?

Only reason I know to get married.

Is he a cowboy?

He's a southern gentleman.

If he lived in Bakersfield more than a week, he qualifies as a cowboy.

Well, I prefer to think of him as a southern gentleman.

That means he must have money.

Tabby looked at me and laughed. None he's told me about, she said.

Roxy said, Shit, Tabby, you people from Bakersfield are fucking crazy. Anyone ever told you that?

Tabby sat down on the marble paving stones beside her cousin and put an arm around her shoulder. You told me that, once or twice, Roxanne Cochran, she said.

Roxy did the same with her arm, putting it around Tabby's shoulder and then she handed Tabby the joint, and this time Tabby took it. They sat there for a while, then Roxy said, Let's go for a walk on the beach. Just you and me. Do some girl talk. You don't mind if I take away your wife for a while do you, Cowboy?

Hell yes, I minded. I didn't want to be left sitting alone on the terrace, but I sure wasn't going to whine and say I wanted to tag along while Tabby and Roxy did their girl talk thing—whatever the hell that was. It had been bad enough having to sit here on the terrace listening to them talk about me.

So Roxy and Tabby left, and as they did, Roxy handed me what was left of the joint. I was a little bit flustered, but I took it. What the hell else was I supposed to do?

The rest is for you, Cowboy. It's good shit. Enjoy.

So I was left alone. In one hand, I held an empty Christmas cider mug painted with angels and baby Jesus, while in the other hand, I held a joint of what Roxy called good shit that I was supposed to enjoy. Talk about fucking crazy.

So I smoked what was left of the joint. I couldn't really say why I did. Not after all these years of just saying no to drugs. But, hell, for that matter, I couldn't say why I had just up and left Bakersfield either, or why I had out of the blue asked a girl to marry me who, at the time, I had known for less than two weeks.

Must be that damn B movie again. Maybe that was my life permanent from now on.

B movie.

Crazy.

As I smoked the joint, I knew it was something I wasn't supposed to be doing, and I felt a little bit like I had that time when me and Bobby Plumber snuck off and smoked almost a whole pack of Camels up at Fuller Ridge. Except this time I didn't get sick and vomit up a coke and a half-digested slice of pepperoni pizza.

By the time the sun had finished setting out over the gray Pacific, I was stoned, wasted, toked, roped out, smashed, baked, fried, toasted, lobotomized and, definitely having a nice daze. First time ever, Llewellyn Trout, and holy shit, this wasn't anything like the terrible, confused state of mind I had been led to expect by the *Drugs Are for Losers* videos they showed us during Red Ribbon Week back at Waynesburg High.

Hell, this was fanfuckingtastic. Something you should have done a long time ago, Llewellyn Trout. A long, long time ago. But damn, a cold beer would sure taste good. And some popcorn, too.

The breeze off the ocean was cold, and I went inside and sprawled out on the bed, flipping through channels on the flatscreen mounted on the wall.

CNN News—terrorists in Afghanistan.
Lucy reruns.
Football bloopers.
Dueling banjos.
Elmo and Big Bird.
Tale of Two Titties.
California Gold with . . .

Wait, wait, wait, what was that? Go back. Go back.

I flipped back a channel. Damn, I hadn't been mistaken after all. Bigger than life on plasma flatscreen, there it was,

Tale of Two Titties.

What the hell was this? So Reverend Jimmy Cochran subscribed to porn channels? He didn't allow beer, cigarettes, or swearing in his house, but pot was okay and porn channels, too? Shit, life didn't get any stranger than this.

Little did I know.

When Roxy and Tabby returned from their girl-talking on the beach, it was dark, and I was lying there six-quarters stoned and two-quarters asleep, and the room was dark, and I was in bed and had pulled the blankets over me due to having opened the window because I like the sound of the waves, and I had never heard anything like that before because the Arkansas Ocean had dried up in the global warming, and was that true or was I just imagining it because I was stoned.

And I was lying there with my eyes closed, and my thoughts seemed a little bit jumbled, and I figured it was on account of me having smoked a joint, and I heard the door open and I mumbled hi to Tabby. She was moving about but not turning on the light. I was lying there, not so much pretending to be asleep but more just being too stoned and too lazy to open my eyes, when I felt a hand reach under the blanket and gently stroke my chest, and it didn't stop at my chest, and I was about to throw my arms around Tabby and drag her into the bed with me, but then she walked away and I heard the door open and someone said, Goodnight Cowboy, and, holy shit, I opened my eyes, and sure enough, it wasn't Tabby, it was her fifteen year old cousin, Roxy who was standing there in the doorway, and she said, Sleep tight, Cowboy, and then she closed the door, and I looked around to see if Tabby was in the room, but she wasn't, and I thought, Holy shit, Llewellyn Trout, what the hell is going to happen next in this crazy movie?

Tabby came in a few minutes later, and I opened my eyes this time to make sure it was her, and I thought, Should I tell her what had just happened? But then I thought, No, don't say a word. Why go opening a bag of worms? Or was it a can of worms? Or maybe a can of sardines? I was too stoned to remember, or care, and besides, it's sometimes best for things to remain unsaid. Let sleeping dogs lie, or was it lying dogs sleep, goddamnit, whatever the hell it was, it's best sometimes if you just don't say a word. Some things are best kept secret.

But Roxy with her spike collar and pierced belly button and the "Jesus Saves" tattoo just above the top of her low-cut jeans and who knows what piercings there might be below that had gotten things started and I sure as hell wasn't going to let them stop now, so me and Tabby picked up where we had left off the night before, and tonight there was no noise from the room next door.

April 16

WHEN I WOKE the next morning, I found Tabby seated out on the terrace. The morning was chilly, and Tabby had the hood of her sweatshirt pulled up over her head. She said Roxy was still asleep and had warned that no one had better wake her until she was damn well ready to wake herself because she was ditching school today and sleeping in.

So we're alone, the two of us, Tabby said. Come sit with me, Llewellyn Trout. I'll share my coffee with you. Tabby held out a large Starbucks.

Jacob brought it back for me. If you want something for breakfast, just let him know and he'll get it for you.

Steak and hashbrowns? He'll cook them for me?

He won't cook anything, but he'll bring back something for you to eat—so long as it's Starbucks or Chinese take-out. They don't do much cooking here at Uncle Jimmy's house. Mostly just bring food in.

I told Tabby, Holy shit, your Uncle Jimmy lives like a goddamn movie star. I think I'm going to be a preacher when I grow up.

Tabby said, You just go ahead and do that, Llewellyn Trout. But till then why not come with me down to the beach and we'll walk in the waves.

Tabby held my hand as we walked along the beach. Where's all the seashells? I said. That's what you find scattered along the beach in California, right? Hundreds of them just lying there, ready for you to pick up and put to your ear so you can hear the roar of the ocean.

Tabby just looked at me like I was maybe a bit crazy, and to change the subject, I said, Doesn't it irritate you that your uncle calls you Tabby Cat?

No, not really. Why should it? It's my name, after all. Cat's my middle name.

I thought, Holy shit, here I am married to this girl and I don't even know her middle name, but what came out was, Cat? Your middle name is Cat? What the hell kind of name is that?

Llewellyn Trout, you're a goof. The name is Catherine. Tabitha Catherine, but Uncle Jimmy likes shortening it to Tabby Cat.

Well, I still don't like the way he says it, I told Tabby.

Tabby said, You're, a goof, Llewellyn Trout. It's what he's called me ever since I was a little kid.

I shrugged and said, Well, whatever.

Tabby had been right about the ocean being cold. I didn't think I would stay walking in the waves for very long.

I said to Tabby, You know what cold water does to guys, don't you? and I gave her a playful nudge with my shoulder. It wasn't a hard nudge, but it seemed to throw her off balance, and it happened at just the time a bigger-than-usual wave came in. Anyhow, Tabby ended up falling into the ocean, and I put out my hand to help her up, but instead of her letting me help her up, she pulled me down instead.

So that's where I went. Down. Down into the next wave, and, for the first time in my life, I tasted salt water of the ocean. Not so different from the salt water I would swish with when Pop would hit me because I deserved it, but the ocean water had only the salt taste and none of the blood taste.

I said, Shit, Tabby, what the hell did you do that for? and she answered, Seemed like fun. Didn't it to you?

Jesus, Tabby, you're goddamn crazy. I think I'm married to a crazy lady?

You're just confused because you're in love, Llewellyn Trout.

By this time, me and Tabby had both scrambled out of the waves, and we threw ourselves onto the sand and were lying there, face to face beside each other.

You ever see that *Jane Eyre* movie? I asked her.

No. But I read the book.

Well, I think I'm going to have to lock you up in the goddamn attic, Tabitha Catherine Trout. I think I'm going to have to lock you up for good.

What attic are you going to lock me in?

Don't need an attic. I got handcuffs.

You're not locking me up with handcuffs, Llewellyn Trout.

Why not? You might find it exciting.

Did you ever read *Gerald's Game?*

What are you talking about? I asked, and Tabby said something about that I should read more Stephen King novels, but I was getting cold so I just said, Holy shit, Tabby. Let's go get out of these soaking sweats. I'm freezing.

April 17

THAT AFTERNOON, TABBY got a phone call from her Uncle Jimmy, and she put it on speaker, and her uncle said to her, Hey, Tabby Cat, why not come on down to Green Branch Ministries, and I'll give you a tour of our new media center. So Tabby said, Come with me, Llewellyn Trout, we're going over to see Uncle Jimmy's church.

When we got there I said, Holy shit, Tabby, what kind of church is this?

Tabby explained that when her Uncle Jimmy started out, he was a preacher at a church not much different than Santa Margarita back in Bakersfield, but now his Green Branch Ministries included a retirement community, an elementary school, and one of the largest churches outside of Texas.

Tabby said, That's the difference between Tina and her brother. The two of them grew up in a trailer park. Same home, same schools, same everything. Only difference is one had ambition and the other one didn't. Me, I've got ambition, Llewellyn Trout. How about you?

I didn't even answer because I was so amazed that, holy shit, the church grounds even had a miniature golf course and a gift shop.

I said, Who ever heard of a church having a gift shop? As we passed by, I stopped at the window display to see what the hell kind of stuff would they be selling at a church gift shop.

Holy Bibles in simulated black leather, $32.99. Praying hands key chains in your choice of brushed stainless or genuine sterling silver, $6.99 or $18.99, respectively. A round stained glass of the holy family with Mary and Joseph bundled up all warm and cozy but baby Jesus naked and probably freezing his butt off, and a dove flying around in the sky above them with a stick in its mouth, $18.99. And for only $25.99 you could own a framed and autographed photograph of the Reverend Jimmy Cochran, himself—dressed, as you might guess, in a white silk suit and open-collar shirt in your choice of colors. Everything else remained the same in all the pictures: the broad smile and big white teeth, the fake tan, the white silk suit. The only thing that changed from one picture to the next was the color of the shirt, and

163

even that was obviously done with the magic of Photoshop. Maybe some people wouldn't have been able to tell, but I could. Blue shirt. Green shirt. Purple shirt. Red shirt. Even pink. All done with Photoshop.

I said to Tabby, Goddamn, a person could buy a picture of your uncle to match colors in every room of the house, and she said, I think that's the idea, Llewellyn Trout, I think that's the whole idea. You sell more pictures that way. Uncle Jimmy didn't get where he is today without taking things like that into account.

Tabby took me to a long, two-story building with lots of tinted glass windows, and inside was a receptionist with bright red lips and poofy hair that looked like it came off some plastic made-in-China doll.

Reverend Cochran is expecting you, the lady said when Tabby explained who we were. The lady pointed with a finger that had a long red nail and said, Just down the hall and to your left.

So we went to the office just down the hall and to the left, and when we went in, Uncle Jimmy said, Well, well, well, if it ain't my Tabby Cat and that handsome-dansome young husband of hers, and it pissed me off the way he said it because even if he laughed away as if it was only a joke, it was still irritating. I got even more pissed off when Reverend Cochran gave Tabby a big bear hug as if he hadn't seen her for years instead of it having been just the previous afternoon that he had given her the very same kind of hug, and I thought, Why does this asshole every time have to hug her like that?

Reverend Cochran told us there was a new building he wanted to show us. Still smells of paint and fresh carpet, he said.

Down a shady, eucalyptus-lined walk, we came to what Uncle Jimmy said was Green Branch Ministries' new media complex. Enough electronics here to make a geek die of brain hemorrhage, he told us, and he must have thought it was a funny joke because he laughed and slapped me on the back.

I wanted to say, Stop hitting me, goddamnit. But how can you say something like that to a man of God, especially one who is smiling all big and with white teeth.

Still smiling away, Uncle Jimmy told us that this newly-constructed building, smelling of paint and fresh carpet, was where the word of the Lord went out each day through the Green Branch television and radio ministries. On the internet too, these days, of course, he added.

But, of course, we certainly haven't neglected the traditional printed media, Uncle Jimmy said as he handed me a glossy magazine from a stack by the door in the reception area. Take it as a souvenir, Lewie. It's just another example of how Green Branch Ministries is bringing the Gospel into the 21st Century.

I wanted to say Fuck you, shithead, but, instead, I said, Thank you, sir.

Uncle Jimmy showed me and Tabby room after room, some busy with people working and others filled with nothing but racks of new electronic equipment.

When everything is fully set up, we'll have better equipment than most Hollywood studios, Uncle Jimmy said. There's no reason the Lord God should take second place to Hollywood, isn't that right, Lewie?

Goddamn, this guy knew how to irritate me. Nobody called me Lewie. Nobody who wanted to remain my friend, at least.

You know, Uncle Jimmy went on without waiting for me to answer, From my pulpit, I can only reach a handful of people for the Lord; ten to twelve thousand on a typical Sunday. But with our new media center, my ministry reaches the entire country and, pretty soon it'll spread God's good news across the entire world. So tell me, Lewie, what do you think of this place?

This time he waited for me to answer, so I said, It's very impressive, sir.

Well, Lewie, I hope to see you and your beautiful bride at our Sunday morning service.

I glanced at Tabby because I sure as hell didn't want to go to any Sunday morning service, but she winked at me and nodded, so I said, Yes, I would look forward to that, sir, and I hoped Uncle Jimmy hadn't seen me roll my eyes.

Then Uncle Jimmy said, Tabby Cat, why don't you take Lewie on home and then come back; I have some things I'd like to discuss with you.

So Tabby drove me back to Reverend Cochran's house, and as we drove I said to her, I still don't like your uncle, and she said to me, Why not, Llewellyn Trout? and I told her, I don't know; I guess he just rubs me the wrong way.

You'll find he's really a nice guy when you get to know him, Tabby told me, and I said, Yeah, maybe, but I don't think so. Anyhow, what is it he wants to discuss with you?

Tabby didn't know, and she said the only way to find out was for her to go back and talk to Uncle Jimmy, so why didn't I just hang out at the pool for a while. The water's heated, but if you want something warmer, you can kick back in the hot tub instead.

So that's what I did. It was early evening and a chilly wind was bringing a heavy fog in from the Pacific, but that only made the hot tub seem all the more inviting, and I was sitting there, relaxing, breathing in the chlorine, listening to the bubbling water and, further off, the sound of the waves, and I was almost dozing, when someone splashed water in my face. I opened my eyes, and there was Roxy standing at the edge of the hot tub. She was wearing a red bikini, not yellow polka-dot but sure enough itsy bitsy teeny weenie, and she was kicking water at me with her foot.

Why the hell did you do that? I asked, wiping water from my face, and somehow it came out sounding like I was really pissed, and I didn't want to sound like a poor sport, so I said, Sorry, I really didn't mean for it to come out that way. I was just a bit startled.

Well, then let's start over again, Roxy said, and she grinned that part-elf-mostly-gremlin grin and then splashed me again.

I should have right then gotten out of the hot tub and walked away. Not just walked, I should have run. Run like hell.

But, instead, I just smiled and splashed her back.

Roxy said, Better stop splashing me or I'll tell on you, and it made me laugh because it was such a little-kid thing to say.

Then she stepped into the hot tub and stood there right in front of me, and she said, What do you think, Cowboy? Do you like my newest tattoo? and I said to her, What newest tattoo? and she said, Which one do you think, Cowboy? The one you're always having such a hard time not staring at, of course, and she pointed to the tattoo that I had thought said "Jesus Saves" because I had been too embarrassed to look at it real careful, but there it was, now, smack dab in front of my face and right above it, a belly button pierced with a silver hoop that had a gold cross hanging from it, and all of a sudden it was, holy shit, because the tattoo didn't say "Jesus Saves," but instead said "Jesus Shaves."

I didn't know what the hell to say, and I was a bit flustered, so I said to Roxy, I don't pay much attention to tattoos.

Roxy said, Sure you do. Especially to that one. You should get one, yourself, Cowboy. How about a little red devil tattooed on your chest right about here, and as she said it Roxy reached out and used a finger to trace the outline of a devil on my chest and the pointy end of its tail ended right on my goddamn nipple.

It would look good on you, Cowboy. All the women would think you're hot.

They already do, I said.

I guess Tabby does at least, Roxy said. Tell me, Cowboy, why would that sweet cousin of mine go and marry someone like you?

She married me for my money, I said, and I could hardly believe I was carrying on like this with my own wife's fifteen year-old cousin, and I thought, You better run, Llewellyn Trout. You better run like hell. But instead I just sat there and let Roxy string me along.

Is that all she married you for, Cowboy? Did she marry you just for your money?

That and my good looks.

Not because you're good in bed?

Oh, yeah, that, too. Mostly that.

I don't believe it.

That don't mean it ain't so.

Want to come up to my room and prove it?

I said, Goddamn, Roxy, I'm a married man and you're just a fifteen-year-old kid.

Roxy sat down beside me there in the hot tub and put an arm around my shoulder, and it was making me feel really uncomfortable, but I was even more uncomfortable when she took my hand and put it on her breast, but somehow I didn't stop her, and she said, Just a kid, huh, Cowboy? Tell me, does that feel to you like just a kid?

I pulled my hand away and said to her, What the fuck, Roxy? What are you doing? What's Tabby going to say if she sees something like that going on?

Roxy shrugged. Don't know. You'd have to ask her, Cowboy. But you know where my room is if you change your mind. Roxy let her hand slip off my shoulder and into my lap, and she left it there too long for it to be just an accident, far too long, and I sat there thinking, Oh shit. Run Llewellyn Trout, Run like hell and don't look back.

But I didn't run. I just sat there, and then Roxy stood up right smack dab in front of me with that goddamn tattoo right back in my face again, and she said, Come on up any time, Cowboy. I'll even roll you a joint.

April 18

I WAS STILL in the hot tub when Tabby came back from talking with her Uncle Jimmy. I could tell right off, from the way she was walking, almost skipping, that Tabby was sure as hell excited about something.

Come with me, she said. I've got something to show you. She put out a hand to help me from the hot tub.

I said, It's cold out of the water; why not just tell me what it is. What is it? and Tabby said, You're going to have to come see for yourself.

So I went with her to the front of the house, and Tabby said, There it is, Llewellyn Trout. You like our new car?

I said, What are you talking about, Tabby? because the only car in the driveway at the time was a silver Porsche Boxster.

Tabby kept bouncing up and down from being so excited. Can you believe it, Llewellyn? she said. It's our very own. Uncle Jimmy gave it to us.

Tabby explained that, well, officially, the car was registered to Green Branch Ministries, but that was just for tax purposes. So long as Tabby remained one of her uncle's employees, the Porsche would be ours to drive. A Porsche, Tabby said, still jumping up and down like an excited kid. Can you believe it, Llewellyn Trout? A Porsche of our very own!

You're working for your uncle? I said. And he gave you a car?

Tabby said, Yep. Let's go for a drive and I'll tell you all about it.

I just stood there, trying to figure out what crazy thing might happen next in this movie.

Tabby said, Come on, Llewellyn, let's go. You want to drive?

I said, No I don't have my license on me, which was true enough, but, fact is, I didn't want to tell Tabby I didn't know how to drive a stick shift.

Seeing as I was still wet and the wind was cold, the thought of sitting in a car with the heater on seemed like a good idea, so I said, You go ahead and drive.

Tabby got in on the driver's side, and she made me put my towel down so my wet swimsuit wouldn't ruin the leather seat. Tabby couldn't stop talking. I had never seen her so excited. Not even when I asked her to marry me.

She said, Can you believe it, Llewellyn? I have a job working for Uncle Jimmy.

What kind of job? I asked.

Tabby said, You know that receptionist lady, the one with the red lips and poofy hair, the one who directed us, down the hall and to your left? Well, she's retiring, and Uncle Jimmy said I could take over for her.

Pay might not be the greatest, Tabby told me, but the benefits—perks is what Uncle Jimmy called them—the perks more than made up for that. And one of those perks was a rent-free apartment at Green Branch Villas.

I asked, Green Branch Villas? What's that?

Tabby told me it was an apartment complex owned by her uncle's Green Branch Ministries. Lots of people who work for Uncle Jimmy live there, she said.

Tabby went on to say that me and her would be moving into the new apartment sometime next week.

I said, What the hell, Tabby, don't I get a say in where we're going to be living? Besides, I don't like the idea of you working for your Uncle Jimmy. I don't like him. I don't trust the man.

Oh, come on, Llewellyn, Tabby said. Don't be such a jerk. We need a place to live. You should be happy Uncle Jimmy has offered us an apartment at The Villas. Rent free, no less. And it pisses me off when you're so ungrateful and go talking like that about Uncle Jimmy when he has been so generous with us.

I could tell I had kind of pissed Tabby off, so I told her, Sorry, about what I said. Then, to lighten things up a bit, I said, Just don't go starting to wear poofy hair and red lipstick.

Tabby said, Llewellyn Trout, you're a goof.

April 19

W ELL, THERE WAS some painting to be done and some carpet to be replaced, so it ended up being almost a week and a half before me and Tabby moved into our new apartment at Green Branch Villas. Not that there was much moving to do. The apartment already had furniture, appliances, and that kind of stuff. All me and Tabby had to move in was the few things we had brought with us from Bakersfield.

I was still a bit pissed about Tabby not having asked me where I thought we should live, but I had to admit our new apartment was beautiful. Besides, I was glad that me and Tabby were moving into a place of our own. Happy that the two of us were moving away from Uncle Jimmy, who seemed to take never-ending delight in finding new ways to irritate me. His newest amusement was to sing that *Louie Louie* song every time he passed by me, and what most irritated me was the way he would always give Tabby a hug in a way an uncle just isn't supposed to hug his niece.

I was also glad to be moving away from Roxy because over the past almost two weeks every time I saw her, I couldn't help but remember her standing there in the hot tub with the bottom of that little red bikini right smack dab in my face and the "Jesus Shaves" tattoo right above it, and Roxy standing there, gremlin-grinning down at me as the water bubbled up blue and white all around her, and then her sitting beside me in the hot tub and putting my hand on her breast and saying, Tell me, Cowboy, does that feel to you like a little kid? And every time I thought about it, I wondered what the hell would have happened if I had gone to her room and she had rolled me that joint. What then? I couldn't get it off my mind. It kept me awake at night.

And that wasn't the only thing Roxy had done. Sometimes I would think, Goddamn, does she do this shit intentionally just to tease me and get me all worked up, or is she just clueless about what she's doing to me?

Mornings, I would have to take a deep breath and tell myself, Don't go there, Llewellyn, don't even go there, because I would see Roxy shuffling around the house in that little pink nightie of hers, as if she was the only one at home and it didn't matter how she dressed.

I would blush and get flustered when Roxy would lean over so you couldn't help but see right down her shirt to that breast she had put my hand on and said, Just a kid, huh, Cowboy? Like I say, I would blush and get flustered, but at the same time I couldn't tear my eyes away.

And then there was the day Roxy was sitting there by the pool and she was wearing nothing. Not one thing. Jacob was off somewhere, and so was Uncle Jimmy, and Tabby, too, and it was just me at the house, me and Roxy, and she knew damn well I was there, but in spite of that, she was lying out there by the pool, naked, and she was smoking a joint and I thought, Goddamn, I know she knows I'm still here at the house, and she knows damn well that I'm likely to see her. Then she glanced up and saw me at the window and smiled at me, pretending to be embarrassed but not putting on her clothes and, instead, just slipping into the water.

I knew she was playing games with me, and I knew I should run like hell, but I couldn't, and it was driving me crazy, and Roxy would do that gremlin grin and raise her eyebrow at me like she was saying, I know what you're thinking, Cowboy. I know exactly what you're thinking.

So, now, even if I wasn't running like hell, at least I was moving out of the house where just down the hall was Roxy's bedroom with the joint she would roll for me and the breast she would put my hand on just before I discovered if there were any piercings down there below that "Jesus Shaves" tattoo.

Yes, I sure was glad me and Tabby were moving into a place of our own. It was a good thing. Yes, definitely it was. It was a good thing. No doubt about it.

I told myself that over and over. You know it's a good thing, Llewellyn Trout. You know damn well it's good you're moving with Tabby out of that house and into an apartment of your own.

The next Sunday morning I wanted to sleep in, but Tabby said, Come on, Llewellyn Trout, get dressed up nice; we're going to church today, and I told her she sounded just like Mom when she used to tell me to get dressed up real nice for Sunday service at Waynesburg Baptist.

But as I should have expected from any church run by Reverend Jimmy Cochran, the Green Branch House of Worship was not the least bit like Waynesburg Baptist.

Green Branch House of Worship was more a cross between sports stadium and fancy movie theater. And like a theater, there was a screen down front, but it was bigger than any movie screen I had ever seen. Way bigger. And like in a high-class movie theatre, the seats reclined to suit the comfort requirements of the occupant, and they were wide, so I guess, they were built with fat people in mind.

I remembered what Uncle Jimmy had said about his media complex having equipment every bit as good as any Hollywood studio, and I whispered to Tabby, Goddamn, I know where your uncle gets his ideas. No wonder I feel like a movie star when I'm at his place.

I was wondering, When will someone say, You may be seated like Reverend McKey always did after a song at Waynesburg Baptist, but nobody did say it, and the music just kept on going and going and getting louder and louder. I whispered to Tabby, You should see if your Uncle Jimmy will let you play piano in his church. Tabby looked at me like she hadn't heard what I said, but I think she heard perfectly well but was just ignoring me so I would shut up.

Then Reverend Jimmy Cochran came out on the stage and people cheered like he was some rock star or a politician or, what he more likely would have liked for himself to be thought of—a movie star.

After the music stopped, the lights went dim, and there on the giant screen in front of all ten or twelve thousand or so of us, and larger than life, way larger than life, was the Reverend Jimmy Cochran in a white silk suit and this time an orange shirt that matched his tan.

Reverend Cochran said, Praise God, and wasn't it wonderful, praise the Lord, to think that this morning's service was being broadcast live all across the country and when just a bit more equipment was in place, broadcasts would go out weekly via television and radio to thirteen different countries, and, also via the internet where it could reach every man, woman, and precious child who has access to the world wide web on the internet, praise Jesus.

Everyone clapped again and some bald-headed guy in the seat just in front of me put two fingers in his mouth and let out a whistle. I guess it was a whistle for Jesus, or maybe it was for the world wide web on the internet, or maybe for Reverend Jimmy Cochran of Green Branch Ministries, I wasn't quite sure, but I thought, What the hell kind of church is this, anyhow? Almost as crazy as Santa Margarita in Bakersfield. I glanced over at Tabby, but she didn't seem to think it was the least bit unusual. I guess she had been to Uncle Jimmy's church enough times to know what to expect.

April 20

THE NEXT MORNING, Tabby went off to start her receptionist job at Cochran Green Branch Ministries, where she would park her brand new Porsche in a special reserved parking spot that would soon have her name painted on it, and she would greet her Uncle Jimmy with a hug, and all day she would pleasantly smile and say, Down the hall and to your left.

After she left the apartment, I took her beat-up old truck to get a battery and some new tires.

Tabby had told me that, seeing as now she had a Porsche, the old truck of Tina's would belong to me.

Well, ain't that fucking sweet of you, I felt like saying.

Get some good tires, Tabby had told me. After all, I get paid on Friday. Big bucks, Llewellyn Trout. Big bucks.

So that's what I did. I got BFG All-Terrains, and when Tabby got home, I told her, Come on, Tabby, come on out and see the tires I got for the truck, but she told me, Not right now Llewellyn, I've got to go to the mall and buy some new clothes for my work. I'll bring us back Chinese take-out for supper. Anything special I can get for you?

I said, Would you like for me to come along? But Tabby told me, No, don't bother, Llewellyn, you'd just get bored following me around. All I'm doing is buying clothes.

I said, Goddamn it, Tabby, it's not about your clothes, I just thought maybe you'd like my company. Or maybe you'd prefer to have your sugardaddy uncle come along to keep you company.

As soon as I said it, I knew I had pissed Tabby off. She said, Well, then, Llewellyn, I guess I'll be leaving. The mall's open late tonight, so don't feel you have to wait up for me. And then she went off, squealing her goddamn tires, like always.

Goddamn Porsche.

So fuck it all. Tabby had said not to wait up for her, and I damn well didn't.

Buy your new clothes, Tabitha Trout. Go to the mall and buy your goddamn clothes. I'll just lie here alone and have lustful thoughts, and it won't be about you, that's for damn sure. So you just go ahead and buy your fancy-dancy clothes, and I'll have my lustful thoughts about someone else. Maybe about someone who calls me Cowboy.

April 21

WHEN TABBY GOT home that night I pretended I was asleep. I felt her kiss me gently, and then she whispered, Sorry about getting mad and going off and leaving you alone, Llewellyn.

But I just kept pretending to be asleep.

The next morning I hardly saw Tabby. She got a phone call, and she was urgently needed down at Green Branch Ministries, and I wanted to say, Goddamn it Tabby, what the fuck. Just slow down and at least say a proper good morning to me, but she was hurrying around trying to get her hair dry, and then getting into those fancy new clothes of hers so she could wobble down the stairs on those fucking high-heels and then drive her goddamn Porsche to her Uncle Jimmy's office so she could be a kiss-ass receptionist.

Well, I sure as hell wasn't going to sit around the apartment waiting all day for Tabby to return. So I got on Craig's List, looking for a job opening, and then I got in the pickup that had so generously been given to me and even had new tires and battery, whoop-dee-doo, and I drove down to Anderson Rod and Gun and asked if they still had an opening.

They did, and, would I like to fill out an application?

When they found out how much I knew about guns, they hired me on the spot. Minimum wage to start, but there would be quarterly performance reviews.

And there's no reason a young man like yourself shouldn't double his salary within a year if he proves his worth by making a lot of sales. So if you think you'd like to give it a go, welcome aboard, Llewellyn.

I did think I would like to give it a go, and, holy shit, I made my first sale within the hour. A good one, too.

In walked Uncle Jimmy—the last person I would have expected to see at Anderson Rod and Gun, and I said to him, Good morning, sir, can I help you.

Well, I'll be doggone, said Reverend Cochran. Lewie, that wife of yours never told me you had got yourself a job.

I wanted to tell him, Well, goddamn it, that's because she doesn't know, herself, due to her always being so busy kissing your ass at Green Branch Ministries.

But saying that sort of thing to a customer isn't a good way to keep a job you just started, so I smiled and said, What can I help you with, Reverend Cochran?

Well, Lewie, it's my birthday. Fact is, your Tabby Cat and a few other gals that work at Green Branch came in early this morning and put up balloons and streamers to decorate my office. Mighty nice of them, wouldn't you say?

I thought, So that's what Tabby was in such a hurry to do this morning and why she wouldn't even take time to eat breakfast with me. I guess she would rather spend her time decorating her sugardaddy's office for his goddamn birthday. Well, fuck both of you.

That's what I thought, but what I said, of course, was, I'm so glad they decorated the office for your birthday, sir.

Reverend Cochran smiled. Of course he smiled. Did he ever not smile? And he said, Well, Lewie, it's a tradition of mine on my birthday to take the afternoon off and buy myself something to celebrate the day, and this year I'm thinking of buying myself a handgun. Is that something you can help me with? Is that something you know anything about?

Oh, I knew about guns, alright, and my first thought was to sell the Reverend Jimmy Cochran a used Lorcin .380. It's a gun no one in his right mind would want to own, and it would have given me a good feeling to know that I had sold a piece of steel shit to this man of God with his big white teeth and his fake tan. But then I figured that in consideration of those quarterly reviews and potential subsequent pay raises, it might be better if my first sale was something a bit more substantial. Something more expensive.

So what Reverend Cochran ended up buying was a Smith & Wesson 357 revolver. Near ten times the cost of the Lorcin. He was disappointed that he would not be allowed to take it home with him.

State of California requires registration and a ten day wait, I told him.

Well, Lewie, he said, I guess we have to follow the law, and I told him, Yes, sir, we do.

But what I meant, of course, was, Fuck you, shithead.

After Uncle Jimmy left the store, the manager, Mr. LeMar, said, Well done, Lew, well done, and he gave me a thumbs up.

I was proud of myself. But I was a fool. Selling that gun was one of the biggest mistakes of my life.

April 22

THAT EVENING WHEN I got home, Tabby wasn't there yet. And why would that surprise me? She was probably still eating birthday cake with her sugardaddy, I figured.

But I was wrong. When she got home a few minutes later, Tabby had a surprise for me, and she said, Close your eyes, Llewellyn Trout. Sit down and close your eyes till I tell you to open them.

So I did, and it sure did take a long time, but finally Tabby said, Okay, Llewellyn, you can look now, and there in front of me was a brand new Webber grill and a bag of mesquite charcoal, and on the grill, but still wrapped in plastic, were two fat steaks.

I should have said, Thank you, or something like that, of course, but I was surprised and what came out was, How the hell did you get that home in your Porsche?

Tabby looked kind of hurt, and I was sorry I hadn't said the right thing.

A friend of mine from Green Branch brought it in her van, Tabby told me. If you don't like it, Llewellyn, we can take it back.

But I gave her a hug and told her it was the perfect gift.

I was feeling bad, because, here, Tabby had given me a sweatshirt at Christmas and now a barbecue grill, and I had never once bought a single thing for her, and I thought, With my first paycheck, I'll go out and buy a wedding ring for her. At least I'll make a down payment for one because that's probably all I'll have money for.

I put that grill out on our patio and started cooking up those steaks, while Tabby changed out of that ridiculous skirt and the wobbly heels and into the Levis and flannel shirt that she looked so much better in.

As I tended the steaks, I told Tabby about getting a job at Anderson Rod and Gun. Minimum wage, I told her, but I like working there. I explained about quarterly reviews and about there being plenty of opportunities for salary increases. Then I mentioned about Uncle Jimmy being my first customer.

Tabby said, Well, what a coincidence, and how wonderful it was that I had found work so quick, and how great it was that I was going to enjoy working there at, what did I say the name of the place was? Andrew's Gun Shop?

Anderson Rod and Gun, I said, and I was kind of pissed that Tabby hadn't been listening to me more carefully, but I was also hoping it was going to be an evening that me and her would enjoy together—first a good meal and then Tabby maybe dropping the remote control down her shirt or something like that. And if she didn't, I could try sticking it down the front of my Levis again. Worth a try, right?

But then, and I don't know why, I went and said something really stupid about, why had Tabby gone off early this morning with hardly even a hello for me, and had she really done it just to put up decorations for her uncle's birthday?

Jesus Christ, Tabby. Balloons and streamers? That's what's important to you? Your uncle's birthday is more important than your husband?

Tabby snapped back for me to, please, for god's sake, stop this continual complaining about her Uncle Jimmy. I'm new on the job, Llewellyn, she said. I'm just trying to fit in smoothly and make a good first impression. What's so wrong with that? Besides, Uncle Jimmy has done so much for us. You know that as well as I do. Just look at this beautiful apartment we live in. And how about us having a Porsche to drive? How about that, Llewellyn? I don't suppose they offered you even a Chevy when they gave you a job at the gun store, did they?

Oh fuck!

So Tabby wanted to light a fuse, did she?

She wanted to firebomb Dresden?

Waste My Lai?

Wreak carnage at Columbine?

Well she sure as hell knew how to do it.

Enough of me beating around the goddamn bush.

So I said it.

I said, No, Tabby, they didn't offer me even a fucking Chevy, but I hear sugar daddies always buy fancy cars for their whores.

For a while Tabby just stood staring at me. Jesus, Llewellyn, why the fuck are you doing this? Is the Porsche your problem? Is that it? Is it? Are you jealous that I'm driving a Porsche? Well I'm tired of your whining, goddamn it. I've got ambition, Llewellyn. Not ambition like some folks, who will walk all over the other person, but I'm damn well not going to be like Tina and spend all my life just scraping by and living in a single-wide trailer and driving some crappy truck. I'm damn well not going to be trailer trash all my life, Llewellyn. You may be satisfied with some minimum wage store clerk job, but I'm on my way somewhere, and if you're not coming along, at least stay out of the way.

By now, Tabby wasn't just talking. She was pretty much screaming.

Go on, Llewellyn, go ahead and drive that goddamn Porsche tonight. See if you can even fucking figure out how to shift. Do you think I don't know that you can't drive stick? Well, I'm taking the truck, and I'm leaving. And I'm not stopping till I get to the top of fucking Alaska. Hell, for that matter, I may go south, and I won't stop till I get to the bottom of Argentina.

Well, I sure as hell hope you won't stop at Argen-fucking-tina, I said. For all I care, you can just keep right on going.

Jesus, Llewellyn. Why are you doing this?

I said, What the fuck, I'm not the one leaving. But go ahead if you want. I won't stop you. I just hope you don't stop driving when you come to the goddamn ocean. You can just keep right on going. And I hope the water's deep.

Tabby threw down the bag of frozen onion rings she had taken out to nuke and sent them scattering all over the floor, then she stormed across the room. She was crying, and I knew she didn't want me to see.

And I hope the ocean's full of fucking sharks, I called out as she slammed the door.

Right then, all I wanted to do was go out after her and drag her back inside and slap her around a bit like I would have if I had been a real man like Pop.

But instead, I let her walk out on me.

I spent the evening chewing on a tough, overdone steak and watching the *Weather Channel,* and hoping they would report blizzards and hurricanes in Argentina.

Argen-fucking-tina.

I thought, right now I sure wish I had a bottle of Comfort, but I didn't even have a six-pack of beer, and then I started crying, just like I did that night I told Tabby how I had killed Mom and Misty.

Just like a baby, I sat there, sobbing and blubbering.

Jesus Christ, what have I done? Don't leave me, Tabby. Oh, please, please, please don't leave me. You can work for your fucking uncle if you want. You can wear your fancy clothes and high heels. You can drive your Porsche. I don't mind driving the truck. I don't care, just please come back, and come back safe.

179

Yep, I sobbed and blubbered just like a crybaby.
Pop would have been ashamed.

Late that night Tabby came in, and this time I did not pretend to be asleep. I could tell she had been crying, and I'm sure she could tell that I had been, too.

How was Argentina? I asked.

Cold.

The ocean?

Deep.

Sharks?

Had to fight them off.

You must have drove fast to get back so quick.

I always drive fast.

I'm glad you're back. Glad you're safe.

Me, too, Llewellyn Trout.

Let's not argue ever again.

Not ever.

April 23

I T WAS SEVERAL months after our argument that Tabby took me out for breakfast. She woke me real early. Get up, Llewellyn Trout, she said. Haul your lazy ass out of bed. We're going out for some pancakes, and this time we'll find a place where they have blueberries. Real blueberries. Fresh, not frozen.

So that's what we did, and as we sat eating those pancakes with blueberries—fresh, not frozen—Tabby said, I'm going to the mountains for a couple days, you want to come along?

I said, What are you talking about? You're forgetting I have to go to work.

No you don't, Tabby said. I already called Mr. LeMar at Anderson Rod and Gun. I told him about you and me never having had a honeymoon, and I told him I wanted this trip to be a surprise for you. He said he would be happy for you to go. He won't even dock you any pay. He said for the two of us to have a good time because you've been working hard and you deserve to take a few days off.

Tabby said she had already made overnight bed and breakfast reservations for us in a town called Idyllwild. Think of it as our honeymoon, she said. Our honeymoon five months late.

I could tell from the tone of her voice that Tabby was a little worried I might be upset that she had gone and made arrangements without asking me.

I told her, Goddamnit, Tabby, do you remember that morning on the beach when I said I was for sure married to a crazy lady?

Tabby nodded kind of hesitantly, and I knew she was hoping this wasn't the start of another fight.

Well, now there's no longer any doubt about it, I said. I should have locked you up, Tabitha Trout. I should have locked you up for good. Locked you up before it was too late. Locked you up before you do more crazy things like this.

Tabby grinned at me and said, Llewellyn Trout, you're a goof, and she told me that last night she had packed an overnight bag with stuff for the both of us, and it was already in the trunk of the car.

Well, I said, In that case, I guess we're both of us set to go.

And so we went.

When we had walked to the far end of the parking lot, that being where Tabby liked to park her car so it wouldn't get dinged, she went and got in at the passenger side, and I told her, I think you're forgetting something.

I'm not forgetting anything, she told me. Llewellyn Trout, you're going to learn how to drive stick shift. This car stays in this parking lot until you drive it out.

Come on, Tabby, I said. I'll crash the damn thing.

Maybe. But you got to learn stick sometime, and there's only one way to do that.

So I got in on the driver's side of that silver Porsche Boxster, and Tabby handed me the keys.

Other than the fact I pretty near ran over an old lady who was pushing a grocery cart as I was backing out of the parking space, and if you ignore the damage done by me putting probably the equivalent of ten thousand miles of wear and tear on the clutch during the next few hours, things went pretty well, and it was a beautiful drive through the hills out of San Juan Capistrano along Ortega Highway, and then up to the small town called Idyllwild. Tabby said it was a place her and Tina had sometimes visited for a weekend getaway.

As we pulled into the little town, Tabby pointed and said, Look up there. The top of that mountain is where we're headed.

I said, Is there really a road all the way to the top? and Tabby told me, No, you goof, but there's a trail.

That means we're walking?

You like climbing mountains, don't you?

I said, I don't know. I never climbed one. That one looks pretty high.

Top's at about nine thousand feet, Tabby said, and I looked at her like she was crazy. She told me not to worry; the trailhead where we would park was at over six thousand, so all we had to hike was less than three thousand. I looked at her like she was still crazy. I'm locking you up as soon as we get home, I said.

April 24

T HERE WERE ONLY a few other people on the trail that day—mostly
fat folks, red-faced and out of breath. But there was also this guy
with a bushy white beard and a walking stick, and he looked a bit
like a Hobbit wizard or probably a more accurate description would have
been hillbilly mountain man, and he said to me and Tabby, Be careful
about staying out too long, my young friends, be real careful; weather's
changing.

Once the guy had passed us, Tabby looked at me and rolled her eyes. I
pointed a finger at my head and made the twirly crazy sign because the sky
was clear with only a few clouds.

When we got to the top, I said, Goddamn, you can see half way round
the world, and then I asked Tabby why the hell had someone put a building
way up here at nine thousand feet.

It's a fire lookout, Tabby told me. It's empty, though, except at fire
season. By now, Tabby had started climbing the rickety steps that led up
the outside of the lookout.

I don't think you're supposed to go up there, I told her. Look at the
sign, it says, "No Trespassing."

Tabby shrugged and said, Llewellyn Trout, do you always follow rules?
Forget about that sign. Just come on up here.

So I did.

At the top of the stairs there was a deck that ran all the way around the
lookout building, and there were windows that went all the way around
as well.

This place is magical, Tabby said. Tina used to bring me up here when
I was a kid, and I used to pretended I was on top of Mount Everest, but
I couldn't remember that name so I called it Mount Everlasting, and I
imagined that everything I could see from here was my domain and I was
the princess of it, and it all belonged to me—to me and only me, and then
galloping up the trail would come a handsome prince on a white horse, but,
instead of being dressed in lace and fancy clothes like those pansy princes in
the fairy books, my prince was always wearing cowboy boots and a cowboy

hat. When he arrived, he would swoop me up with him onto his white horse, and, together, the two of us would ride off to one of those faraway places you can't see from anywhere in the world except from right here at the top of Mount Everlasting.

I said, Tabby Trout, I'm not going to let you ride off with any cowboy. Not even if he's a prince. Then I said, Are you sure no one lives here? I was looking through those windows that went all the way around, and inside the lookout there was a small wood stove and a card table with an empty glass salt shaker on it along with a dog-eared paperback, a candle, too, and a butter dish but no butter. Off to the side, there was a cot with couple blankets neatly folded and stacked, and on top of them was a pillow. On the floor beside the wood stove was a small pile of firewood.

Tabby told me people live here 24/7 but only during the fire season. Look, she said, and she pointed to a hand-written note that was taped to the inside of the door. Sure enough, it said, *Closed until next fire season.*

I suddenly realized that the wizard guy with the white beard must not have been crazy after all because, just about then, it started to rain. At first just a few sprinkles, but within a couple minutes it was coming down hard. And, goddamn, it scared the shit out of me when the hair on my head frizzled from static electricity and then lightning flashed and the thunder was so loud the windows of that fire lookout rattled like they were about to break.

We're kind of exposed here, aren't we? I said.

Tabby said, I suppose we are, but there's a lightning rod on top. Let's see if we can get inside, and she tried the door handle, and, sure enough, it opened and we went in.

I think we're stuck here for a while, I told her, pulling the door closed.

Tabby stood beside me, and she said, Put your arms around me, Llewellyn Trout. Put your arms around me and keep me warm. Hold me and don't let me go. Don't ever let me go.

So I did.

And she said, Give me a kiss, Llewellyn Trout. Give me a kiss just like you wanted to that first night you walked me home back there in Bakersfield.

I said, How do you know I wanted to give you a kiss that night, and Tabby shrugged and grinned up at me, and she said, Women just know.

I said to her, Tabitha Catherine Trout, I'll give you a lot more than a kiss because, frankly, my dear, I'm a southern gentleman, and I don't give a damn how long we're stuck here in the rain.

Tabby said, Llewellyn Trout, you're a goof. I know what you've got in mind, and we can't do that kind of thing here on the top of Mount Everlasting. Especially not in a lookout that has windows all the way around.

I said, And why not, Tabby Trout?

Because someone might see us, that's why.

And who might that someone be? Would you please point them out.

Tabby shrugged and she said, Stop, Llewellyn, stop. And I told her, What's the matter, Tabby Trout, where's your sense of adventure?

Well, I don't think it's there, if that's what your hand is searching for, Tabby said.

Well, then, It'll just have to search somewhere else, I told her, and it was good I did, because Tabby whispered, I think you found it, Llewellyn Trout, I think you found it.

I said, Found what, my dear? Your sense of adventure?

And Tabby said, Yes, I guess. I suppose that's what it is. Yeah, I'm pretty sure that's what it is. Does it feel like that to you?

I said, Well, I don't know, so I'll have to check and make sure.

Just then there was more lightning and more thunder, and the rain started coming down even harder. It wasn't just pitter patting on the roof or splish splashing down those windows; holy shit, it was pounding away on that tin roof like a punk drummer strung out on methamphetamine, and water was pouring in sheets over the windows like it does in one of those automatic drive-through car washes.

By the time I finished making sure I had found Tabby's sense of adventure, it was getting toward evening, and the rain had still not let up. I said to Tabby, We better get going or it'll be dark before we get down the hill.

Tabby said, It's too late for that already. I think we better stay here for the night. I don't want to end up like those people on the evening news who have to be rescued because they do stupid things in the wilderness and end up lost or getting hypothermia, then the search parties have to go looking for them, and everyone who hears about it on the evening news says, What the hell kind of idiot goes and does something stupid like that?

So, even though Tabby had made reservations for us at a bed and breakfast down in Idyllwild, the two of us spent the night in the fire lookout at the top of Tahquitz Peak. We sure were glad someone had left blankets. The cot wasn't designed for two, but Tabby said that just meant we would have to cuddle up all the closer.

I found matches and finally got a fire going, using the small stack of firewood someone had been kind enough to leave at the end of last fire season.

The dog-eared book lying there on the table was Stephen King's *The Girl Who Loved Tom Gordon,* and me and Tabby lay there, cuddled up warm under the blankets, and I read to her from the book, but I didn't get even quarter way through before the candle burned out, and I said to Tabby, Well, I guess that's that. There's not much more we can do now.

Tabby said to me, Llewellyn Trout, I bet even in the dark I can find your sense of adventure.

I said, I bet you can't.

Oh, yeah? What do you bet? Tabby said

A blueberry pancake breakfast when we get back to Idyllwild.

The next morning the sky had cleared, and me and Tabby left the lookout at daybreak and walked back to Idyllwild.

Don't forget you owe me a blueberry pancake breakfast, Tabby said.

April 25

ME AND TABBY had a wonderful vacation in Idyllwild, and the months that followed were wonderful, too, but when Tabby one day came back from work at Green Branch Ministries, saying she was going on a trip with her Uncle Jimmy, it was more than I could take.

I didn't care how excited she was to have been invited to go, and I didn't care that her uncle had asked her to be part of what she called the Initial Planning Team, I just wasn't going to allow her to go. End of discussion

I was pissed in the first place that evening when she told me about the trip. It was my twenty-first birthday, and Tabby hadn't even remembered to wish me a happy one. So that afternoon when I got off work at Anderson Rod and Gun, me and a couple of other guys who worked there had gone out and got shitfaced. Pissed and drunk as a skunk, as Pop would have said. Then on my way home I had stopped at the A&M Liquor and got myself a fifth of Southern Comfort so I could celebrate my twenty-first all by my lonesome back at the apartment because I knew damn well Tabby wasn't likely to be there.

And I was right, of course. The apartment was empty. Tabby was still at work.

So I sat there with my bottle of Comfort, staring at the blinking display on the coffee maker timer.

Why the fuck did Tabby always have to work late? Maybe it was true that her Uncle Jimmy needed to work late, but what the hell did he need a receptionist for after closing time? Tell me that.

He didn't of course. I wasn't that naïve. Not that big a fool. I knew damn well what that asshole preacher was after, and it was hard for me to believe Tabby couldn't see it just as well as me. Whatever the case, it pissed me off that her job was more important to her than I was. After all, it was no longer a new job. There wasn't any need for Tabby to feel she had to go out of her way to fit in smoothly. No need for her to go the extra mile to make a good first impression. Hell, it was obvious she simply preferred spending her evenings at the office with her Uncle Jimmy rather than at home with me.

Even on my goddamn twenty-first birthday.

Fuck it all, and I was damn glad I had brought that fifth of Comfort home with me. You don't fucking turn twenty-one every day of your goddamn life.

When Tabby finally got home, sometime around 9:30, I had already made pretty good progress on that bottle of Comfort.

Isn't it exciting? Tabby said after she finished telling me about the trip she would be going on with her Uncle Jimmy. The arrangements had already been made. She had even applied for an expedited passport.

I said, Fuck it, Tabby. You're not going on any goddamn vacation with your asshole uncle.

Oh, please, Llewellyn, let's not start this again. It's not a vacation. It's more like a business trip. There's a team of five of us going, and we're doing it for such a good cause.

Tabby explained how Uncle Jimmy was launching what he called the Global Rescue Foundation, which was going to be working through local and international agencies to make it easier for people in America to adopt orphaned children from Third World countries.

There's such a need, Llewellyn, and I can help, Tabby said, and I asked her, What the hell does your Uncle Jimmy need a receptionist for when he's on a trip?

Goddamn it, Llewellyn, do you think I can't do anything but take phone calls and give people directions?

I said, Fuck it, Tabby, I just don't like being married to someone who finds her job more important than her own husband.

You know that's not true, Llewellyn. Besides, I've asked Uncle Jimmy if you could come along, and he said you're welcome to. So why not come along with us? All expenses are paid. We'll have some fun.

Yeah, like hell. I poured myself more Comfort. What did Tabby think I was going to do, just quit my job at Anderson so I could tag along on some goddamn project of her Uncle Jimmy's? No fucking way I was going to do that. No fucking way.

I've got a job, too, you know, I said. Don't you think it's just as important to me as yours is to you?

Oh, Llewellyn, I know. But please try to understand. It's not as if I'm leaving you forever. It's for less than two weeks. And afterwards, Uncle Jimmy wants me to be assistant director of the Global Rescue Foundation that he's starting up. I'll be doing something to help make the world a better place. And it will be so good for the two of us, as well, Llewellyn. I'll be paid more than three times what I'm being paid right now, and it'll be a job I like so much better than the one I have. Is two weeks really too much to ask? I'm so excited about it. Can't you try to understand?

I said to Tabby, You do what you want. Go ahead and get your big pay raises. Go ahead and get your fancy assistant director's job. I bet your Uncle Jimmy will even give you a fancy new car to go with your fancy new position, won't he? What will it be, Tabby, a Rolls? Or maybe a Bentley? Something fancier than a fucking Porsche, I'm damn sure. And something with a back seat big enough for both you and your Uncle Jimmy. So go ahead, Tabby. Go off with that sugardaddy of yours; let him fuck you all night long if that's what he wants, because that is what he wants, believe me. Go with him if you want to, Tabby, but don't expect to find me waiting for you here when you come back.

And that's when I hit her. Hard. With the back of my hand right across her face. There was blood at the corner of her mouth, and I knew there would be swelling the next day, maybe bruises. I had seen the aftereffects of Pop's backhand often enough to know how much damage a backhand can do.

But Tabby didn't wait to rinse with salt water. She didn't wait to put ice on the sore spot.

There was no changing what had been done. No changing what had been said.

Tabby was gone.

She had left me. Left me to finish up that bottle of Comfort all by my lonesome.

And I did.

Fuck it.

April 26

TABBY DIDN'T COME back that night, and she wasn't home when I left for work at Anderson the next morning, hungover and asking myself, How the hell did Pop used to drink so much of that shit, and my god, right now even the thought of it made my stomach heave.

About mid morning I was feeling a bit better, and I thought maybe I should call Tabby. But then I figured, No, goddamn it, if she wants to talk to me, she knows my number.

She still wasn't home when I got off work. But that wasn't unusual. Often as not, work would keep her at Green Branch Ministries late into the evening. So there was nothing to worry about. Right? Nothing at all.

When I finally went to bed, once again pissed and drunk as a skunk, but this time on Jack Daniels, not Southern Comfort, Tabby still wasn't home, and I said, To hell with it, who gives a flying fuck, but, fact is, I was starting to get worried. Maybe something bad had happened to Tabby. Maybe she was hurt. Maybe she had been in a car crash. Damnit, why did she always drive so fast.

When she still wasn't home the next morning, I called over to Green Branch Ministries and was told that Reverend Jimmy Cochran and his team had already left the country. And, yes, Tabby was with them.

I said, How the hell can that be? She doesn't even have a fucking passport. The lady at the other end said, Please watch your language, sir, and she said, Tabby obviously must have gotten her passport because Reverend Cochran and his team were in the air at this very moment. In fact, their departure time was just, let's see, about half an hour ago out of Los Angeles International.

I was so shocked I didn't even know what to say. I just hung up.

My god! Tabby wasn't even in the country anymore? She really had left me? Sweet fucking Jesus.

After I hung up, I didn't bother going in to work at Anderson. That Jack Daniels had left me feeling every bit as sick as the Southern Comfort had the night before.

Last time Tabby left me, I had cried and blubbered like a baby. This time I just went out and bought myself a twelve-pack of Coors. No more of the hard stuff, I told myself. No more Comfort. No more Jack.

Next morning I did the same. And the next. About noon, I got a call asking why hadn't I showed up for work two days in a row, and if I wanted to keep my job, I better get my goddamn butt down to Anderson right now. So I went in, but when my boss, Mr. LeMar, realized I was pissed and drunk as a skunk, he told me to go on home, and there would be no need for me to come in the following day. I could collect my final paycheck on Friday afternoon.

Guns and alcohol just don't mix, Mr. LeMar told me. Not in this store, they don't.

I told him, Fuck you, Mr. LeMar, my Pop never had a problem mixing guns and alcohol.

To hell with working at Anderson, I didn't like working there, anyhow. I flipped the place off as I left the parking lot and drove back to the apartment and opened myself another Coors.

I don't know why I went over to Reverend Cochran's place that evening. Or maybe I do. Even at the time, I think deep down I really did know. I guess when you've been drinking for two days straight, you sometimes do stupid things, and I thought, Be careful, Llewellyn; be real careful, but, then, somehow, even after all the years, I remembered sitting there in Flo's Diner, watching Miss Elsa sizzle ants with a cigarette lighter, and I remembered how she had told me, Don't worry, sweetheart, it's okay to play with fire just so long as you're careful. Well, tonight I was going to play with fire. And to hell with being careful.

That's the kind of bullshit you feed yourself when you're wasted on Comfort, Jack, and Coors.

So I put my swimsuit on and got in the truck to drive over to Reverend Jimmy's big fucking mansion, where there was a hot tub and where there was someone who called me Cowboy—someone who had told me, Come on up any time, Cowboy. I'll even roll you a joint.

Holy fucking shit, I was so drunk I scraped up the side of the pickup as I was pulling out of the car port. I thought, Goddamn, now Tabby will really be pissed at me, and then I said, Why the hell should I give a flying fuck about a few scratches because when Tabby gets back, I won't even be here anymore.

When I got to Reverend Jimmy's place, I went to the hot tub, and I punched the electric switches for the bubbles and the lights, and then I stepped right in.

It sounds crazy now, but not at the time, it didn't.

Hell, after a fifth of Comfort, Pop didn't see anything unusual about having shot a scumbag in the back with a whale harpoon, so I figured that after two whole days of drinking why should I feel there was anything unusual about going uninvited over to another person's house and getting into the hot tub.

I was sitting there, wondering where Tabby might be, England? France? Mexico? Argen-fucking-tina? and all of a sudden, there beside the hot tub was Roxy, looking down at me. I guess the bubbling water and the sound of waves from the ocean made it so I hadn't heard her coming.

But here she was, and this time she wasn't wearing that red bikini but, instead, a pair of jeans and a T-shirt that said, *Jesus Loves You. Everyone Else Thinks You're an Asshole.*

What are you doing here, Cowboy? she said.

Waiting for you, I guess, I told her. I got no one else to wait for.

Roxy said, They tell me Tabby went off with my daddy to Vietnam.

Holy shit, I told her, is that where those two assholes went?

Then I said that, seeing as my wife had run off with her boss and I had spent the last few days drunk as a skunk on Jack and Comfort, I had decided that this evening I would ease my bones in a hot tub, but, unfortunately, on the way I had scratched up the side of my truck, pulling out of the car port.

That's what I told Roxy, and, obviously, I guess you sometimes ramble and don't always talk the most clear when you've been drinking too much.

Someone should write a redneck country song about you, Cowboy, Roxy told me, and I said, What the hell do you mean by that?

Well, your wife ran off with a preacher man. You've got yourself shitfaced on Jack Daniels and Southern Comfort. And now you've crashed your pickup. Sounds like a country song to me, doesn't it to you?

Then, after a pause, Roxy said, Mind if I join you in the hot tub, Cowboy?

I told her, Do as you please, it's your hot tub, not mine.

I thought Roxy would go off and change into that red bikini of hers and come back out to the hot tub, but, holy shit, she, right there in front of me, took off her jeans and the *Jesus Loves You* T-shirt, and she wasn't wearing anything under them, and she just stepped into the hot tub and stood there in front of me in the water that was all blue and bubbly, and she said, You ever seen my tattoo, Cowboy?

I said, Goddamn, Roxy, don't you think you better put on a swimsuit or something? And she told me, Don't bullshit me, Cowboy. Don't tell me you came over here and climbed into this hot tub because you wanted to see me in a swimsuit. I know better than that.

Holy shit, what was I supposed to say because of course she was right.

And then she sat down on my lap, and she took my hand and said, Here, Cowboy, feel how smooth that new tattoo of mine is, and I told her, It feels smooth as a baby's bottom, and she said, Yep, it does.

Later on, quite a bit later, she said, You want me to roll that joint I promised you, Cowboy?

I said, Sounds good, and I thought we would go up to her room, but she just reached into the pockets of the jeans lying there beside the hot tub and pulled out everything she needed.

And there we sat in that hot tub with the sound of the white bubbles in the blue water and the sound of the black waves in the darkness of the ocean, and we smoked that joint Roxy had rolled.

And then another.

Roxy was sitting across from me, and I was staring right into those dark gray eyes of hers—so deep, so bottomless—and in that moment I saw what I had never seen there before.

Oh, I had seen it before, just never there.

In that moment, I knew that Roxy was on the dark side. Swept over there long ago. It wasn't like Misty, where you felt you could, if only you had the courage to go out yourself into the dark current, maybe you might be able to bring her back. No, it wasn't like that with Roxy. I knew that she had been on the dark side so long there was no bringing her back.

Holy fuck, Roxy, I said. How long since you got swept over to the dark side, and she looked at me like, What the hell are you talking about, Cowboy?

I guess alcohol and a couple joints can make you say things you wouldn't otherwise, and that evening sitting there in that Dali painting, and for I don't know what the hell reason, I told Roxy things I had never told anyone before. Not anyone. Not even Tabby.

I told about Misty and how she got pulled over to the dark side. I told about Miss Elsa and the switch. About the hide-and-seek games and the chasing games. About the gun with the fucked up trigger that went off by accident. About Pop standing there with his head bowed and praying silently to our father which art in heaven and then blowing a hole in the back of his head.

I wasn't crying this time as I talked. Not like the time when I told Tabby about killing Mom and Misty. I just sat there in the hot tub, talking away nonstop, but not fast, and the whole time, Roxy just sat there and didn't say a word, and she was staring straight into my eyes—every moment into my eyes in a way no one else had ever before looked into my eyes—like she was searching for something there.

Then all of a sudden I ran out of words, and I sat silent and staring into those bottomless gray eyes across from me on the other side of that hot tub of blue filled with white bubbles, and suddenly, with Roxy staring back into my eyes, I knew she saw in mine what I saw in hers, and I realized the dark side wasn't somewhere else but was here—right here, right now—and I was there on the dark side, and I had been for I don't know how long, but why had I never even felt the current dragging me over? Weren't you supposed to dig in with your fingernails to keep from being dragged over? I hadn't felt any current, so maybe that's why I hadn't struggled. Maybe it had just happened without me even knowing.

I whispered, We're both there, aren't we Roxy? We're both of us on the dark side, aren't we?

But Roxy looked at me like, You're crazy, Cowboy, and I realized I was so wasted I wouldn't make any sense even if I tried to explain myself.

Come with me, Cowboy, Roxy whispered, putting a hand on my shoulder, but her touch this time was different, gentle and warm, like she was older than me and wiser and not a kid still only fifteen years old.

Come with me, she whispered. I'll show you the dark side.

We went into the house, and she got us towels to dry off, and she put on sweats and gave me an oversize towel to wrap around my shoulders to keep warm because all I had was my swimsuit. Then she led me down the hallway and into a bedroom. It's my daddy's room, she told me as she opened a closet, and it was one of those big walk-in ones. And there, reflecting white silk suits and colorful silk shirts, was a huge wall-size mirror.

Roxy pressed a small button, and the mirror slid into the wall like a sliding door, and this wasn't a B movie any more but more like a Bond movie—Bond, James Bond.

Come down here, Roxy said to me. Be careful, the stairs are dark.

April 27

I FOLLOWED ROXY down a narrow flight of stairs into a dark, window-less room, lit only by one of those lava lamp things like the hippies had back in the 1960s.

I said, I didn't know this house had a basement, and Roxy told me, Hardly anybody does, Cowboy. Not many folks in California have basements, but my daddy has one, and the only way to get here is those stairs we just came down. No one in California expects a house to have a basement, so no one bothers looking for one. Only a few of Daddy's closest friends know this place even exists.

Roxy flipped a switch and soft lights came on around the room, mostly artificial electric candles with dim bulbs that were supposed to look like flames but didn't.

It was a huge room, and at one end was one of those gazillion dollar home theatres you sometimes see in magazines that show what rich folks have in their homes, and, at the other end of the basement, it was like two separate bedrooms in opposite corners. One bedroom was like from the days of *Gone With the Wind,* and the other one was like a crazy crash pad you see in those movies about the hippies in the 1960s.

In the *Gone With the Wind* corner was a bed with brass posts, white lace, and pink ruffles. Old black and white photographs hung in dark wooden frames on the wall, and, holy shit, most of those pictures were of ladies with old-fashioned underwear and some with nothing on at all, but their hair still all curled up fancy on top of their head.

In the hippie crash pad corner, old rock LP album covers hung on the wall like pictures without frames, and one of them had a picture of a girl with red hair and an airplane and no clothes. On the floor was a mattress with no bed frame and, I figured, probably filled with water, and it was covered with a paisley quilt, and beside it on the floor was the lava lamp that had been the only light that was on when me and Roxy first came down the stairs.

Across the basement from those two beds, almost the entire wall was covered by a giant flatscreen. Not anything like those ones you see but don't ever have enough money to buy in the Circuit Center stores. This screen was much bigger, and there were speakers all around the room—not just little plastic ones but big boxes of polished wood.

In front of the screen was a black leather couch and, behind it, a half dozen leather lazy-style chairs, arranged like some small, luxury theater.

And, holy shit, the ceiling of the entire room was a mirror. Everything you saw below, was reflected above.

Roxy pointed to the leather couch and said to me, Take a seat, Cowboy. She opened a tall wooden cabinet, and inside was shelf after shelf of VHS tapes and DVD discs.

Roxy said, This is what my daddy calls his personal love library.

She spent a minute or two searching through the cabinet, and I sat there shivering because my swimsuit was still damp and the towel around my shoulder wasn't doing a very good job of keeping me warm, and then Roxy put in a VHS tape and after a bit of static and snow on the screen, there was suddenly a picture of a little girl, maybe four or five years old and she was dressed in a fancy, frilly dress with lace, and the girl was seated on that same *Gone With the Wind* bed that was right here in one corner of this basement.

The little girl seemed a bit nervous and maybe even scared, but then there was a soothing voice that said, Don't be afraid, darling. Daddy won't hurt you.

The girl's eyes darted nervously, but the soothing voice said, It's okay, Baby Doll. Won't you smile for Daddy?

And the girl smiled, but it wasn't one of those sparkle-eye smiles kids have when they are happy, but, instead, it was one of those pull-your-lips-back-and-show-your-teeth smiles you do just because the person taking the picture says to you, Cheese.

Then the same soft and soothing voice said, Would you please take off your clothes, sweetheart. Take them off for Daddy.

It was obviously the voice of the person who was doing the recording, and I thought, That sure as hell sounds like Reverend Cochran, and then the voice said, That's a good girl, you know what to do.

And that is when I recognized the timid little girl in the frilly dress—the girl with the bottomless gray eyes; it was Roxy, and she was having a hard time undoing the top button on that dress of hers, and the voice sweet and smooth as Southern Comfort said, Here, honey, let Daddy help you with that, and suddenly there in front of the camera was Reverend Jimmy

Cochran of Green Branch Ministries, and he was gently helping his daughter undo her top button.

And that man of God was wearing nothing. Not even silk underwear.

What I saw in the next minutes made my stomach turn, and after all the drinking I had done over the past few days, my stomach was already uneasy, and this was more than I could take. I vomited, and because I had only been drinking and not eating much of anything, all that came up was clear slime and yellow gunk.

Roxy put in a different video, and this time the girl was a little bit older but not much, and this time she was dressed in some ridiculous costume that made her look like one of those 1960s hippies, and she was this time on the waterbed mattress, and I heard that same soft, sweet voice telling the girl, Oh, yes, that's right, honey, you know how to do it just the way Daddy likes, and this time the little girl didn't have any problems with buttons, and I said to Roxy, Please stop it. That's enough. But she said, No, Cowboy. Tonight you told me about when you were a kid, and I listened the whole time. Now I want you to see how it was for me as a kid. You have secrets you never told anyone until tonight. Well, so do I.

I said, Your father's a monster.

Roxy said to me, No he's not. I love my daddy. But if you want monsters, Cowboy, I'll show you monsters. Oh, yeah, I'll show you monsters.

Roxy took several DVDs from the shelf, and it was true what she said. Some of the things she showed me, on those DVDs made the Reverend Jimmy Cochran really seem gentle, kind, almost loving. I vomited again, and this time there was no yellow gunk, just clear slime.

Those poor little kids, I said, and my voice came out just a scratchy whisper. It's all real, isn't it?

Roxy nodded. Every bit of it, Cowboy. No acting there. You don't see good shit like this on the porn channels, do you?

And then Roxy put in another DVD and I said, Oh holy fuck, because I knew that kid there on the screen. It was David—the little foster kid that came to live with Uncle Stew and Aunt Marge just before I left Waynesburg.

The video showed the little boy lying naked on the same bed I used to sleep on out in the Winnebago, and lying there naked with him was Uncle Stew.

Roxy said, You don't want to see the rest of that one, Cowboy. You've already vomited twice tonight.

Roxy shut off the DVD player, and I just sat there on the couch, shivering and feeling sick to my stomach.

I pointed to the cabinet of videos, and I said, My god, how many of them are there? and Roxy said, Dozens, who knows, probably more like hundreds. I never counted them. Most of them are just regular old every-day porn you can rent at most any video store. But the good ones, the real ones, oh, there's probably only a few dozen, not as many as a hundred, I don't think.

Are they mostly of you?

Oh, no, Cowboy. My daddy has videos from all over the world. It's like a club these guys have. You send one of them a video that you've made, and you get one back in return.

I can't bring myself to tell right now all that Roxy showed me that night. In some of those videos, I don't think she was more than three or four years old, and in others she was older and her body was starting to change. Sometimes she was there alone with her daddy, and sometimes other men were there, too.

By this time I was shivering and my teeth chattering like crazy because it was cold in the basement, and I didn't have a towel for my shoulders because it was full of slime and yellow vomit, and Roxy put all the videos back so that no one would know they had been watched, and then she took me back upstairs.

We went to her bed and we curled up there under the blankets to get warm, but as I lay there with Roxy that night, there were no more lustful thoughts, only a deep, deep sadness, and Roxy lay with her arm around my shoulder, and it was like when Misty would put an arm around me and comfort me as I lay sobbing after the things Miss Elsa would do to us.

I cried that night, but not Roxy. I bet she never once had cried in all those years of her father abusing her. Like Misty, she probably just took all the terrible things that were done to her and didn't fight and didn't cry.

I whispered to Roxy, I wish I had been here, I would have kept you safe, I would have stopped it from happening.

But I knew deep inside it was a lie. Just like with Misty, I wouldn't have done a damn thing.

I am a coward. I always have been.

April 28

THE NEXT MORNING I woke before Roxy, and I looked at her lying there, the piercing on her lip buried in the pillow, and her scraggly hair covering all the piercings in her ears, and she looked so innocent, and I knew this wiseass teenage punk was really just a little kid who right now looked more like thirteen than like fifteen, and I thought, My god, Llewellyn Trout, what have you done? What the fuck have you done?

And I thought about Lindsey Longpoke and how she had been 18 years old back then, and here was Roxy, just fifteen. And I thought of Mr. D and how he had been about five years older than Lindsey, and here, I was almost six years older than Roxy. And I thought, My god, Llewellyn, do you realize that the difference between eighteen and fifteen is only three years, but that difference could land you in prison, and I thought, Holy shit, what on earth have you done? Why didn't you run, you stupid shit? Why the hell didn't you run? You should have run, but, instead, you came over here. And you know damn well why you did it.

When Roxy woke, she smiled at me, and the smile was this time more elf than gremlin, and she said, I'm glad you were here with me last night, Cowboy. I needed someone to hold me, and I thought, My god, Roxy, it was me that needed holding.

I thought about Misty, and about Lindsey Longpoke, and about Miss Veronica, and, like them, Roxy might not show it on the outside, but inside she was just a girl who needed someone to care for her, someone to make her feel safe, someone to make her feel loved. That's what she had wanted from me last night, and, I had gone and taken advantage of her, because taking care of her, making her feel safe, and making her feel loved was not at all what I had in mind when I came over and made myself at home in that hot tub. Not even a little bit what I had in mind.

As we sat on the upstairs terrace, looking out over the Pacific—blue today with no fog—me and Roxy were smoking a joint and drinking Starbucks and eating sweet and sour soup that Jacob had brought back for our breakfast, and I pointed out at the ocean and said, Somewhere over there is Vietnam. Somewhere over there is my wife.

Roxy nodded. Her and my daddy.

I asked Roxy, Do you think he would . . . well, you know, with Tabby . . . your daddy, do you think he would . . .

Spit it out, Cowboy. Are you trying to ask if Daddy would fuck your wife?

I sort of shrugged and nodded at the same time.

If she gives him a chance, Cowboy, no doubt about it. If she gives him a chance. Haven't you seen the way he looks at her? Haven't you seen the way he acts around her?

I said, Do you think they ever have?

How would I know, Cowboy? You'd have to ask Tabby. Hell, for that matter, ask my daddy; he'd probably tell you the truth.

I sat for a while real quiet, and then I said, Roxy, I don't think I want to know.

Are you going to tell Tabby about us? Roxy asked. Are you going to tell her about last night in the hot tub?

I said to Roxy, No, I'll be out of town before Tabby gets back.

You're planning on getting out of Dodge City, are you, Cowboy?

Roxy laughed, but it wasn't an amused laugh. What the fuck are you talking about? she said. Don't give me any shit about you leaving Tabby. You aren't that big a fool. She's crazy about you, and you're a fucking idiot if you're going to throw away something like that.

I told Roxy, Well, if you think so high and mighty of her, why did you do what you did with me last night in the hot tub?

Don't blame me for that, Cowboy, Roxy said. I didn't force anything on you.

Yeah, but aren't you Tabby's friend? I mean, I know you are her cousin, but you're a friend, too, right?

She's the best friend I ever had, Roxy said.

Well, I said, If you are her friend, then why did you do it, Roxy? and I heard her words come right back at me, Well, if you are her husband, then why did you do it, Cowboy?

Oh, god, why the fuck hadn't I run?

How about you? Are you going to tell Tabby? I said, thinking I might still be able to turn the question back on Roxy.

I've got secrets darker than anything that happened in that hot tub last night, Roxy said. I haven't ever had a problem keeping a secret. Some things are better kept that way.

I sat there thinking, My god, Roxy, you're sometimes like an innocent little kid, sometimes you're a smartass teenage punk, and sometimes you're wiser than any person I ever met.

I'm good at keeping secrets, too, I told her. Real good.

April 29

HOW HAD I been so stupid to think I would be gone before Tabby got back? Where the fuck was I planning to go? Bakersfield? Waynesburg? Yeah, like hell.

Besides, this morning there was nothing I wanted more than to have Tabby back again, and I wished I had gone with her on the trip like she had invited me to. After all, here I had gone and gotten myself fired from Anderson Rod and Gun, anyhow, so why shouldn't I have gone along on the trip.

I got in that truck, scraped and dented all down one side, and I drove back to mine and Tabby's apartment, and when I got there, what the fuck, I must not have locked the door when I left, because when I put in the key, it was already unlocked.

I went inside, and I was surprised as hell, because there sat Tabby. She had her head on her arms at the dining room table, and she was crying. At first when I walked in, she just sat there, not even bothering to lift her head, but then I said her name . . . Tabby.

She jumped to her feet and threw her arms around me and said, Oh, Llewellyn, I'm glad you're still here. I was so afraid you really had left me. So very afraid.

I asked Tabby, Why are you here? I didn't expect you back for few days.

Tabby sure wasn't like Roxy or Misty. She had no problem crying. Over and over she kept saying how sorry she was, how very, very sorry she was that she had gone and left me.

I thought, How can you be sorry you left me when the side of your face is still bruised from me hitting you?

Tabby said, You were right, Llewellyn, you were right about my Uncle Jimmy, you were right all along. I'm so very, very sorry.

It took a long time before Tabby was able to pull herself together enough to tell me what had happened.

At first the trip had gone so well. It was all so exciting. Tabby had never been on an airplane before, only a few times even in an airport.

When Reverend Cochran and the other people in his team arrived at Tan Son Nhat International Airport at Ho Chi Minh City, waiting there for them were several Vietnamese men, who knew English, even if not very well, and with their help, everyone on Reverend Cochran's team got through customs real quick and with no problem, and then the team was taken to a seaside resort where Tabby was given a room of her own.

My gosh, Llewellyn, it was so fancy and not anything like a Motel 6, Tabby said. You know, I began to think, maybe you had been right after all, and this really was going to be nothing but a vacation.

After the team got settled in and washed up, all five of them gathered for a meal that was served at tables set up right on the sand of the beach and with big tropical woven-straw umbrellas over the tables. Uncle Jimmy bought drinks for everyone, lots of drinks, even for Tabby because nobody seemed to give a damn if she was twenty-one or not, and Tabby thought, What the heck's going on, because I didn't think Uncle Jimmy ever drank alcohol.

Between having too many drinks and being exhausted from the trip, Tabby had gone to bed right after lunch, but jet lag seemed to have upset her schedule, and she woke in the evening and couldn't sleep, so she went out to walk on the beach, and when she returned, she saw Uncle Jimmy sitting at the outdoor bar by the pool.

She was going to say hello to him, but then she realized maybe she shouldn't because he was with a Vietnamese woman and was buying a drink for her, and his hand was on her leg and stroking it gently under the bar.

Tabby was a bit flustered and not sure what to think, but then Uncle Jimmy and the woman stood up and Tabby thought, My gosh, Vietnamese women are sometimes not so tall, but that one looks more like a girl than a woman, and Uncle Jimmy took that girl's hand, and, together, the two of them walked off together into the night.

The next morning Tabby saw Uncle Jimmy sitting with the same girl at one of the tables set up out on the sand, and now in the light of day there was no doubt that it wasn't a woman, but a girl, probably not more than thirteen or fourteen years old, Tabby guessed.

At first Uncle Jimmy seemed a bit uncomfortable when Tabby walked up to the table, but then he introduced the girl as Huong, and he said she was an orphan and he was interviewing her as someone who might be a potential candidate for adoption back in the U.S.

It wasn't just Uncle Jimmy that was buying drinks for young Vietnamese girls. The other men in the team were doing the same, and other tourists were, too, and Tabby wasn't stupid enough to believe they were all interviewing the girls as potential candidates for adoption.

That evening, Uncle Jimmy said, Hey, Tabby Cat, why don't you come to my room after a drink or two. Huong will be there and I'd like for the two of you to get to know each other.

Tabby hadn't known what to say, so she just turned to walk away, but Uncle Jimmy called her back.

Loosen up, Tabby Cat, he told her. This is a different country. A different culture. People do things differently here. They're not so uptight about these things as we are back in The States. You need to learn to respect their culture and be part of it instead of being some uptight American tourist.

Tabby said, I thought you came here to make arrangements for orphaned children to find homes.

That's right, Tabby Cat. That's right. But we came a few days early for a bit of R&R. Nothing wrong with that, is there?

Uncle Jimmy went on to say that the next day he and his team would be meeting with Vietnamese officials to take care of the necessary arrangements.

And let me tell you, Tabby Cat, Green Branch Ministries has brought thousands of dollars in order to make the necessary bribes. We are very serious about helping these children.

Tabby said, My god, Uncle Jimmy, you're going to bribe government officials? and he told her, Like I said, Tabby Cat, this is a different culture. They expect bribes. It's the oil that makes the machine work. Nothing wrong with bribes. I don't recall them being mentioned in the Ten Commandments, do you?

No, I guess not, Tabby said, and her Uncle Jimmy told her, Well, then, Tabby cat, like I say, loosen up and accept that these people have a different culture, a different way of looking at the world.

The worst part, Tabby told me, was that her Uncle Jimmy had given up even pretending that his friendship with Huong had anything to do with adoption. He knew that Tabby was aware of exactly what was going on, and he thought she wouldn't care.

He had promised to make her assistant director and had given her an apartment and a fancy car, and, because of that, he thought she wouldn't care what he did. He figured he could do anything he damn well pleased. He thought Tabby wouldn't do anything or say anything to stop him.

Anyhow, when Tabby realized what was going on, she had snuck into her uncle's room and taken her return ticket, and her passport, too. She was sorry she had to sneak into his room to do it, but Uncle Jimmy had insisted on keeping the tickets and passports of everyone on his team. Just a precaution, he had told them. We don't want anything getting lost.

Tabby had taken a taxi to the airport, and was on a flight back to LAX before her uncle probably even knew she was gone.

There was an email waiting for her when she got back to our apartment. She showed it to me.

It was from Uncle Jimmy, and it was all casual as if nothing unusual had happened.

Uncle Jimmy was sorry his Tabby Cat had found it necessary to leave early, but he hoped she had enjoyed her flight back home. She wouldn't have had to steal her ticket and passport; Uncle Jimmy would have been happy to give them to her at any time. He and his team looked forward to returning in a few days, but in the mean time, there was so much of the Lord's work to be done.

Uncle Jimmy hoped Tabby was looking forward to taking on new responsibilities as assistant director of the Global Rescue Foundation, and he hoped as well that she was looking forward to the added responsibilities, salary increases, and various other perks that would come with those added responsibilities. How fortunate it was that God had already provided someone to take over Tabby's old position as receptionist.

Last but not least, was the exciting news that the Lord God had worked it out for Uncle Jimmy, himself, to be the first person privileged to adopt a dear Vietnamese child through the newly formed Global Rescue Foundation of Cochran Green Branch Ministries.

As an attachment, Uncle Jimmy had sent a photograph of the darling orphan girl he would be adopting—the dear child he would be lifting from the filth and poverty of the slums of Ho Chi Minh City.

Tabby clicked on the attached picture. And what I saw was kind of the mental equivalent of the time Sergeant Jesus Sanchez hit me in the gut.

April 30

I SAID, MY god, Tabby, that girl looks so much like Misty. My voice came out just a whisper. Holy shit, your uncle is going to adopt a girl who looks just like my little sister. And then I thought about that *Gone With the Wind* bedroom and the hippie crash pad bedroom and little Roxy and all she had gone through, and I knew instantly what would happen to that little girl from Vietnam when she came to live with Reverend Jimmy Cochran, and I said to Tabby, I'll never let your uncle adopt that girl. Never. Not over my dead body.

Not over my dead body.

I meant that. But if I had known what it would really cost me, would I have had the courage to try stopping Reverend Cochran?

Of course not. I'm a coward.

May 1

WITH JET LAG and all, Tabby was so tired she fell asleep late in the afternoon, and when she did, I called Roxy and asked her to come over. When she arrived, she said, Why the hell is Tabby back already? and I told her about what had happened.

Roxy nodded. I knew she'd figure things out, she said. Tabby's not someone who likes to take advice, but she's smart enough to figure things out on her own.

I told Roxy about the Vietnamese girl her daddy was going to adopt, and I said, I'm afraid for her, Roxy. I think your daddy might do the same thing to her that he did to you.

Roxy said, Why do you say might, Cowboy? Of course he will.

I said, What can we do to stop it? Maybe if you bring me one of those videos from your daddy's basement I could take it to the police. We need some kind of evidence so they'll believe me.

Roxy shook her head. No, Cowboy. I don't want you going to the police. I don't want my daddy getting in trouble.

I said, But Roxy, think what he did to you.

I know what he did to me, Cowboy. And I also know that my daddy loved me. I know that he still loves me.

I looked at Roxy like, Are you serious? Are you fucking crazy? Are you bullshitting me?

Roxy said, What's your problem, Cowboy? Of course I love my daddy. Just like you loved yours.

But that's different. Pop was different. He never abused me.

He hit you all the time. You told me so yourself. He hit you. Hit your mother. Hit your little sister.

But that was only when he was pissed off. My Pop loved me. He loved all of us.

Roxy shrugged. And my daddy loves me, Cowboy. What's wrong with my daddy showing me his love? Tell me that. What's wrong with it? Did your daddy often show you his love? Did he often give you a hug? Often give you a kiss? I don't think so. Not from what you told me about him. But

207

my daddy shows me how much he loves me. He shows me all the time. And never once has he hit me, Cowboy. Never once even a spanking.

I could hardly believe what I was hearing. I remembered that night when Pop held me on his lap and put his arm around me and wiped away my tears before shooting himself to keep me from having to take the blame for killing Mom and Misty. I said to Roxy, Yes, my Pop showed me his love, but it was in a different way.

Hitting you? Breaking your teeth? That's how he showed his love?

I shrugged, and Roxy said, Well, like I told you, my daddy never hit me. Never hurt me. Never once. So who's worse? Tell me that, Cowboy. Who's worse, your daddy or mine? Would you have turned your daddy over to the cops?

But, Roxy, think what he did to you.

Like I told you, Cowboy, I know what he did to me. Sometimes he still does it to me. I don't usually stop him. I didn't tell you that part, did I? And let me explain something else to you, Cowboy, there's lots of ways for a person to show love. No one sees anything wrong with a hug. No one sees anything wrong with a kiss. Where do you draw the line, and why should I draw it in the same place as you do?

But Roxy, we're not talking about hugs and kisses. We're talking about your daddy having sex with you.

I know that, Cowboy. What's wrong with sex? Did you ever have sex with Tabby? Tell me that, Cowboy. Have you ever fucked your wife?

I felt myself blushing from embarrassment, but also from anger. Goddamn it, Roxy. Of course. But that's different.

Is it one of the ways you show her your love?

Well, I guess.

Then there you have it. Sex is one way to show love. Why shouldn't it be the same way for me and my daddy?

But it's not the same. It's different.

Then tell me exactly how, Roxy said. Tell me exactly how.

Well, because it is.

Fuck it, Cowboy! That's not a good answer, and you know it. So go ahead, give me a real answer. Tell me exactly how it's different.

And I sat there what I guess you would call dumbfounded because I couldn't think of anything to say.

Finally I spoke. But what about last night. You said you were showing me the dark side.

The dark side is *your* name for it, Cowboy, not mine. But it's true, there are days when I want to kill my daddy. Some days I want to slice him to pieces with my own hands and watch him die real slow while I record it all on video so I can replay it over and over. But most days I love him more than anything in this world. Some days there's nothing I wouldn't do for him. Nothing.

I just sat there shaking my head, and Roxy said, You think I'm pretty fucked up, don't you Cowboy?

I could only shrug, and Roxy said, Well, I guess you're pretty much right. I'm probably about as fucked up as anyone can ever get. I imagine it has to do with what you call getting carried over to the dark side.

You're not fucked up, Roxy. Maybe just confused.

Don't bullshit me, Cowboy. I'm completely fucked up. I know that. You know that. But what's wrong with being fucked up? What's wrong with being on what you call the dark side? What about your little sister, what was her name?

Misty.

Yeah, was Misty fucked up—never saying a word to anyone, off in a world of her own, always in trouble at school? There's nothing wrong with being fucked up, Cowboy. All of us over here on the dark side are fucked up. All of us. You told me last night you thought maybe you had already been carried over to the dark side. Well, I don't think so. I'll tell you something, Cowboy, if you're not completely fucked up, you're not on the dark side.

Holy shit, I would never have believed I would be holding a conversation like this. And the crazy thing is that what Roxy said seemed sometimes to make more sense than what I was saying. I was so upset my hands were shaking and my voice was unsteady, and then I thought of what to say, and for sure Roxy couldn't disagree with me on this one.

I said, What about all those other kids you showed me videos of? What about the girl whose face was so bruised and swollen she couldn't even open her eyes. How about the little boy who got whipped and had his head held in toilet water as punishment for fighting back when some sicko tried shoving a brush handle up his ass? How about the girl who was handcuffed to that iron grate, and was screaming and sobbing while one sick fuck after another did to her whatever the hell they wanted. What about the little boy lying there with my Uncle Stew and you said I better not watch that one because I had vomited twice already. What about them, Roxy?

Was that love? Nothing wrong with any of that, I guess you think. Just people showing their love.

I was surprised Tabby didn't wake up because by now I was almost yelling.

Roxy sat there silent for a long time, and then she said—and I could tell she was pissed when she said it; she said, You weren't talking about turning *those* men over to the police, Cowboy. You were talking about turning over *my daddy*.

I pleaded with her to stay and listen, but Roxy left, and I heard the tires of her Corvette squeal as she pulled into the street.

May 2

TABBY SLEPT LATE into the evening, and she didn't look very comfortable there on the couch, so I sat down beside her, and I shook her gently and said, Wake up sleepyhead, it's time for you to crawl into a real bed, and Tabby grinned kind of sleepy and gave me a hug, and she said, I think you made your first poem for me, Llewellyn Trout. Sleepyhead and bed, they rhyme, I think they do, don't they? and then she was back asleep right there on the couch.

I went into the bedroom and went to bed alone. There was no one tonight to put an arm around my shoulder.

But I couldn't sleep. There was too much on my mind.

I lay there, and I wasn't tossing and turning like you're supposed to when you can't sleep but, instead, I was just lying there still as can be, all curled up in a ball but wide awake.

But my mind was tossing and turning, that's for sure.

I kept thinking of little Misty and the girl who looked so much like her in that picture Tabby's Uncle Jimmy had sent. The girl he was going to adopt. The girl he was going to lift from the poverty of the slums.

Maybe that wouldn't be so bad. The little girl probably lived in horrible conditions, and Uncle Jimmy would bring her to live in his big fucking mansion looking out over the Pacific, waited on by a valet named Jacob, who would bring her Starbucks and Chinese takeout. Then, afternoons and evenings, she would walk on the beach or kick back in the pool or the hot tub.

And, like Roxy, that little girl would probably grow up to love Uncle Jimmy. He would never hurt her. He would never hit her like Pop used to hit me. He would be kind to her and gentle. And when she turned fifteen she would get a brand new Corvette of her own.

That's better than the lice, and the hunger, and the piles of shit in the streets because in the slums over in Vietnam they don't have indoor toilets. Yeah, Mom had told me all about the slums over there. She had lived in a village, not the slums, but she knew about the slums, and they were not a place anyone would want to live.

211

Mom had chosen to come live with my Pop. The man she slaved for. The man who swore at her, insulted her, and beat her when he came home pissed and drunk as a skunk.

But never once had I heard Mom say she wished she was back in Vietnam. Not in her village. Not in the slums.

Maybe the little girl would be better off with Uncle Jimmy just like Mom was better off with Pop. Maybe she would love Reverend Cochran just like Roxy did.

Maybe I should stay out of other people's business.

Finally I slept, and I guess that's when the tossing and turning started, because when I woke the next morning, the blankets and sheets were all tangled around me.

And I was crying, even though I couldn't remember a damn thing I had been dreaming about. Crying in my sleep, for chrissake. Pop would have been ashamed.

When I got up, Tabby was sitting at the dining room table, her laptop in front of her.

She said, Good morning, sleepyhead, and she patted the chair beside her. Sit down, she said. Look what I've got here. She pointed to her computer screen. I think Uncle Jimmy accidentally sent me someone else's email. I don't think I was supposed to get this.

I brushed my hair back from my face because it was a mess after the night, and I looked at that email she had gotten, and the email said,

Stew and Marge,

> *You've both wanted to adopt for so long. I've got a beautiful little boy for you. Praise God for miracles, and praise God that Global Rescue Foundation has found favor with several people in high places here in Vietnam.*

> *For years, the two of you have faithfully supported Green Branch Ministries with your prayers and your generous contributions, and it has been a pleasure to get to know you and to share with you our love of the Lord God.*

God bless all of you in Waynesburg and thank you, again, Stew and Marge, for your generous contributions to the ministry. Stew, I would like to add my personal thanks for your additions to my love library.

I'll be in touch with further details when I get back.

Jimmy

I knew who that email was to. There was only one Stew and Marge in Waynesburg. Yes, I knew damn well who that letter was to. And I knew what Uncle Jimmy was referring to when he talked about his personal love library. Jesus!

I knew I had to do something about it.

I had already talked to Roxy; I had tried to persuade her to help, and that had gotten me nowhere. But there was someone who could maybe get through where I had failed, and that someone was, of course, Tabby. Maybe it would work if she showed Roxy the email addressed to Uncle Stew. Maybe Tabby could say something, do her girl talk, do whatever it might take to make Roxy see how important it was that she help.

Maybe Tabby could make her cousin see that no doubt most of the children helped by Global Rescue would go to good homes, but Uncle Jimmy was also using his so-called charitable foundation to put children into homes where they would be terribly abused.

But how was I going to explain things to Tabby? How was I going to explain the videos I had seen a couple nights ago? How was I going to explain why I had been over at Roxy's house in the first place? How was I going to explain why Roxy had chosen to show me the dark side?

My mind raced, and I thought of all sorts of stories I could tell and all sorts of ways I could explain how Roxy had come to show me those videos, but the will had gone out of me.

All my life I had been so good at keeping secrets.

But no more.

The time for secrets was over.

I was going to tell Tabby the truth about what happened in the hot tub. I loved her too much to do anything else.

So that's what I did.

May 3

I DON'T NEED to go into everything that happened after I told Tabby what had gone on between me and Roxy there in the hot tub. I had hoped maybe Tabby would say she had fucked her Uncle Jimmy so the two of us were even and she was sorry, too.

But that wasn't the case.

Fact is, we had another fight. Worse than any one before. Much worse. And you might think that if it was that bad I probably ended up slapping Tabby around pretty bad, but I didn't. Fact is, she hit me, and I was the one who had to rinse with salt water.

And when it was all over, the two of us were lying on the floor in each others' arms, crying and laughing at the same time, me telling Tabby that I loved her, and her saying to me, Well, in that case, Llewellyn Trout, you're a goof.

That afternoon, Tabby went over to talk with Roxy. I don't know exactly what the two of them ended up doing. I don't know what Tabby said. Maybe they walked on the beach. Probably did their girl talk.

But when they came back late that night, they told me what I had been hoping to hear: Roxy was willing to help.

What had convinced Roxy was the email to Uncle Stew and Aunt Marge. She didn't see anything wrong with children being placed in homes like her daddy's. She wanted to make that clear from the start.

For chrissake, they're called pedophiles, she said. Do you know what that means? A pedophile is a person who loves children. What the hell is wrong with someone loving a child?

I said, Jesus, Roxy how can you say something like that?

Roxy said, Yeah, you think you are so much better than me, don't you, Cowboy? You think your abusive alcoholic Pop was better than my daddy. Well, let me tell you something; looking down on someone like my daddy is like looking down on someone who loves puppy dogs.

I said, But people who love puppies don't fuck them.

Roxy said, Oh for chrissake, Cowboy, we've been through all this already.

We're not talking about people who fuck puppies. We're talking about people who fuck people. You know, Cowboy, people do that; people fuck people and no one gets upset. We all do it. And aren't children people? So where's your problem, Cowboy?

Tabby looked over at me like, Shut up, Llewellyn. Just shut the fuck up. You're going to ruin everything.

So I did; I shut up.

Roxy agreed that Uncle Stew was different. That wasn't love. If there was a dark side, that was it. No other video she had ever seen, and she had seen a lot; no other video could turn her stomach like the one of my Uncle Stew and that young boy.

Because of that, Roxy was willing to help me and Tabby try to stop her daddy. Anything to help keep a kid from having to be adopted by your uncle, she said. Anything. What kind of sick relatives do you have, anyway, Cowboy?

Roxy explained that her daddy had been in trouble with the police a couple times in the past, and always things just got swept under the rug. Nothing was ever done; Reverend Jimmy Cochran had money and he had friends in high places. Capitol Hill, and even the White House, Roxy told us. He always comes out smelling like a rose.

I said, So, what are we going to do, then?

Well, Cowboy, can you imagine if one fine Sunday morning, instead of the Reverend Cochran showing up larger than life on that giant screen at the front of his church, what if, instead, what showed up on that screen was one of those sweet videos he made of me and him sharing a father-daughter moment?

I just sat there, and I think my jaw was hanging open or my eyes were bugging out like in cartoons because both Tabby and Roxy started laughing at me.

All I could think to say was, Holy shit. But then I thought a bit about it, and I said, How are we going to manage something like that?

Roxy said, Don't worry about it, Cowboy. Me and Tabby have it all figured out.

Roxy said she was sure she could get us into the church late at night when there would be nobody there. And if we can just get into the media booth where they control the sound system, the video cameras, all that kind of stuff—if we could do that, Roxy was sure we would be able to figure things out. Then come Sunday morning, all we would have to do is get Mr. Zale, who usually handled all those technical matters, to step out of the booth for even a few minutes and that's all it would take. Sounds easy enough, doesn't it, Cowboy? I think even you can understand that one.

I said, I don't know, I'm not so sure. Roxy's smartass tone of voice was kind of pissing me off.

Roxy looked at me kind of disgusted. She said, What the hell is your problem, Cowboy? Your balls fall off in the hot tub, or something? And that pissed me off even more.

Come on, Llewellyn Trout, I know we can do it, Tabby said, and I knew she was trying to smooth things over—lighten things up—because she knew this whole plan could so easily fall apart if Roxy decided not to help.

So the three of us promised each other that we would work together. Who cares if the whole idea was fucking crazy. Not doing anything was even more crazy.

May 4

THE FOLLOWING NIGHT, all three of us snuck into Uncle Jimmy's sports-stadium-movie-theatre-mega-church.

The media booth had a lock on the door, but it had been left open, and, once we got inside and turned on the electronic equipment, it was surprisingly easy to figure out how to get a DVD to show up on the screen down at the front of the church and how to override the pictures sent by the two video cameras that were mounted at the front of the church and operated by remote control from up in the booth.

Roxy said, Just like I told you, Cowboy. Easier than shit.

We figured that having that father-daughter video show on that big screen for even thirty seconds in front of the ten to twelve thousand people who would be in church on a Sunday morning would be all we needed. Tabby said, That'll get national attention. Even Uncle Jimmy can't sweep something like that under the rug.

We just had to make sure we got in a part that showed Reverend Cochran's face. We couldn't leave any question about who it was in the video.

Anything beyond thirty seconds will be gravy, Roxy said. Pure gravy.

May 5

TWO DAYS LATER, Reverend Cochran and his team returned from Vietnam.

Tabby did not want to go to work that morning, but I told her, You have to Tabby, we can't give that son of a bitch any reason to be suspicious. Go in there and kiss his ass. He'll love you for it.

Yeah, I know, she said, giving me one of those leprechaun grins. That's what I'm afraid of.

So Tabby went in to work, and that evening she came back excited as can be. She told me that she had overheard someone telling Uncle Jimmy that everything was finally in place and working so that next Sunday's church service would be broadcast live not just across the United States but also across the world via the Cochran International Media Network.

Do you realize what that means, Llewellyn Trout? Do you realize what that means? Not only will ten or twelve thousand people in Uncle Jimmy's church see that video. And not just a few million Americans. The whole world will see it. The whole world, Llewellyn Trout. The whole world.

And I said, Holy shit, Tabby. I sure hope nothing goes wrong.

May 6

ON THE FOLLOWING Sunday morning, there was to be a special
addition to the regular church service. Reverend Cochran was
going to show videos of his team's trip to Vietnam, and he would
explain how, with God's help, The Cochran Green Branch Ministries would
soon be helping hundreds of Third World orphans find loving Christian
homes right here in America. Tabby had learned that much at work, and
it fit into our plans just fine.

Roxy said, We'll just substitute one video for another. Things are just
getting easier.

That morning Roxy phoned and said her daddy had left home early. I
guess he wanted to make sure everything is working smoothly for his first
world-wide television broadcast, she said.

So me and Tabby drove over to Roxy's.

On the way, Tabby said, Let's just hope this is one of the days when
Roxy is pissed off at her daddy. If it's one of the days when she's in love with
him, this whole thing might just fall through.

And, yep, we were lucky. Roxy was plenty pissed at her daddy. The
night before he had told her she wasn't allowed to get another piercing.
Roxy was really pissed. That was good.

Let's go nail the son of a bitch, she said. So that's what the three of
us set out to do.

From Roxy's house, we had planned on driving two cars over to Green
Branch Ministries House of Worship, but it ended up that Roxy's car had a
flat tire. Piece of Chevy shit, Roxy said, and I grinned and said, Watch your
language, young lady, that's a Corvette you're talking about.

Unfortunately, it meant the only car we had was Tabby's two-seater
Porsche, and obviously there was no way all three of us would be going
to Uncle Jimmy's church.

Go on, the two of you, Tabby said to me and Roxy. You don't need
me. You go do what you have to do. I'll be here waiting for you when
you get back.

219

And that made sense. At the time it made perfect sense. But what a mistake it was. Sweet Jesus, what a mistake it was.

I went with Roxy.

This was going to be easy, right? Flat tire, no problem. I mean, sometimes little complications arise. That never stopped MacGyver.

So, like some kind of heroes, me and Roxy drove off in a two-seater Porsche and left behind the thing that was most precious to me in the whole world, and I was foolish enough to believe that when I got back she would still be waiting for me.

After all, she had told me she would be waiting, hadn't she? Isn't that what she said?

May 7

ROXY WAS WHAT Pop would have called cool as a cucumber, but I was nervous as hell, and Roxy said, Relax, Cowboy, relax. Even if things go wrong it's not the end of the world. We'll figure out some other way to stop him.

You have the DVD? I asked, and Roxy said, Of course I do, Cowboy. I recorded just the juiciest highlights of my favorite episodes. And I added a few pictures that Tabby took with her cell phone during her trip to Vietnam.

A minute later I asked the same stupid question. I guess I was nervous. Yeah, no shit, I was nervous.

Roxy just shook her head like, What kind of idiot are you, Cowboy? But she was nice and only said, I told you, Cowboy, I've got the DVD. And I've got my daddy's cell phone, too.

I asked her, Why the phone? and she said she was going to use it to get Mr. Zale out of the media booth. I'll send him a text message that he's needed down at the front of the church for just a moment, and he'll think the message is from Daddy, so he'll take it seriously. That should give the two of us a chance to get into the media booth.

I said, Goddamn, Roxy, you've got everything thought out. And it's good she did because I obviously didn't.

When we got inside, we took seats right up at the top near the media booth—nosebleed area, Roxy said. It was an area where hardly anyone wanted to sit and there were lots of empty seats.

The service started out pretty much like the one I had been to when me and Tabby first moved down from Bakersfield. There was loud music and singing that was led by none other than the Reverend Jimmy Cochran, himself. There he was, bigger than life on the giant screen, all smiling with white teeth, and his face glowing orange from that fake tan, and his lime green shirt unbuttoned too far, and his silk suit so white it seemed almost to glow against the dark midnight blue that was the background on the screen.

I sure hoped Uncle Stew and Aunt Marge would be watching the live broadcast and not just waiting for the replay later on.

I'm sorry I have been away for the past few Sundays, Reverend Jimmy Cochran said, smiling out at all ten or twelve thousand of us from behind his Plexiglas pulpit.

Well, he went on, My friends, you will recall that before I left, I told you that, with your prayers and generous contributions, Cochran Ministries has established a charitable foundation that will save countless orphaned children from deplorable conditions in Third World countries. Many hundreds will receive care and education at orphanages in their home countries and many others will find adoptive parents and loving families here in America, God bless it.

He went on to say how pleased he was that God had given him an opportunity to take a team of dedicated workers with him to Vietnam these past few weeks, and in that country they had met with officials and government agencies, and with the good Lord's help and grace, great progress had been made. Reverend Jimmy Cochran hoped that, within the next month or two, he would be bringing the first precious orphans out of Vietnam. With God's help, and the generous support of all those listening both here and across the world via television, Green Branch Ministries would continue to grow, and within a few years would, undoubtedly, be rescuing innocent children throughout Asia and Africa.

Just then, the cameras faded to black and the image of Reverend Jimmy Cochran up on the screen was replaced with video footage obviously shot during his trip to Vietnam.

Quick, now's the time, Roxy whispered, and I saw her madly texting away with her daddy's cell phone. Goddamn, her thumbs moved faster than her eyelashes.

A few moments later, I saw Mr. Zale hurry out of the control booth, and Roxy whispered, Now, Cowboy, now.

In seconds, we were in the media booth and Roxy locked the door behind us and handed me the DVD she had tucked between the pages of the *Holy Bible* she was carrying.

My hands were shaking like crazy as I slipped that disc into the machine. Wait, Roxy whispered. I'll tell you when.

On the big screen up front, Reverend Cochran was walking down some muddy alley over in Vietnam, and there were raggedy children swarming around him, and as he sat down on a door step, he lifted one of those little children onto his lap, and it reminded me of the picture in *Bible Stories for*

Young Children where Jesus is holding little children in his lap, but those kids are clean and have bright, colorful clothes, whereas these Vietnamese ones were filthy and had raggedy clothes.

Smiling into the camera, Uncle Jimmy sat stroking the child's head, and that is when Roxy whispered, Now, Cowboy, now!

I hit the Play button at the same moment she hit the Stop on the other machine.

All of a sudden the image on the big screen wasn't Reverend Cochran on a doorstep in a slum with a raggedy Vietnamese child on his lap. Instead, it was Reverend Cochran sitting on a hippy waterbed with a lava lamp on the floor beside it, and on his naked lap sat a young girl with dark gray eyes that darted, nervous and scared.

Then came a more recent picture of Reverend Jimmy Cochran, a bit fuzzy, like one from a low-megapixel cell phone because that's what it was, but it was clear enough that you could see the man of God stroking the thigh of a Vietnamese girl who couldn't have been more than thirteen or fourteen years old.

The media booth was pretty much soundproof, but monitor speakers let me and Roxy hear what was going on out in the auditorium. It was as though every one of those ten or twelve thousand people in Reverend Cochran's Green Branch House of Worship let out a gasp all at once. And then a silence fell on the place, and it reminded me of the silence that fell when Mr. D was taken away in handcuffs.

And then things got crazy. Women started screaming. Some tried to cover the eyes of their children. I heard one of them screaming, Jason, you close your eyes. I told you Jason Fredrick Hansen, you close your eyes. Jason! Jason!! Jason!!! Do you hear me? You're a naughty boy, Jason Fredrick Hansen! You close your eyes right now. Close them now or I'll tell your father when we get home.

I'll bet Jason gets a licking when he gets home, Roxy said with a grin. What a naughty boy.

Mr. Zale was back by now and he was pounding on the glass door and motioning for us to unlock it, but Roxy just grinned at him and shook her head like some little kid taunting a substitute teacher or something.

Down front, I saw Reverend Cochran slip quickly off the stage and I wondered where he was going, and I said, You son of a bitch, you can run but you can't hide.

People were milling about now, some surging toward the front as if they wanted to get a better view, Jason Fredrick Hansen, among them, no doubt, the naughty boy, and other people were trying to get out of the place as if it was on fire, Jason Fredrick Hansen's mother among them, no doubt.

Me and Roxy had figured that if we got to show thirty seconds of the DVD it would be enough, but we got in lots more than that. Lots of pure gravy, as Roxy called it.

By this time Mr. Zale had gotten the help of a few other men, and together they were pounding the thick glass door of the media booth with a fire extinguisher.

Roxy said, Okay, Cowboy, we've done enough. Let's go.

But there was no going. As soon as Roxy unlocked the door, Mr. Zale and the men with him lunged at us and threw us to the floor. I struggled to get away, but they held me down, and I noticed Roxy was just sitting there and not struggling, and because of that they were leaving her alone, so I stopped fighting them, and when I did, they let me up, but then they made me sit back down.

You stay right there, young fellow, said Mr. Zale. You stay right there until the police come for you, and I thought, Holy shit, does this idiot really think it's me and Roxy that cops will be coming for?

Mr. Zale had his attention on getting the video stopped and then he started talking real loud into a microphone, and he was trying to get the people calmed down and he was saying, Don't panic, folks, don't panic. Everything is under control. Everything's under control.

But Roxy wasn't under control. She said, Come on, Cowboy, and she grabbed my hand and pulled me to my feet and out of the media booth. I followed her into the middle of a mass of people and Mr. Zale's men couldn't get to us, and I guess the crowd thought those men were the bad guys or something because they started beating them up, and me and Roxy slipped out of the church just as the cops were pulling up with their sirens and flashing lights.

And this is when I did such a foolish thing. Actually, it's not so much what I did, but more what I didn't do.

May 8

I DIDN'T GO back to Reverend Cochran's house. Instead, me and Roxy just stood there in the parking lot outside the Green Branch House of Worship, watching everything that was going on.

I want to be here to watch them take him away in handcuffs, I said.

It was maybe twenty minutes or so we stood there watching. By the looks of things, pretty much everyone had come out of the church by now. But instead of driving off in their cars, people were standing around like me and Roxy, watching to see the cops haul Uncle Jimmy off to jail.

Me and Roxy were standing not far from one of the cop cars that was sitting there with its lights still flashing and its window half down, and we could hear what was being said over the radio in the car, and what we heard made us look at each other in surprise.

That's affirmative. One of the perpetrators is reportedly a juvenile female approximately 15 years old, break.

Go ahead.

Pierced lower lip. Multiple ear piercings. The accomplice is reportedly male, approximately 20 to 25 years of age, possibly wearing blue jeans and a yellow sweatshirt, break.

My god, Roxy said. The cops aren't looking for my daddy, they're looking *for us*, and I said, We better get out of here.

So we did. We got out, and as we were leaving the parking lot, Roxy pointed to an empty parking spot that had a sign with the words "RE-SERVED, Reverend Jimmy Cochran" on it, and Roxy said, Daddy's gone already. That's his spot.

I said, Holy shit. They let a child molester drive off, and, instead, they're looking all over the place to arrest the two of us.

Keystone cops couldn't do better, Roxy said, and she laughed, but I didn't know what she was talking about.

When we got back to Roxy's house, I expected Tabby to meet us at the door, and when she didn't I should have known right away that there was something wrong, but I wasn't at first alarmed, and then I got a sick feeling in my stomach because Roxy said, I wonder if my daddy's here. We should have checked to see if his car is in the garage.

So we did check, and sure enough, there in the garage was Reverend Jimmy Cochran's orange Lotus Exige, and Roxy said, Oh shit, and I said, I wonder if Tabby's still here, and I was beginning to be scared because what if Uncle Jimmy had figured out it was Tabby that had taken the video of him with his hand on that Vietnamese girl's thigh, and, I knew, of course, he would have figured it out; who else could have done it other than Tabby, and holy shit, I suddenly was afraid like never before.

I said to Roxy, We've got to make sure Tabby's not still here.

So we went back into the house, and there was still no sign of Reverend Cochran, and no sign of Tabby either.

But then I found her in the kitchen. She was lying on the Italian marble tile and all around her was blood, and it was one of those times when the darkness and the nausea came over me, and I whispered, Oh, please Jesus, don't let her be dead.

Tabby was alive. As I lifted her from the floor and sat there in a pool of her blood, still warm, I held her in my arms, and she whispered, Stay with me, Llewellyn Trout. Stay with me and don't let me go. Don't ever let me go.

But I couldn't keep her. Oh, my god, I tried. I held her so tight. Dig-your-fingernails-in tight I held her. But I couldn't keep her, and she quietly slipped away.

Tabby died in my arms.

May 9

I WAS STILL sitting there when the cops arrived and came bursting into the house with their guns drawn because Roxy had called *911* and told them there had been a murder. They tried to take my Tabby from me, but I wouldn't let them, but then the ambulance people came and took her from me, and I was still just sitting there in the pool of blood and with blood all over that yellow sweatshirt Tabby had given me for Christmas and the color of the blood that was all over it was almost the same color as the words that said *Hello LA.*

Roxy was sitting beside me, and she put her arm around my shoulder. But believe it or not, I wasn't crying.

I just sat there trying not to get pulled over to the dark side. A few nights back in Roxy's hot tub I had thought I saw the dark side, but I had only imagined it because I was drunk and stoned. Right now, though, the dark side was very real, and it was more terrifying than anything I had ever imagined, and the dark current was pulling at me, trying to drag me over. And maybe it had already done that because I could hear the police talking, but it was like their voices were echoes from somewhere far away.

The perpetrator has apparently vacated the premises. All rooms of the residence have been thoroughly searched. Call backup and cordon off the perimeter.

And from far away I heard Roxy tell them, No, he hasn't fucking vacated. I know where he is. And she said, Follow me, I'll show you. Then she took my hand and she told me, Come on, Cowboy, we can't sit here forever. So I got to my feet but it was like watching someone else, and I was on the dark side and watching myself from over there, and I watched as Roxy took my hand and helped me to my feet. And I knew why I wasn't crying, and it was because I was on the dark side, and when you are on the dark side, you don't cry.

I went with Roxy as she led the cops to her daddy's bedroom and to the walk-in closet with the mirror that slides into the wall, and the cops went down the dark stairs first with their guns drawn, but there was no need for those guns because when Roxy turned on the lights, there, lying on the leather couch in front of the bigscreen and reflected in the mirrored ceiling, was Reverend Jimmy Cochran, and clutched to his chest with one hand was a black *Holy Bible,* and there was a dark hole in his forehead where the bullet had gone in, and on the floor beside the couch was that beautiful Smith & Wesson 357 revolver I had sold him.

Roxy walked over to him and knelt down beside the couch. She gently lifted that bloody head into her arms, cradling it like a baby. Then gently, ever so gently, she kissed the lips where blood was just beginning to seep out, and she whispered just one word—*Daddy.*

There were tears in her eyes.

May 10

I ALWAYS WONDERED what it was like to be on the dark side, and now I know. Roxy was right. You don't go to the dark side without being fucked up.

I wake in the midnight and there's no Tabby beside me. I'm alone. Not even the spook man in the corner, and I wish there was someone, even the spook man, but there's no one. Just me.

And when I wake in those midnights, I sometimes pray to our father which art in heaven, hallowed be thy name, if only you would give me courage, oh, please, please, father which art in heaven, give me courage, because if I had it, if only I had the courage, I would put a goddamn bullet through my fucking head.

But there's no answer from the darkness. The courage never comes, and I know there is no god on the dark side. There's just me. Just me and the darkness.

Just me, the darkness, and the Southern Comfort bottle that sits empty on the bedside table, glowing in the light of the red alarm display that's blinking because I haven't bothered to set it since there was a power failure a month ago, maybe two, who knows, maybe it was three months. Who cares?

Mornings, I wake to the downstairs sounds of Mrs. Castro's goddamn soap operas, and I drag myself into another day, bleary eyed, fuzzy tongued—cursing whoever the hell it was that invented the liquid headache they call Southern Comfort, and swearing never again to touch a drop of the sweet liquor that last night slid down smooth as a copperhead through marshy backwaters but this morning twists the gut like a condemned man's last meal does in those moments when the sodium thiopental begins to flow.

It's not just that I lost Tabby. What makes it worse is knowing that it was all for nothing. Well, almost for nothing. Sure, we stopped Jimmy Cochran, but we didn't stop any of the others.

229

Those videos of Jimmy Cochran's contained enough evidence to put dozens of people behind bars. The videos were there in the basement. I know they were. I saw them. But the cops took them away and they disappeared. There was never an investigation.

I inquired about it once at the police station. I told them there had been videos showing people all over the country abusing little kids. All over the world, in fact. Why aren't the videos being used to put those people behind bars? I asked.

The cops told me the only videos they had recovered from the premises of Jimmy Cochran's residence were run of the mill pornography. You can see for yourself, Mr. Trout. It's right here in the report. Would you like to read it?

Nothing illegal about owning pornography, they told me. They had no record of incriminating evidence of any sort. Everything was spelled out clearly in the report. Jimmy Cochran had allegedly abused his daughter. He had committed suicide. End of story. Investigation closed. Is there anything else we can help you with, Mr. Trout? Well, thank you for coming in, and we appreciate your concern.

I remember Roxy saying that her daddy had friends in high places. Well, I guess one or more of those friends wanted those incriminating videos to simply disappear because that's what happened.

Uncle Stew should be behind bars and wearing a prison uniform for his abuse of a young child. Instead, he's still wearing his chief of police uniform and harassing people for parking illegally, smoking pot, and shoplifting candy bars. Fuck Uncle Stew.

I don't live at the Green Branch Villas any more. Now I'm living in a small room I rent from an old lady named Mrs. Castro. But my money's almost gone, and I won't be here long if I don't get out and find myself a job. I had lots of money after Tabby died because she had life insurance as one of those perks she got from the Green Branch Ministries. But it has been a year, now—more like a year and a half, and my bank account is pretty much empty.

A few weeks ago—actually, it was probably more like a few months ago, who knows, Roxy stopped by. She said, Cowboy, get your ass out of this fucking room and find yourself a goddamn job. Find something to get your mind off your troubles, and for godsake stop feeling sorry for yourself because Tabby sure as hell wouldn't want you moping about, and I told her, Fuck you, Roxy, what do you know? and then I thought about the videos and her with her big gray eyes, uncertain and fearful, and how if you looked carefully into them you could see the dark side, and I said, Sorry, I didn't mean to say that, and she smiled at me and put her hand on mine and said, Tell you what, Cowboy, why don't you come with me on Tuesday and I'll introduce you to Dr. Kent.

I told Roxy, I'm not sick, I don't need any goddamn doctor.

She told me Dr. Kent wasn't a regular doctor but a psychiatrist that she goes to because, seeing as she was still a minor, the judge had required that she visit a court-appointed psychiatrist who would help her deal with the trauma of her father having shot himself and also come to grips with the abuse she had suffered as a child. Last but not least, it would help Roxy cope with the fame and publicity that came about as a result of that video of her and her famous daddy. After we showed that video, Roxy had been on lots of TV talk shows, and someone had helped her write a book. She had made lots of money, but, seeing as she already had plenty, she had given most of it to some organization that helps kids who have been abused.

I told Roxy, I'm not crazy, I don't need a goddamn psychiatrist.

But Roxy came by that Tuesday anyhow, so I said, What the hell, and I went with her.

Dr. Kent told me, Come back every Tuesday and Friday at 10 a.m., and don't worry about the cost.

So I went to see him, and he had me sit in a chair because he didn't have one of those funny couches, and he told me to talk about myself, but, for some reason, I couldn't say hardly a word.

He said, Talk to me, Llewellyn. If you won't talk, I can't help. So I tried, but I couldn't. I just sat there feeling stupid. Dr. Kent said to me, Llewellyn, have you ever written a journal? Maybe a blog?

I told him, No, never.

He said to me, Why don't you try writing a daily blog. We'll keep it a private. I'll be the only other person with the password.

So I have been writing a blog pretty much every day, and, like Dr. Kent suggested, I started by writing about the earliest things I can remember. Things like me sitting in that claw-foot bathtub with me and Pop having a good laugh about me turning that bath water into bubbly champagne.

I guess Dr. Kent was right about it being easier for me to write about things than to talk about them. Each time I go see Dr. Kent we go over what I wrote since the last visit. At first, I thought, This is crazy shit because what the hell difference is writing a blog going to make.

But I think maybe it has been helping after all.

May 25
(I'm Back From My Trip!)

I WAS SITTING in my room upstairs at Mrs. Castro's house, watching an infomercial about some space-age vacuum cleaner that's more powerful than a Kansas tornado, when I heard a knock at my door. I answered it, and I said, Holy shit! because standing there in front of me, wearing a green bowtie and yellow sunglasses, was—you guessed it—there in front of me was Mr. D. But what you wouldn't guess is that he had shaved his head. Yep, completely bald.

He didn't just shake my hand but, instead, put his arms around me and gave me a hug. Lew, he said, It's good to see you again.

When I asked Mr. D what was he doing here and how the hell had he found me, he said, Well, I'm here to see you, of course, Lew, and I found you by searching on Google; how else does a computer geek find an old friend?

I was surprised to see Mr. D and not entirely happy about him showing up like this, but I didn't know what else to do, so I said, Come in, Mr. D; come in. Take a seat. Make yourself comfortable. Let me pour you a drink. It was one of those times when I sounded real formal as if I was talking to some elegant southern gentleman, and I felt kind of stupid, but I thought, You've got nothing to feel stupid about, Lew Trout because this bald-headed guy standing in your doorway is wearing a green bowtie and yellow sunglasses.

Anyhow, Mr. D came in, took a seat, and, once I had poured him a few shots, he made himself comfortable. And, holy goddamn shit, he told me he was going to be spending the night.

That is if you don't mind, of course, he said. You don't have much space here, but I don't mind sleeping on the floor.

What the hell else could I do but shrug kind of helplessly and say, Well, of course, Mr. D; you're welcome to stay overnight if you need a place to sleep.

Before the sun had set, the two of us were pretty much wasted.

I said, Mr. D, I think we're drunk. Smashed, sloshed, plastered, fucked

232

up, kerschnickered, and blitzed. Or like my Pop would have said, I think we're pissed and drunk as a skunk.

Mr. D said, no, we were nothing of the sort; we were merely mildly inebriated. But from the way he slurred his words, it was obvious he was as shitfaced as I was.

I said, Why did you come see me, Mr. D? Aren't you still mad at me for what I did to you back there at Waynesburg High?

Mr. D said, Lew, I was never mad at you. I know you did it because you were concerned for Lindsey. How could I be mad at you for being concerned for the person I loved more than anything in the world.

I said, You seemed pretty mad at me there in Las Vegas at the wedding chapel.

That was hard for me to take, Lew. It's true. It was very hard. There you were, so happy and getting married to a beautiful girl, and all I could think about was my Lindsey and how much I loved and missed her. I almost didn't make it through that ceremony, but it wasn't anger I was feeling. Anyhow, let's not dwell on that. Where is that wife of yours, anyhow? You're not apart already, are you?

I told Mr. D a bit about what had happened, and believe it or not, there were tears in his eyes when I got to the part about Tabby getting killed. So thinking I would turn things more cheerful, I said, Tell me, Mr. D; what's the real reason you've come to visit me?

Mr. D said to me, Well, Lew, like I said, I'm here to see you, but aside from that, I've come here because I'm dying and I have a favor to ask of you.

Sweet Jesus shit! Mr. D was dying?

I said, You can't be dying, Mr. D. You're not old enough.

Mr. D said, Age has nothing to do with it. The doctors all try to say it politely and not be too blunt, but fact is, I'm dying. Expiring, meeting my end, passing away, giving up the ghost, snuffing the candle, tailgating with Jesus, and boldly going, going, gone.

Mr. D started laughing, and I started laughing, too. Laughing really, really hard. Goddamn, we both were wasted. I mean, how else do you sit around laughing about someone dying.

You're shitting me, I said.

No I'm not, said Mr. D. I have cancer of the pancreas. The doctors say I've got probably a few weeks. Maybe a few months. Not likely more. But who can really say? It's not as though the grim reaper keeps a calendar app on his iPhone. When he said this, Mr. D started laughing again, but this time I didn't laugh along with him. This time his joke didn't seem funny.

I said, Holy shit, Mr. D, I don't even know what a pancreas is. I know you've got one somewhere inside, but I don't know why it's there. I don't know what it does.

Me, too, said Mr. D, I didn't used to know anything about a pancreas, either. But mine went bad. I tried the chemotherapy. It made me lose my hair and made me feel like poop. So I stopped it.

I wasn't laughing. Any more, Mr. D wasn't laughing, either. He told me that having only a short time left in this world had made him rethink his life.

I mean, when it comes down to it, he said, How important is Elvis? Not that The King isn't important to folks like me who really love him, of course. But in the big picture, how important is he? Do you understand what I'm talking about, Lew? It's just not important.

I wasn't sure I did understand, but I told Mr. D, Yeah, sure; how important is Elvis, anyhow? Probably not important at all, and as soon as I said it, I knew from the look on Mr. D's face that I had hurt his feelings. What the hell. What was I supposed to have said? I guess it was one of those cases where you're damned if you do; damned if you don't.

Anyhow, Mr. D told me he wanted to visit the grave where Lindsey Longpoke was buried.

She was the only person I ever really loved, he said. And then Mr. D asked me to go along with him to Waynesburg. Come with me, Lew, he said. It's a long drive, and I would enjoy your company.

I told Mr. D that Waynesburg Arkansas was the last place on earth I wanted to visit. I'd rather go to Bumfuck Egypt, I said. Maybe even to Bakersfield, California. You might have fond memories of Waynesburg, Mr. D, but not me.

Come along for the ride, Lew. We'll have some good times. We'll shove a few Elvis CDs into the stereo; we'll crank up the volume; we'll crank down the windows; and we'll cruise Route 66 in my Cadillac. What do you say, Lew? Come along with me.

So, still hung over, me and Mr. D left for Waynesburg early the next morning. We were driving a 1954 pink Cadillac.

It's just like the one Elvis bought back in 1955, said Mr. D.

The two of us didn't talk much as we drove, but, like you might imagine, we played Elvis CDs pretty much the whole way.

234

Elvis was singing *Blue Hawaii* as we changed a flat tire somewhere out the other side of Flagstaff. Mr. D cursed the cop who sped by without bothering to stop and see if there was anything he could do to help. Gosh dang those cops, said Mr. D. The son-of-a-guns are supposed to protect and serve, but, fact is, about all they do is harass and intimidate. Well, they can darn well kiss my sweet patootie.

Elvis was singing *Are You Lonesome Tonight* as a desert sun scribbled sloppy orange and yellow on a purple New Mexico sky, while Mr. D snored in the back seat and I sang along with the music real loud so as to keep myself awake.

Elvis was singing *Release Me* as we passed an Oklahoma stockyard, where cows stood hoof-deep in brown muck, staring at us from their guantanamo pens—bored, sullen, and distrusting.

And, you guessed it, Elvis was singing *The Green Green Grass of Home* as me and Mr. D pulled up in front of Waynesburg's Sandman Motel—just $69 a night for a single.

But a room with two beds will be $75 per night, sir. You'll find it very comfortable, and just like the sign out front says, every room has a 27-inch TV with cable and a free movie channel. Complimentary continental breakfast is served in the lobby between the hours of 6:30 and 8:45. So I'll just need a credit card and picture ID, if you don't mind, sir, and if you happen to know your license number, it would save me a trip out to your car.

Me and Mr. D had planned on sharing the driving. One of us would sleep while the other drove. We had figured if we did that, we would be able to drive straight on through. According to MapQuest, the trip should have taken just a bit over twenty-four hours. But fact is, I ended up doing most of the driving. Mr. D did most of the sleeping. I guess it was the cancer. We had stayed at a couple motels along the way, and the twenty-four hour trip ended up taking us three days.

In spite of us having taken our time, me and Mr. D, were both tired, and neither of us bothered to stay up and watch that 27-inch TV with cable and free movie channel.

We went to bed.

When I woke in the morning, Mr. D had already gone out. To where, I had no idea.

I went down to the lobby, but the continental breakfast had already been put away. Put away or eaten, I didn't know which. Didn't much care.

I poured myself some coffee—strong, black, murky, and lukewarm. I drank it from a Styrofoam cup, not noticing till half way through that there was lipstick on the rim; goddamnit, the cup had obviously been already used by some lady who wore clothes that no doubt matched the pink color of the lipstick on that Styrofoam cup.

Across the street from the Sandman motel was Blue Bottle Liquor, and that was convenient for me. I walked over and bought myself a bottle of Comfort. Then I paused in the parking lot, walked back inside, and bought a second.

You can never have too much Comfort, I told the guy behind the counter.

He shook his head and looked at me like, What the hell is a young fellow like you doing, buying two bottles of Comfort? and, don't you know if you keep on like this, you're going to end up an old drunk.

You've started early, Mr. D said when he returned to the motel and found me drinking Comfort from that same Styrofoam cup with the pink lipstick.

I asked him where he had gone out to so early, and he told me he had been over to the cemetery where Lindsey was buried.

I wanted the first rays of morning sunlight to find me visiting her grave, Mr. D told me. He said he had expected it to be a sad time, But it wasn't that way at all. In fact, it was an uplifting and edifying experience.

First rays of sunlight? An uplifting and edifying experience? Who else but Mr. D would use words like that to describe a visit to some one's grave?

Here, I said to him. Why don't you join me? I held out my bottle of Comfort, but Mr. D shook his head. None for me, he said.

I shrugged and told him, Suit yourself.

I was pretty much wasted by the time noon came around, and like lots of times happens when I'm wasted, I was getting really pissed. Mostly because Mr. D was grinding on my nerves. Grinding real hard.

Don't get me wrong, Mr. D was a nice guy, but he had some really irritating habits, like whistling Elvis songs and pausing occasionally to say, Thank you very musch.

I said, Goddamnit Mr. D, would you please shut the fuck up. Don't you know how irritating you are?

Mr. D turned all red—even his bald head—and he looked so very sad. I couldn't help but feel sorry for what I had just said. So I decided to get the hell out of the motel and leave Mr. D alone to whistle away all he wanted.

I walked over to Pixley Park, where Waynesburg Baptist had held a picnic to celebrate sending me off to the Air Force, and, holy shit, when I got to the park, there they were having another one of their church picnics.

A bunch of folks, most of them fat, were waiting politely in line with paper plates as Reverend McKey stood behind one of those park barbecue grills, flipping burgers and dabbing barbecue sauce on the body parts of dead chickens.

Some of the men were playing a game of Frisbee. One of them was Uncle Stew. Yep, instead of being behind bars for molesting a little kid, that son of a bitch was free and having a great time playing Frisbee in Pixley Park—all on account of the cops in Orange County having accidentally misplaced the incriminating videos left behind by Reverend Cochran.

Accidentally, like hell.

I sat down on the grass not far from where the people were gathered. No one paid me any notice. No one recognized me. I guess people see what they expect to see and seldom anything more, and, since no one was expecting to see Lew Trout at Pixley Park that day, nobody did see Lew Trout at Pixley Park. To those good Christian people from Waynesburg Baptist, I was just some stranger who had no business watching their picnic, and the best thing to do was ignore me—maybe I would go away.

But I didn't go away. I just sat there on the grass, and a few of the ladies, who had finished piling their paper plates with food, came and sat on a park bench not far from me.

On the opposite side of the park, there was a raggedy old homeless guy who was going through the trash containers, pulling out aluminum cans, plastic bottles—anything that could be sold at the recycling center for a bit of cash.

It was obvious that Blue Bottle Liquor was where the guy had spent the better part of yesterday's cash from the recycling center; he was so out of it he just shuffled his way right into Uncle Stew's Frisbee game, clueless that he was interrupting anything.

One of the ladies seated there on the park bench said something about it being disgraceful for someone to be publically intoxicated. And, goodness me, at such an early hour of the day, no less. Disgraceful, just disgraceful.

Another one of those ladies said, Whenever I see old drunks like that it reminds me of Henry Trout come back to life. She laughed like she had told a funny joke.

Well, it really pissed me off when I heard the sweet Waynesburg Baptist woman talk like that about my Pop, but it was the things that happened next that really set me off.

Uncle Stew sent the Frisbee flying directly at the old homeless guy, hitting him square in the head. It was obvious Uncle Stew had done it on purpose.

All those good Christian folks from Waynesburg Baptist laughed.

Good shot, Stew, one of them called out.

The old homeless guy seemed confused, and when he realized everyone was laughing at him, he seemed embarrassed.

One of the women sitting there on the park bench yelled out, Get yourself out of the way, Henry Trout. Can't you see you're interrupting a Frisbee game? Once again everyone laughed.

And now those fine Christian ladies of Waynesburg Baptist began to gossip. I could hear everything they said, and it was me and my family they were talking about. That's right; those ladies had to have something to gossip about—even if it meant dragging up people and events from way in the past.

God only knows why that old Henry Trout even bothered attending our church, one of them said.

If you want my opinion, he had no business in any church whatsoever. He certainly wasn't a Christian. Not a true born again one, at least. Of that much I'm sure.

And that poor wife of his. Goodness me, Gladys, I swear I'd rather have stayed in Communist Vietnam than live in America with an old drunk like Henry Trout.

I'm sure you heard what happened to that son of theirs.

Did I hear he was dishonorably discharged from the military?

Indeed he was! Well, you know, they say the apple doesn't fall far from the tree.

Dishonorably discharged, was he? I hadn't heard.

Well, I'm sure it's true, but I've always wondered what the details were. Being drunk while on duty, no doubt, if the young man's anything like his father.

No, Martha, I'm sorry to say it was nothing like that. Not that it would surprise me one bit if he was drunk on duty more than once, but the young man was discharged for molesting a child.

Oh, goodness! You don't say! A child molester? Are you sure?

I swear, Gladys. I heard it from Marge, herself. She was so hurt, God bless her. It just broke her heart. I mean, after all she and Stew did for that boy, bringing him up as if he was their own son. Then he goes and repays them by bringing disgrace on himself and on those who loved him by molesting a child.

A little boy, no less. That's what I heard.

Well, good heavens, I would never have imagined. No doubt Marge prefers to keep the whole affair quiet, poor dear.

No doubt the young man inherited his perversions from his father. I always suspected old Henry Trout was molesting that little daughter of his. I mean, the way she wouldn't speak and was always in trouble of one kind or another at school. Those are sure symptoms of child abuse, if you want my opinion.

Oh, I know what you mean, Gladys. I don't want to sound un-Christian, but it really was a blessing in disguise that Henry killed his wife and daughter as well as himself. I mean it's tragic, of course, and very sad, but you just can't help thinking that maybe folks like them are better off being in the next world, even if they have never experienced the saving grace of our Lord.

It's better not only for themselves, but for others as well. Just look at what happened. That Llewellyn boy lives, and how does he repay the world? He goes and molests an innocent child. It would have been better for all involved if he had died along with the rest of his poor family. Jesus forgive me for saying it, but I have to tell you it's how I feel, Margaret. It's just how I feel. I can't help it.

On and on they went with their gossip. I didn't do a thing. Didn't even move. I just sat there on the grass. But inside me something snapped. I think I felt a lot like Pop must have that evening when he found those three Greyhound tickets Mom had bought.

I'm sure you've heard of Eric Harris and Dylan Klebold. How about David Burke, Patrick Sherrill, or Seung-Hui Cho? I know you've heard of Misty Trout. They were all people who got pushed beyond their limits. Pushed to a point where they snapped.

Well, those Christian ladies from Waynesburg Baptist had just pushed Llewellyn Trout to his snapping point.

I don't know if there's a word for what I felt as I sat there in Pixley Park, watching those Waynesburg Baptist men humiliate the old drunk and listening as their wives gossiped about me and my family. But maybe the word rage comes close.

Rage. You've probably never experienced it. I suspect most people go a lifetime without experiencing it. I, myself, had never experienced it before that day in Pixley Park.

I can tell you this: if you have ever experienced rage, you've probably done time in prison. When you experience real rage, the people around you had better take care because someone's likely to get hurt. Get hurt real bad.

May 26

THAT NIGHT I broke into Uncle Stew's house. All evening, I had sat drinking Comfort, waiting for Mr. D to fall asleep. Then I took the car keys from his pocket. I didn't like taking his Cadillac without permission, but I knew he would never let me use it if he knew what I was going to do. It was only a few miles to Uncle Stew's house, and I wouldn't have minded walking, but you can't walk through town carrying a shotgun and not attract attention. Not that there would likely be many people out so late at night, but if anyone happened to be, it would be just as well not to be seen carrying a shotgun.

Breaking in wasn't hard. I remembered Aunt Marge and Uncle Stew never locked their back door. Uncle Stew used to say he didn't mind if someone broke into his house.

It'll give me an excuse to shoot the sorry son of a bitch, he said.

Anyhow, I walked right in. It was easy, but I was nervous as hell that Uncle Stew would wake up, and, if he did, I didn't doubt for a moment that he really would shoot me—sorry son of a bitch that I was.

But I didn't for a minute feel bad about what I was doing. After all, I wasn't stealing anything because how can you call it stealing when a man takes only what already belongs to him.

The Weatherby 12-gauge I got from Pop is what I was after, and I found it easy enough even in the dark. And along with it, I found the Colt revolver with the fucked up trigger. Yep, the same one I had killed Mom and Misty with. I hadn't planned on doing so, but I decided to take the Colt as well as the Weatherby. It didn't exactly belong to me, but it sure as hell didn't belong to Uncle Stew, either. It had belonged to Pop, and if anyone had a right to the gun, it was me. Along with taking the guns, I took a box of ammunition for the Colt and several boxes of shotgun shells for the Weatherby. Mostly slugs and 00 buckshot. Eric Harris and Dylan Klebold would no doubt have considered me under-armed, but I figured I had what I needed for my purposes.

Anyhow, I took the gun and the ammunition, and I snuck out of the house, but I didn't go directly back to the motel. I had a couple more stops to make, and the first was the old Winnebago. I still had a key for the door, so once again, I walked right in. And once again, I was after only what belonged to me.

Before going off to the Air Force, I had packed my few belongings in a cardboard box, and I was hoping the box would still be out there in the Winnebago. I found it in the closet, right where I had left it. I loaded the box along with the guns and ammo into the trunk of Mr. D's pink 1954 Cadillac.

There was a shed out back of the house where Uncle Stew kept his lawn mower and things like that. He refused to store the mower in the garage.

It's a fire hazard to store anything with gasoline in it within the confines of a garage that's attached to a residence, he had once told me.

I had asked him why, then, did he store his cars in the garage. They have gas in them, I said. Uncle Stew had looked at me real angry, and I could tell he was pissed at me for my smartass remark. I don't think cops have a sense of humor.

Anyhow, alongside the lawn mower in that shed were two five-gallon gas cans, and I was happy to find them both almost full. I put them in the trunk of the Cadillac along with the other stuff.

Then I drove back to the motel. But on my way I stopped at Waynesburg Baptist, and I hid the Weatherby behind some bushes. I didn't want to be seen walking through town tomorrow morning with a shotgun in my hands. I hid the five-gallon gas cans as well.

Back at the motel, the clock on the table between my bed and Mr. D's said 2:14 a.m., but I didn't want to sleep. I was afraid if I did I would wake in the morning and not have courage to do what I had planned. This was the first time I had experienced rage, and I didn't know if it was something that stuck with you through a night of sleep or if it was something you had to keep working on 24/7.

I sat there drinking Comfort and thinking about that evening at Flo's Diner when Miss Elsa had told me, Lewie, it's not dangerous to play with fire just so long as you're careful. Well, tomorrow morning I was going to play with fire. But I wasn't going to worry about being careful because I didn't much give a damn if it was dangerous. I remembered the smell that came from those burning ants. The smell and the crackling noise. I wondered how Baptists smelled when they burned. I wondered how they sounded. Not much like ants, I figured. They probably smelled more like stakes on a barbecue grill, and they probably sounded more like—well, they probably sounded like people screaming. It made me laugh to think about it.

Anyhow, drinking Comfort isn't a smart thing to do if you want to stay awake the whole night, and before long I fell asleep. But there was no need for concern: the rage was still there when I woke.

Mr. D was sitting on his bed, staring at me. What are you planning to do with that thing? he asked, pointing to the Colt revolver that lay on the table beside me.

Goddamnit, my head hurt and I felt like I was about to vomit up what little Comfort might still be in my stomach. I was in no mood to tell Mr. D some long, made-up story about how I got hold of the gun or what I was going to do with it. So I just told him the truth. The words sounded crazy as they came out. Crazy but not at all insane.

I'm going to church this morning, I said. I'm going to shoot me some Baptists. I'm going to shoot me some Baptists, and then I'm going to shoot myself. I've got nothing left to live for, Mr. D. Nothing at all. And by getting rid of those Baptists, I'll leave this world a better place. Hell, I'll be a hero. Kids will write essays about me in school and read them aloud to the class and everyone will clap.

Mr. D's reaction wasn't anything like what I would have expected. For a long time, he sat there real quiet, and when he finally spoke, Mr. D said, You want some help?

What the fuck! Was Mr. D bullshitting me? I said to him, You're not serious, are you?

Mr. D said, Of course I'm serious, Lew. Do you think you're the only one who hates the people in this town? Have you forgotten what they did to me? What they did to Lindsey?

I told Mr. D I was going to set the church on fire. I was going to pour gasoline at the two doorways and most of the windows. I would leave just one small window. People would have a choice. They could stay inside and burn or they could climb out that one small window—and I would be there outside the window with my Weatherby, ready to pick them off one by one. Not that I was going to kill everyone. Some of those folks, especially the kids, I had nothing against. But the one I was for sure going to kill was Uncle Stew.

That's the cop who arrested me, said Mr. D. I'd like to get even with him. Let me help you, Lew.

Uncle Stew belongs to me, I said. Don't you dare shoot him.

So you'll let me come with you?

I suppose, I said. I've got two guns. You can use this one. The trigger's pretty fucked up. But it'll kill people just fine. I know that for a fact. Have you ever shot a gun?

Mr. D shook his head.

I made sure there were no bullets in it and then handed the Colt to Mr. D. He took it, and I could see his hands were trembling. I told him, Don't let it scare you. It's just a piece of metal.

I showed Mr. D how to use the gun and how to load it.

Just make sure you leave one bullet for yourself because I'm not coming out of this alive, and I don't want you coming along unless the same is true for you.

Mr. D nodded. I have no problem with that, Lew, he said. Today with a bullet in my head. A few weeks from now with a body full of cancer. What difference does it make? I've got nothing to lose.

So the two of us got ready.

You would think that when you are about to shoot a bunch of people sitting in church you wouldn't much give a damn about any of the usual morning stuff, but that wasn't the case with me and Mr. D.

We showered, and shaved. Did all that kind of stuff. Mr. D put on a fresh white shirt that he pressed real neat with the motel's iron and ironing board. Then he even put on a red bowtie. When I was ready, I sat watching him as I cleaned under my nails and finished off that bottle of Comfort. Neither of us said hardly a word. I figured Mr. D was trying to keep busy, trying to keep his mind off what we were about to do.

As the time approached, I finished off that bottle of Comfort. I offered Mr. D the last swallow, but he shook his head.

I said, Come on, Mr. D, we're running late.

Okay, he said. Just let me say my last prayers. I sighed and said, Well, just keep it short. You'll be talking to God in person within the hour. But Mr. D didn't seem in any hurry. When he finished his prayers, he apologized for having to take a shit—he called it putting fruit in the bowl. It made me laugh when he said that. What the hell, maybe it was a phrase Elvis used or something.

Anyhow, I told him, Hurry up, Mr. D.

As we pulled out of the motel parking lot, I said, Goddamnit, Mr. D, you're going the wrong direction.

He told me he knew, but he wanted to one last time drive past the cemetery where Lindsey was buried.

I told him, Mr. D, we don't have time for that. We need to turn around right now. That church service only lasts an hour, and that means it's already near half over. We're running late.

I expected him to turn around, but Mr. D just kept on driving. Driving in the wrong direction. We passed the cemetery and then turned onto the highway. I figured Mr. D was losing his courage.

Just take me back, I told him. You don't have to stay. Just drop me off and then leave. I won't be needing a get-away car.

' But Mr. D didn't turn that Cadillac of his around, and by now we were on the highway, heading out of town.

It was beginning to be obvious that Mr. D had no intention of turning around. He just sat there driving and not saying a word. I was getting pissed. Really pissed.

I didn't give a flying fuck if Mr. D had lost his courage. I didn't care if he didn't want to help me. But if he was going to try stopping me—well, that just was not going to happen. No fucking way that was going to happen. Nothing was going to stop me.

You were lying to me, weren't you? I said. You were lying about wanting to help. All morning you've been stalling and trying to make us late, haven't you? Goddamn it, Mr. D, you're a real cocksucker.

Mr. D nodded. I'm sorry he said. I didn't want to lie to you, but I couldn't let you do this thing you've got planned, and I couldn't think of any other way to stop you. I'm sorry, Lew.

Fucking-A, you're sorry, I said. You're a sorry-ass son of a bitch. But you're not near as sorry as you're going to be if you don't turn this goddamn car around and drive me back to Waynesburg Baptist.

Mr. D shook his head. I can't Lew. I'm sorry, but I just can't do that.

I pulled out that gun with the fucked up trigger and cocked the hammer. I said to Mr. D, Turn this cocksucking car around right now. Turn it around right now, Mr. D, do you hear? Do it now or I'll blow your fucking head off.

Mr. D just kept on driving.

Up till now, I had felt all calm and not nervous one bit, but suddenly all that changed. My hands were shaking just like they had that night years ago when I pointed that same gun at my Pop.

Mr. D didn't look at all afraid. Just sad. I said to him, You need to start taking me seriously, Mr. D, but he kept on going straight and, in fact, sped up.

Then Mr. D shifted his Cadillac into neutral, he pulled the key out of the ignition, and he tossed it out the window as far as he could.

I said, What the fuck, Mr. D. Why the hell are you doing this to me?

It's over now, Lew. There's no going back to Waynesburg now. By the time you find that key and drive back, there won't be anyone left at the church.

The car was coasting to a stop, but I knew Mr. D was right. By the time I walked back and found that key it would be too late.

And that's when the Colt revolver with the fucked up trigger went off. But at the moment I wasn't aiming it at Mr. D. I had taken the barrel away from his head and was in the process of turning it on myself when we hit a pothole as we came to a stop at the side of the road, and the jolt made that gun with the fucked up trigger go off. But it did no more harm than put a hole through the top of Mr. D's 1954 pink Cadillac.

Well, Jesus fucking Christ! We're not talking bunker busters. We're not talking RDS-202s. Something even bigger is what happened inside me. But it didn't come out like what I would have expected. It was kind of like those buildings they demolish with explosives. There's just a few small puffs of smoke and then the whole building crumbles onto itself.

No one got killed. No one even got hurt. I just started crying. Yep, Pop would have been ashamed of his crybaby son. He would have sworn at me. Probably hit me because I deserved it. But Mr. D didn't hit me. Instead, he reached out and put an arm around my shoulder. My ears were still ringing so loud I couldn't hear what he was saying, but his arm was comforting, just like Pop's had been all those years ago in the bedroom of that house out on Warner Road with the bloody bodies of Mom and Misty lying arm-in-arm on the floor.

I leaned over and put my head on Mr. D's shoulder.

And I cried.

May 27

M E AND MR. D spent the better part of a week at a motel in Little Rock. Mr. D was gone most of the time. I didn't know where. I didn't care. I was pretty much the whole time wasted on Comfort.

One day Mr. D told me I needed to get my act cleaned up.

I said, Fuck you, Mr. D; fuck you, and he said to me, Lew I'm just trying to help.

Well, I don't want your fucking help, I said. Don't want it. Don't need it. Not your help. Not anyone's.

Mr. D said, I don't blame you for not listening to me. But what would Tabby say to you if she was here? I don't know anything about her except for what little you told me as we were driving out here, but it doesn't seem to me like she would have wanted to see you moping about like this.

I said, Fuck you Mr. D because you're right; you don't know a goddamn thing about Tabby. Not about her, not about me, not about anything. So stay the hell out of my business. Stay the fuck out of my life.

This isn't about the people at Waynesburg Baptist, Mr. D said. You realize that, don't you, Lew? Those people aren't what's making you so angry.

They're assholes, I said.

No doubt, but they don't deserve to be burned alive.

Well, Mr. D, you seem to know pretty much everything, don't you? So why don't you tell me, then. What is it, Mr. D? What is it that's making me so angry if it isn't those assholes at Waynesburg Baptist?

I think you're angry at yourself, Lew. You hold yourself responsible for what happened to your sister. For what happened to your parents. And most of all for what happened to Tabby.

I said, Fuck you, Mr. D. What the hell do you know about me?

I know you mean well. That's what I know. Just like with what happened to Lindsey. You meant well. You wanted to help her. So how could I hold it against you? And you meant well with the others, too. So you have to stop holding yourself responsible. You've got to forgive yourself. If you can't do that, things will eat away at you from the inside until they destroy you.

I poured myself another shot of Comfort. Hell, it wasn't a shot I poured. It was a whole goddamn glass. A glass full to the top. I didn't say anything more to Mr. D. Just fuck you, then I sat there thinking about my Pop and what he had done over in the Nam back in '69. He never forgave himself for killing that officer, and maybe Mr. D was right that something like that could destroy you from the inside out. It had destroyed my Pop.

The next morning I was still vomiting up stomach secretions. Mucus, pepsin, acid, rennin. Mostly slime. Slime and Comfort.

All night I had been doing it. Drinking Comfort, vomiting it up, drinking, barfing, drinking, puking, drinking, heaving, drinking, spewing, and then drinking still more—finally passing out.

I lay in bed all the next day.

All the next night.

By the following morning I was sober.

Sober but still hungover.

I was exhausted. My will was broken. The rage was gone. I guess Comfort had washed it right out of me.

May 28

M R. D SAID to me, I don't think I have much more time, Lew. My strength is gone. My strength and my desire to live; they're both gone. I'm going back to Waynesburg. There's an empty plot in the cemetery not far from Lindsey's. I drove back there the other day while you were sitting here getting drunk. I purchased the cemetery plot, and I made funeral arrangements for myself. I'm going back to Waynesburg. It's where I want to die. It's where I want to be buried.

I said, Mr. D, don't be crazy. You're not going to die. Not any time soon at least. But I knew it wasn't true. I could see it in his eyes. Something there had changed. Kind of like the way Misty's eyes changed when she got taken over to the dark side. But the look in Mr. D's eyes wasn't scary. Just sad. Sad but not unhappy—if that makes any sense.

Mr. D said, I want to give you my car, Lew.

I said, Holy shit, your pink Cadillac? You're crazy, Mr. D. That's your pride and joy.

Well, it's no further use to me. I figure pretty soon Elvis, himself, is going to be driving me around the golden streets in his own pink Caddy. Anyhow, I can't think of anyone I'd rather give the car to. I hope you'll take it; I hope you'll enjoy it.

Mr. D handed me an envelope. All the paperwork's in there, he said. The car's already signed over to you. It belongs to you, Lew.

I said to Mr. D, I really can't accept it. A car like that's worth a lot of money.

Well, like I told you, the paperwork is already done, Mr. D said. The car already belongs to you. You don't really have a choice. I hope you'll keep it and take good care of it. I hope you won't sell it off to someone else.

The following day I drove Mr. D back to Waynesburg and helped him get settled in at the Sandman Motel.

Don't you want me to take you to the hospital? I asked him.

He said, Lew, I don't want to die with a bunch of tubes stuck in me.

I'll stay with you, I told him, but he said to me, No, Lew, you go on home; I don't want to be a bother.

I said, Of course I'm going to stay with you, Mr. D. I'm not going to let you die all alone here in this goddamn motel room.

So I did stay with him.

But it wasn't for long.

When I woke the following morning, Mr. D was dead.

They buried him two days later, just a bit after 12 noon. I was the only one at the graveside as they lowered him in.

I had made sure they dressed Mr. D in an Elvis T-shirt he had brought along on the trip. At first I thought of trying to find an Elvis suit with jewels, but where the hell do you find something like that? Besides, I figured, maybe the T-shirt was a better idea anyhow. I didn't believe in god or heaven or hell or any of those things anymore—not even angels, but if maybe, just maybe, they were true, then I was pretty sure Mr. D was right about now probably standing around talking to Elvis, and he probably would feel stupid if he was dressed up in an Elvis costume when it wasn't even Halloween.

On the keychain Mr. D had given me—the one that had the keys for the 1954 pink Cadillac—there was an Elvis Presley guitar pick. I pulled it off the keychain and dropped it into the grave. Good bye, Mr. D, I said. Say hi to Elvis for me, and, Mr. D, I'm sorry about what happened to Lindsey Longpoke and you. I'm so very sorry.

I had nothing holding me in Waynesburg; that's for damn sure. So I figured it was time to head on back to Orange County. Not that there was anything waiting for me there.

The 1954 pink Cadillac Mr. D had given me was at the far end of the parking lot, and I began walking to it, but then I turned back.

I had been to the graveside service when Mom, Pop, and little Misty were put in the ground. I had never been back. But I went back now.

It took me a while to find the graves. As I stood staring at them. I didn't feel anything. Not even sadness. Not for Pop. Not for Mom. Not even for Misty.

What the fuck are you supposed to do when you go visit someone's grave? Put something on it, right? Flowers, something like that.

Well, I didn't have any flowers. It did cross my mind to take some from other graves, but a person would have had to be pretty much wasted on

Comfort to think something like that was a good idea, and, for a change, I wasn't wasted.

So, instead, I walked to the 1954 pink Cadillac Mr. D had given me. There in the trunk was that box of things I had saved from when I went off to the Air Force. Out of it I took the *Bible Stories for Young Children* book. I started walking back toward the graves, but then I stopped and went back to the car. There in the trunk, between the suitcase and the box of things I had saved was a half-empty bottle of Comfort. I took it, too.

I went first to Mom's grave, and on it I placed that Purple Heart of Pop's that I had been keeping on my keychain. I said, This is yours, Mom. Pop got it for losing an arm, and he lost that arm in order to save you from some fucked up Marine Corps officer who was going to do I don't know what to you, and then Pop brought you here to Waynesburg, and even if he treated you not so good, I think he loved you. I know he did.

Next I went to Pop's grave, and you probably know exactly what I did. I sprinkled what was left of that bottle of Comfort all across it. I wanted to say something, but nothing came, and there was a pain down the side of my face just in front of my ears like there always is when I'm about to cry like a crybaby.

Then I kneeled down beside Misty's grave, and I spent a long time thumbing through the *Bible Stories for Young Children*. Finally I opened it to the page where a star shines down on the place where an innocent child lies with both a Mom and a Pop standing over, keeping watch, making sure no harm comes. I placed the book on Misty's grave, open to that page. Again, I wanted to say something, but nothing came. Just tears.

I started walking back to that pink 1954 Cadillac, but, suddenly, something caught my attention, and it was a grave headstone that had on it the inscription

Miss Elsa Hammerstein
1960 - 1992

I paused because, holy shit, there, right next to it, was a headstone engraved

Veronica Esteban
1975 - 2001
Beloved Daughter, Light Of My Life
Ever Forgiving a World that Treated Her Cruelly

For a long time I stood staring at those two graves and thinking about the days when Miss Elsa lived in the apartment above the garage. The baths in the claw-foot tub, the games of hide-and-seek, the games of chase, the nipple I bit off Miss Veronica, the switch tree, the scream counting, the wolf in the book from Mrs. Euston's library, Miss Elsa lying on the kitchen floor with her eyes and forehead gone but her mouth moving like a bluegill's does when you pull it from the water. And I thought about little Misty and how she never complained, never cried, and how she got carried over to the dark side.

I didn't any longer believe in a god, and I hadn't been to church in a long time, so I'm not sure why I did it—especially since I didn't remember all the words, and I'm not sure I got them right—but I prayed, Our father which art in heaven, hallowed be thy name. Forgive us our trespasses as we forgive those who trespass against us. And lead us not into temptation but deliver us from evil.

Then I walked back to my 1954 pink Cadillac. Rain was starting to fall, but hardly any was coming in through the hole I had put in the top with that bullet from the Colt with the fucked up trigger. Mr. D would have been pleased.

May 29

IT HAS BEEN a few days since I got back from my trip to Waynesburg. Yesterday I drove up to Idyllwild. I took with me the box thing they gave me that had Tabby's ashes in it, though I had a hard time believing it was all of them because how the hell can you fit a whole person's ashes in a box so small? Anyhow, I took those ashes, and hiked up to the top of Tahquitz Peak—the place Tabby, when she was a kid, used to call Mount Everlasting. It was a bright, clear day, and there was a breeze, and I was pretty sure it wasn't legal to do something like that, but I remembered Tabby saying to me, Llewellyn Trout, do you always follow rules? So I opened that box with Tabby's ashes, and I emptied them slowly into the wind, and it carried them away to places I don't know where, and I remembered Tabby telling me about her handsome prince in a cowboy hat who would someday carry her away on his white horse to far-off places you could see from nowhere else in the world except right there at the top of Mount Everlasting.

I had told Tabby I would never let her go off with that prince of hers.

I guess I'm not real good at predicting the future.

May 30

WHEN I WENT to his office yesterday, Dr. Kent told me he had been worried about me. For a while there you stopped writing your blog and then you didn't show up for your weekly appointment. I hoped you were okay.

I told him, Yes, I'm doing real good. Did you read the blogs I wrote about my trip?

Dr. Kent nodded. I did, Llewellyn. And I think it's best if you stay away from Waynesburg for a while.

I grinned kind of sheepishly. I think folks there will breathe easier if I do.

What about the guns? Dr. Kent wanted to know. I also think it's best if you don't keep any of those lying around. Especially when you're drinking.

I told Dr. Kent I hadn't touched a drop since I sobered up there at the motel in Little Rock. And I don't have any guns. And I'm not likely to go buying one, seeing as I don't have any money. But the good news is I hope that will soon change, I said. Tomorrow morning I'm going for a job interview.

Dr. Kent said, Why, Llewellyn, that's wonderful.

I told him, I'm not so sure. It's for a janitor position at a hospital, and I don't think it'll be much fun, but I got to do something or I won't have money for rent and groceries.

May 31

I WENT TODAY for that job interview. I took the bus over to Highgrove Hospital, and when I got there I told the lady at the front desk, I'm here about the janitor job, and she said, Fill that out, and she gave me a Bic pen and an application form on a clipboard, and when I finished it, the receptionist lady took it and told me to please wait. She came back a minute later and told me that I would be called in shortly.

But it didn't seem shortly to me, and I was about to leave because I was getting nervous, but then the receptionist's phone rang, and she said, Miss Moreno is ready to see you. Down the hall, last door on your right.

So I went there, and when I opened the door, holy shit, behind the desk was someone in a lime-green dress and embroidered on it was "Mermaid Services," but there wasn't any embroidered picture of a topless mermaid, only the words "Mermaid Services," and the person wearing the dress was Calli.

I didn't think she recognized me, and I wanted to get the hell out of there before she did, so I said, Sorry, I think I have the wrong room.

But Calli said, Llewellyn, have a seat.

I noticed that her eyes were a little red and maybe she had been crying. I said to her, Let's not waste our time. I'll be going.

She told me, No, please, Llewellyn; please have a seat. I thought it might be you when I saw the name on this job application. But I never knew your name was Llewellyn. I always thought it was Lewis.

I just shrugged. I mean, how the hell are you supposed to have pleasant small-talk with someone who screwed up what you thought was going to be a career in the Air Force? How do you smile at someone who falsely accused you of molesting her child?

Calli said, I owe you an apology, Llewellyn. An apology and so much more. Won't you please sit down. And now Calli was definitely crying, and she kept wiping her eyes with a tissue, but she had that mascara stuff on them and it was making her face a mess.

She looked at me pleadingly, so I sighed and did as she asked, and sat down in that chair across the desk from her.

You remember Patrick, don't you, Llewellyn? she said.

I nodded.

Well, Patrick's father's name was Jose, and he left me before Patrick was born. He went back to Mexico, which is where he was from. But after Patrick was born, Jose decided he wanted a part in his son's life, after all, and he phoned and told me he wanted Patrick to come live with him in Mexico.

Jose threatened that if I didn't let Patrick go, he would come and take him from me because, after all, he was the father and he had a right to take his own son if that's what he wanted. But I couldn't let Patrick go, Llewellyn. His father was a violent, abusive person, and I couldn't bear the thought of Patrick having to grow up with him.

So Calli had moved away from home because she was afraid Patrick would be taken from her, and she might never see him again.

It happens more often than you think, Llewellyn, she told me. Kids just disappear down to Mexico and they are never heard from again. Mexico is a big place and you could look all your life and never find someone if that person didn't want to be found.

So Calli ended up out in the middle of the Mojave Desert. She figured it was a place where no one was likely to find her.

And she was pretty much right, but then, out of the blue, Sergeant Jesus Sanchez showed up, and Calli recognized him as someone who had known her husband, Jose.

Calli had to do whatever Jesus Sanchez told her because if she didn't he threatened to tell Jose where she was living, and she was terrified that Patrick would be taken from her and disappear down into Mexico.

Can you understand, Llewellyn? Calli said to me. When Jesus told me I had to say those things about you, I felt I had no choice. It tore me to shreds, but a mother will do anything, anything at all, to protect her child. Can you understand, Llewellyn? Can you ever forgive me?

I remembered Miss Veronica saying words similar to that back at Waynesburg High, and I had told her, No, I will never forgive you, and the next day she slashed her wrists in a restroom.

But today I said to Calli, Yes, I think I understand. Yes, I forgive you.

Calli tried to smile at me, but it was a crooked, funny smile because she was crying and it was hard for her to make her mouth go right.

I said to her, Whatever happened to that Sanchez guy, anyhow, and she told me, Do you remember that car he sold you?

I nodded.

Well, after you left, he decided that he may as well take it back, seeing as you obviously didn't want it. A few days later he had a crash. They say the brakes went out on him. The master's cylinders or something like that. He didn't die, but last I heard he was still in a coma and no one had much hope he would ever pull out of it.

I said, Serves him right. I should feel happy, I guess. But somehow I feel sorry for him.

Calli nodded. Anyhow, Llewellyn, regarding this job, I just can't give it to you.

I shrugged and said, Well, I figured as much. I may as well be on my way, and I picked up the application from Calli's desk because I wasn't going to leave my personal information with her if she wasn't going to hire me, and I was about to walk out the door, but Calli said, Stop, Llewellyn. Please stop. Sit back down.

So I did, and Calli told me the Mermaid Service had grown and now employed twenty-seven people and had cleaning contracts at three different hospitals in the area. She even had a few men working for her, and I said, Holy shit, do they have to wear a green miniskirt?

Calli smiled and shook her head. We're not just maids anymore, she said. And, no, I don't ask the guys to wear the Mermaid uniform. She smiled again and wiped her nose with a Kleenex.

I guess the mermaid uniform hasn't changed much, I said, motioning to Calli's lime-green dress, and she said, Oh I think it has changed a bit since you saw it last.

She stood up and stepped out from behind the desk and, holy shit, the dress went all the way down to her knees, and she wasn't wearing go-go boots.

And we don't embroider our panties any more, Calli said with a smile. Not the guys or the girls. This time her smile was back to normal and not a half-crying one.

Calli asked me, How are you doing these days, and I said to her, Like shit.

She wanted to know more, but I couldn't bring myself to tell her much. Not about Tabby. Not about hardly anything. Only that I didn't have much money and I needed a job.

I didn't talk much, but Calli talked plenty. She said her company was getting too big for her to handle everything on her own, and she said to me, I would love it, Llewellyn, if you came to work with me.

I thought you told me you couldn't give me the job, I said.

I didn't say I wanted you to work *for* me, Llewellyn. I said I would love it if you would come work *with* me. *With* isn't the same as *for*. I want you to be an equal partner with me in the business, Llewellyn. It's the least I can do after all the pain I brought you.

I just sat there, and I guess I looked sort of stupid because Calli laughed. Well you don't have to make your decision right here on the spot, she told me. Take your time. Think it over.

All I could think to say was, Thank you. Thank you so much. And usually when I am at a loss for words I say the wrong thing, but I think this time it was the right thing.

Well, how about if you think it over and let me know by the end of the week. If you have any questions, feel free to call. Calli handed me a business card that had printed on it a picture of a mermaid. But it wasn't topless.

I was leaving and about to close the door when Calli said, Wait, Llewellyn, one more thing. Patrick and I are going to Disneyland tomorrow. You want to come along?

Author's Note

Finding Comfort

The world outside the home has always been the wolf's domain. It always will be. But most of us find comfort in knowing that once we make it home, we can latch the window, lock the door, and spend the night in peaceful sleep.

It is terrifying when we lose that last safe refuge—when we discover that the wolf is in the house already. It's no use latching the window, no use locking the door.

For many abused children, there is no safety at home because home is precisely where most child abuse takes place. To make matters worse, the abusing adult is often someone near to the child—a parent, a close relative, a trusted acquaintance. The child has no one to turn to, no place to go for comfort.

Abuse can be devastating, and it often casts a shadow that stretches far beyond childhood.

Unfortunately, abuse has another dark side that gets less media attention but can be equally devastating. False accusations of child abuse have destroyed lives, relationships, careers, friendships, and more.

Learn More

Want to contact the author?
Want to learn more about child abuse?
Want discussion questions for a reading group?
Want to learn more about this title?

Please visit

http://www.nocomfort.com

Keep Reading

There are numerous works of fiction that deal with child abuse. Here are just a few of them. Beware: some are not for the faint of heart.

A Wolf at the Table by Augusten Burroughs.
The End of Alice by A. M. Homes
Lolita by Vladimir Nabokov
Lisey's Story by Stephen King
Gerald's Game by Stephen King
Bastard Out of Carolina by Dorothy Allison

Also by Dan Pietsch

The Greatest Happiness

A tale of love and revenge set in an alternate world and in a different time, somewhere between the Oxus and the Jumna

The greatest happiness is to scatter your enemy, to drive him before you ... to see those who love him shrouded in tears.
~Genghis Khan

Turn the page for a preview

Chapter 1

Ashenn wiped enemy blood from his hands. Then he picked a small, over-ripe plum and took a bite.

The night before, his father had told him his favorite bedtime story—the story of how King Daerah and his army defeated the alien hordes. This morning, from a vantage point high in the plum tree out front of his house, the young boy was busy slaughtering the hordes, who, after a winter-long siege, had stormed the city's wall.

On the ground below, Ashenn's sister, Oyera, tended the wounded.

"Stop, Oyera! Stop! You can't do that. You have to shoot arrows at the hordes."

"No, Ashenn, don't be silly. Princess Disia didn't fight the hordes. She helped the wounded and the dying amidst a rain of arrows from the alien hordes." Oyera paused briefly, looking up at her twin brother. "What's an alien horde, anyhow?"

Ashenn continued firing arrows as he shouted back his answer. "Hah! Don't you know? An alien horde is a warrior who doesn't even know how to talk our language."

The children were intent on their play, and they hardly noticed when their parents emerged from their mud-brick house.

"Okay, you two. Your mother and I are leaving for a while. We're depending on you to keep the enemy at bay."

"Get back inside! Keep to the safety of the palace! The hordes are attacking."

"Ashenn, I want you to get out of that tree right now. And Oyera, don't you go ripping holes in that new tunic of yours."

Ashenn and Oyera were too busy to respond.

"I don't think King Daerah and Princess Disia are listening."

"No, they're having far too much fun to pay us old folks any attention. Still, don't you think we should maybe take them with us?"

"How can we do that, my dear? Think about what we're going to be doing. It's not a thing for children. We don't want tears and nightmares, after all."

"I suppose you're right."

"I'm sure of it. Besides, what mischief could those two precious little children of ours possibly get into?"

"Well, then, listen, you two, I don't want you leaving the house while we're away. And Ashenn, I told you to get down out of that tree. I don't want to come back and find you with a broken leg."

The children paid no attention as their parents walked off down the dirt road.

A short time later, they were still busy fighting the hordes, and they didn't at first notice the small, disfigured man who emerged from the cold shadows still lingering damp and colorless amongst the granite boulders at the far edge of the yard.

The stranger paused under the plum tree, wincing and leaning on his walking stick. "My! What brave warriors," he said.

Ashenn looked down from his branch. "I'm not a warrior. I'm mighty King Daerah, and I'll shoot you with an arrow."

"Ah! I see. Well, I hope you won't mind if I stop for a while—here in the shade of your tree. I've brought a bit of a picnic, so I'll just have a bite to eat, and then I'll be on my way."

The stranger sat down under the tree and spread out a white cloth embroidered with colorful birds and flowers.

By this time Ashenn had climbed down from the branches, and he stood beside his sister, watching as the stranger unpacked his lunch.

Reaching into a canvas pack, the man removed several colorfully-decorated sweetcakes. Then he unwrapped a cluster of sugarcoated dumplings. Finally, he pulled out a small wax paper packet and removed a wedge of a light brown substance. A thick liquid oozed from it, and the man put out a long finger, catching a golden droplet on his fingernail.

"What's that?" Ashenn asked, pointing.

"Honeycomb is what it is, my young friend. Sweet, delicious honeycomb."

Reaching into his pack, the man pulled out a knife and carved off a slice of honeycomb, put it into his mouth, and then licked his fingers.

"Ah! Delicious! Once you taste it, there's no going back, you know."

The stranger smiled at Ashenn. His thin lips were shiny, and he licked them again for any last traces of honey. "No, my little friends, there'll be no going back."

A small, dark red spot appeared on the white of the embroidered cloth . . . then another . . . followed by a larger.

"Careless, careless," the man said as he put a finger to his mouth and sucked blood from the small wound his knife had left as he sliced the honeycomb.

There was a short pause as Ashenn studied the sweets laid out in front of the man.

"Could I please have a little taste? And my sister would like one, too, please. Just a little taste of your honeycomb."

"Of course you can have a taste, my little friends. I made sure to bring enough for us all." The stranger carved off a dripping slice for each of the children.

When the honeycomb was gone, the man shared the remainder of his lunch with Ashenn and Oyera. The three of them chatted as they ate, and when the sweets were gone, the man got up to leave. He gave a hiss of pain as he put weight on his crooked legs.

"Perhaps you'd carry this pack for me, young fellow," he said, turning to Ashenn. "You can see it's hard for me with my crippled ankles."

Ashenn looked questioningly at his sister.

She shook her head.

"I'll pay of course," the stranger went on. He held out several coins. "Look at those shiny copper pieces, my little friend. I polished them only this morning. Shined them up just for you."

"I'm not allowed to leave the house," Ashenn said hesitantly. "I want to wait till my mommy and daddy come back."

"No, my dear, you'll come with me. You'll come with me right now." The kind stranger held out two polished copper coins and folded Ashenn's small fingers around them. "You can use them to buy honeycomb for your sister."

"Yes, she'll like that!" The boy's face brightened. "Can she come with us?"

The stranger hesitated—for just a moment he hesitated. "Why, yes, of course she can," he said. "We wouldn't want to leave little Oyera with no one to watch over her, now would we?

CPSIA information can be obtained
at www.ICGtesting.com
Printed in the USA
BVHW052157200223
658866BV00012B/750